CAMBRIDGE LIBRARY COLLECTION

Books of enduring scholarly value

Polar Exploration

This series includes accounts, by eye-witnesses and contemporaries, of early expeditions to the Arctic and the Antarctic. Huge resources were invested in such endeavours, particularly the search for the North-West Passage, which, if successful, promised enormous strategic and commercial rewards. Cartographers and scientists travelled with many of the expeditions, and their work made important contributions to earth sciences, climatology, botany and zoology. They also brought back anthropological information about the indigenous peoples of the Arctic region and the southern fringes of the American continent. The series further includes dramatic and poignant accounts of the harsh realities of working in extreme conditions and utter isolation in bygone centuries.

Narrative of an Expedition to the East Coast of Greenland

In 1828 a Danish expedition was sent out from Copenhagen under the command of the naval officer and explorer Wilhelm August Graah (1793–1863). Its goal was to locate lost Norse settlements on the coast of Greenland, which had existed in certain places from around the turn of the millennium until their collapse some centuries later. The Danes did not find any settlement where they searched on the eastern coast, and the men endured harrowing conditions and near starvation during three winters. First published in Danish in 1832 and reissued here in its 1837 English translation, Graah's work opens with a brief history of the exploration and colonisation of Greenland before recounting his own expedition. Observations on the Greenlandic Inuit are incorporated as well. Addressing what was known about the Norse settlements at that time, the appendix also contains the expedition's scientific observations.

Narrative of an Expedition to the East Coast of Greenland

*Sent by Order of the King of Denmark,
in Search of the Lost Colonies,
Under the Command of
Captain W.A. Graah of the Danish Royal Navy*

WILHELM AUGUST GRAAH
TRANSLATED BY
GEORGE GORDON MACDOUGALL

CAMBRIDGE
UNIVERSITY PRESS

CAMBRIDGE
UNIVERSITY PRESS

University Printing House, Cambridge, CB2 8BS, United Kingdom

Published in the United States of America by Cambridge University Press, New York

Cambridge University Press is part of the University of Cambridge.
It furthers the University's mission by disseminating knowledge in the pursuit of
education, learning and research at the highest international levels of excellence.

www.cambridge.org
Information on this title: www.cambridge.org/9781108075145

© in this compilation Cambridge University Press 2014

This edition first published 1837
This digitally printed version 2014

ISBN 978-1-108-07514-5 Paperback

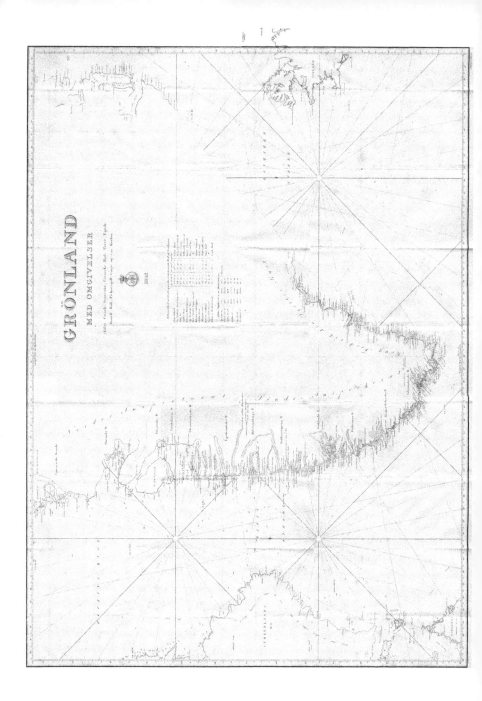

The material originally positioned here is too large for reproduction in this reissue. A PDF can be downloaded from the web address given on page iv of this book, by clicking on 'Resources Available'.

NARRATIVE OF AN EXPEDITION

TO THE

EAST COAST OF GREENLAND,

SENT BY ORDER OF THE KING OF DENMARK,

IN SEARCH OF

THE LOST COLONIES,

UNDER THE COMMAND OF

CAPT^N W. A. GRAAH, OF THE DANISH ROYAL NAVY,

KNIGHT OF DANNEBROG, &c.

———

TRANSLATED FROM THE DANISH,

BY

THE LATE G. GORDON MACDOUGALL, F.R.S.N.A.,

FOR THE

ROYAL GEOGRAPHICAL SOCIETY OF LONDON.

WITH THE

ORIGINAL DANISH CHART COMPLETED BY THE EXPEDITION.

———

LONDON:

JOHN W. PARKER, WEST STRAND.

M.DCCC.XXXVII.

PREFACE.

THE death of MR. MACDOUGALL, the Translator of the following pages, who was unfortunately drowned at Largs, in Scotland, in October, 1835, having unavoidably delayed the publication of this work, advantage has been taken of the delay, to profit by the kind offer of CAPTAIN JAMES CLARKE ROSS, Royal Navy, to add a few notes to the work; which, from his experience on the Coast of Greenland, and in the Arctic Seas, cannot fail to enhance its value.

It has been considered better to allow the homely style in these pages, probably attendant upon an almost literal translation of the Danish, to remain unchanged, rather than risk the chance of error, by substituting the more usual forms of expression.

THE EDITOR.

CONTENTS.

WINTERING AT NUKARBIK ; WITH SOME REMARKS ON THE CLIMATE, POPULATION, &c. OF THE EAST COAST.—1829—30.

FRUITLESS ATTEMPT TO PENETRATE FURTHER NORTH— RETURN.

APPENDIX.

OFFICIAL INSTRUCTIONS

TO

W. A. GRAAH, Esq., First Lieutenant, Royal Navy.

His Majesty the King having been graciously pleased, by Royal
Mandate bearing date the 18th of last December, to nominate you
to the command of an Expedition having for its object to explore
the East coast of Greenland, from Cape Farewell to lat. 69° North,
We, the undersigned Commissioners specially appointed to direct
the preparations for, and subsequently to superintend, the same,
communicate to you the following Instructions for your government.

The Expedition will consist, besides yourself, of Mr. Vahl, as
Naturalist, and Mr. Matthiesen, Superintendent of the Colony of
Frederick's-hope, in Greenland. Copies of the Instructions given
to these gentlemen, are herewith furnished you, for your information. You are, further, authorized to take with you a Danish
sailor, to serve as cook. The choice of the individual is left wholly
to yourself: we would, however, recommend you to select for this
office, some person already familiar with the navigation of the
Greenland seas. The rest of the persons to be attached to the
Expedition will be native Greenlanders, of whom you will engage
a sufficient number, men and women, to man two women's-boats,
and two kajaks, these being the sort of vessel in which we deem it
most advisable for you to perform your voyage.

You will, in company with Mr. Vahl, and the sailor above-
mentioned, take a passage in the vessel destined to sail, about the
middle of March, for the Colony of Juliana's-hope. Arrangements
to that effect have been concluded with the Greenland Board of

Trade, and preparations will be made for reception in it of whatever articles it may be necessary for you to take with you for the
purposes of the Expedition, and concerning which you will apply—
with regard to provisions, stores, and other like necessaries, to
the undersigned the Councillor of Justice Gede;—and as far as
regards the Instruments you may require, to the undersigned
Captain Zahrtmann.

On your arrival at Juliana's-hope, you will communicate with
Mr. Matthiesen, and we judge it most expedient for you thereupon
to set about exploring the coasts in the immediate vicinity of the
Colony, particularly in the direction of North, by which means
you will the sooner meet with him. On his reaching Juliana's-
hope you will, in conjunction with him, determine on the measures
to be taken with respect to the building of your women's-boats,
the engaging of crews for them, and whatever else may be necessary
towards the furtherance of your Expedition. You will perceive
from the copy furnished you of the Instructions given Mr. Matthiesen, that we have thought it most conducive to the interests of
the Expedition to intrust to him especially the charge of these
preparatory measures, as being the individual most likely to be
possessed of the requisite local knowledge. Though we, however,
thus exempt you from this duty, we still leave it to your discretion,
as commanding the Expedition, to determine whether, or not, it
may be expedient for you to take steps towards these preparations
previously to his arrival.

We presume that, on being joined by Mr. Matthiesen, you will
be able to determine at what time your preparations at Juliana's-
hope will be completed, and this ascertained, you will decide upon
the place which you may think best adapted for you to winter at.
We are of opinion, that Nennortalik or Friederichsthal are best
suited to this purpose, as you will there be able to take advantage
of the first opportunity that may offer in the Spring of 1829, for
setting out upon your Expedition. As, however, the preparations
above referred to, and various other circumstances, may create
obstacles that we are here unable to foresee, we leave all this to your
discretion, advising only that you employ the year 1828 in such a

manner as to enable you to seize the very first occasion that may present itself in 1829 of setting out; with a view to which, you will, as soon as Mr. Matthiesen shall have joined you at Juliana's-hope, at all events transmit, by women's-boats, to Nennortalik or Friederichsthal, the various articles you may design to take with you upon your Expedition.

Whatever leisure time may be at your disposal between the date of your arrival in Greenland and your going into winter quarters, you will employ in drawing up a chart of as much as possible of the coasts of the district of Juliana's-hope, determining by astronomical observation the latitudes of the principal points, and their longitude, as well by means of the chronometers with which you will be provided, as by lunar observations whenever an opportunity for making such may offer. These observations you will enter regularly in a register to be kept for that purpose, and in which you will be careful to specify in every instance the data on which your calculations have been founded, as also, in a separate section, whatever magnetical observations you may make, as well of the dip and variation of the needle, as of the intensity of the magnetic force. At the place where you may winter, and whither, we take it for granted, you will have had your larger instruments conveyed, you are further directed, besides the above, to neglect no opportunity of accurately determining the longitude by observation of the occultation of fixed stars, and the eclipse of satellites, with a view to subsequent comparison with simultaneous observations made in Europe; and you will therefore combine with the meridian of said place the various points where, in the course of the year, you may have made observations of longitude. Among your other magnetical observations, you will, still further, be careful to note the diurnal changes of the magnetic needle, and specify the same in your register, which, on your departure for the East coast, you will leave, under a sealed cover, in safe keeping, together with such of your instruments as you cannot conveniently take with you. You will, moreover, annex a copy of the observations you may make next Winter, for determining the positive longitude, to the Report you are to address to us before setting out for the East

coast, which Report we expect to receive with the homeward-bound
ship of 1829. As early as possible in 1829, you will set out on
your Expedition, whose limit is to be the southernmost extremity
of the land seen by Captain Scoresby in 1822, the same called by
him Cape Barclay, and said to be in lat. 69° 13′ N., and long.
24° 25′ W. of Greenwich, beyond which you will in no case proceed. We judge that you will be obliged to pass one Winter on
the East coast, but not more than one; and we enjoin you, therefore, on no account to turn back without having reached the object
in view, be the difficulties you may encounter what they may, until
the year 1830 be so far advanced that it may be absolutely necessary
for you to do so, in order to reach Friederichsthal before the setting
in of Winter, and thus avoid the necessity of spending another
Winter on that desert coast. The only event in which you are
authorized to deviate from the rule here laid down, is the following.
As the aim and end of the Expedition is to seek for traces of the
old Icelandic colonists supposed to have inhabited these coasts,
every effort should be made by you to sail along the whole extent
of them as high as lat. 69°, and this, accordingly, we recommend
you to do, without stopping to make any special researches on the
way, the more so as you will doubtless be furnished with abundant
time for so doing, by the stoppages which the nature of the navigation will, from time to time, compel you to make.

Now, as you will perceive from the Manuscript Chart accompanying these Instructions, this coast, according to the old tradi-
tions handed down to us, never was inhabited so high up; if, therefore, between the 62nd and 63rd degrees of latitude, you meet with
any vestiges of ancient colonization; if you discover fiords, with
regular vegetation on their banks, like those in the district of
Juliana's-hope; if you observe any conformity between the face of
the shore and the ancient charts; or fall in with a race of people
different from the natives of West Greenland; and, if on proceeding further, you find no longer any actual, nor any vestiges of a
former, population, you will, in such case, turn back without proceeding to the above-mentioned Cape Barclay, in order that you
may devote the more time to a close and careful examination of

the traces thus discovered.   You will learn from the Instructions drawn up for Mr. Vahl, what the points of Natural History and Philosophy are, to which his attention is to be especially directed, and with regard to which, you will afford him all the facilities and assistance in your power,—an injunction which it is the less necessary for us to urge, as we are well assured that you will feel disposed yourself to take part in such scientific pursuits, as well as encourage others to assist in them, whenever practicable.   To your especial care we recommend the drawing up of a chart of the East coast, in so far as may be possible on a voyage like that on which you are about to enter, not doubting that you will make the best use of your small collection of instruments, which, for your Expedition to the East coast, should, in our opinion, comprise but a pocket chronometer, a small sextant, a small azimuth-compass, an artificial horizon, and a couple of good telescopes.   Yourself, as well as Mr. Vahl and Mr. Matthiesen, will enter, in a day-book, full and copious notes of all the observations and remarks you may make in the course of your Expedition, with a view to their being reduced to order, and extracts made from them when a fitting opportunity may offer.

The above comprises all that we here, and at this moment, are capable of furnishing in the form of Instructions, for an enterprise of so peculiar a nature as that in which you are about to engage. The rest we leave to your skill and discretion, our unqualified confidence in which is best attested by our recommendation of you to this important trust.   We take, however, occasion to remark, that there is no way in which you can more advantageously display these qualities, than by maintaining that perfect good understanding among the members of the Expedition, which we look upon as absolutely indispensable to its ultimate success.

We take this opportunity of informing you, that a yacht, belonging to Messrs. Svendsen and Thorlacius, of Œnundafiord, in Iceland, is expected to make an attempt at reaching the coast of Greenland, in the Summer of 1829, or 1830.   If, therefore, you should see a vessel of this description, you may conclude it to be the one here spoken of, and, if practicable, you will place yourself in communication with it, in order to transmit to us, by this channel, intelligence of your condition. For the rest, you will furnish us with information of your progress and proceedings as often as may be practicable; and especially if, as we suppose will be the case, you should spend the Winter of 1829-30 on the East coast, you will be careful to send intelligence to that effect, to Nennortalik, in order that it may be transmitted to us by the ship that may be sent to Juliana's-hope, in 1830. All such reports you will address to the undersigned Count Moltke.

We presume that you will spend the Winter of 1830-31, at the same place, and occupied with the same employments, as that of 1828-29, and, as no further attempt is contemplated, whatever may be the result of your Expedition, you will, in the Spring of 1831, resume your hydrographic labours in the district of Juliana's-hope, taking care, however, to return to that colony by the time that the ship destined to sail from thence is ready to put to sea, when you will embark in it, together with Mr. Vahl, and the sailor you take with you, and repair hither. Mr. Matthiesen, on the other hand, after having rendered you the account referred to in his Instructions, may, in the Spring of 1831, at once proceed to resume his ordinary functions at Frederick's-hope.

With respect to your means of conveyance and subsistence in Greenland, both before and after your Expedition to the East coast, orders have been given to the Superintendent of the Colony of Juliana's-hope, who, as well as his subordinate functionaries, has been commanded by the Greenland Board of Trade, not only in this, but likewise in every other respect, to furnish promptly, yourself and companions with all the aid you may require, and they may be in condition to afford.

Having thus made every provision which we have judged calculated to promote the success of your enterprise, and having touched here on all the points to which, circumstanced as we are with respect to the distant country where it is to be prosecuted, we have thought ourselves justified in calling your attention, leaving the rest to your own conduct and discretion, we have now but to express our earnest hope, that, by a propitious combination of events, you may be so fortunate as to attain the object of your enterprise,—an object that has been sought in vain for centuries, and that involves national interests of such great importance.

A. W. MOLTKE,   J. W. HORNEMANN,
COPENHAGEN,   GEDE,   ZAHRTMANN.
Feb. 21, 1828.

INSTRUCTIONS

FOR

MR. VAHL, AS NATURALIST TO THE EXPEDITION.

HIS MAJESTY THE KING has been graciously pleased, by Royal Mandate dated the 18th of December, 1827, to order that an Expedition, under command of W. A. Graah, Esq., First Lieut., Royal Navy, and to which Mr. Matthiesen, Superintendent of the Colony of Frederick's-hope, will be attached, shall, in the Spring of 1829, set out from the district of Juliana's-hope, in South Greenland, with the view of exploring the East coast of that country; and His Majesty has been further pleased to appoint you Naturalist to the same.

Although the undersigned Commissioners entertain no doubt, that, as a man of honour, and lover of science, and one aware no less of the importance of the object at which the Expedition aims, than of the necessity that must accrue to those who participate in it of a sacrifice of the ordinary conveniences of life, your conduct will be marked by a strict attention to the duties incumbent on you, they nevertheless, feel it to be their duty, in obedience to His Majesty's command, to communicate to you the following Instructions, the observance of which is of importance to the success of the Expedition.

I. As the successful issue of the enterprise contemplated

depends not only on the correctness of its original plan, and the courage of those engaged in it, aided by a propitious combination of events, but likewise on their tact and prudence in their intercourse, as well with one another, as with the natives of the country; it is incumbent on you to maintain, as far as may depend on you, unanimity and concord among the members of the Expedition, and, with respect to the natives, uniformly to observe such a line of conduct as is calculated to gain their confidence and good will.

II. Immediately on your arrival at Juliana's-hope, you will proceed to explore the various large fiords in its vicinity, particularly such as have not hitherto been visited by naturalists, and as you judge, either from your own observation, or on the information of others, most likely to yield results important to science. The women's or other boats, with their crews, provisions, &c., which may be required by you for the purpose of prosecuting these researches, will be furnished you on application to the Superintendent of the Colony.

III. You will make out a list of the various specimens you may find, adding a description, where requisite, of such as are new, or rare. Of such as are unusual here, you will, as far as may be practicable, make a collection,—of animals, namely, and minerals for the Royal Museum, and of plants and seeds for the Botanic Garden. Should there occur among these specimens any of which we do not possess correct delineations, and which it may be impossible for you to transport, you will, if time permit, make coloured drawings of them, with a view to their insertion in the Flora Danica.

IV. As some of the mountains of Greenland are accessible, you will endeavour, by barometrical observations, to ascertain their height, as also to determine the limit of the snow-belt and the glacier, and of the various vegetable productions at different altitudes. We could wish, further, to be furnished with your observations on the temperature of the earth and of springs.

V. Should you discover any ruins, or other vestiges of ancient colonization by Icelanders, particularly any not already described by other travellers, you will take notes thereof, and make search for stones with Runic inscriptions, which stones, should you find any, you will have conveyed to Juliana's-hope, or, should this be found impracticable, take accurate copies of the inscriptions on them.

VI. You will keep a journal on which the incidents of the day, and whatever else you may observe worthy of remark, in the course of your excursions, shall be regularly registered, a copy of which journal you will, on your return, deliver into our hands.

VII. As you will be furnished with proper instruments for the purpose, you will be enabled to make meteorological observations. These, likewise, registered in a separate journal, you will deliver, on your return, into our hands.

VIII. On setting out for the East coast, you will take with you no more books, instruments, &c., than are absolutely necessary. As you proceed, you will endeavour to collect as many specimens of Natural History as there is room for in the boats. As measures will be taken to establish, if possible, a communication between the different inhabited places on the East coast and the nearest Danish establishment, you will endeavour, from time to time, to have whatever you may thus collect transported to Juliana's-hope, in order to make room in the boats for more.

IX. What has been already observed at §§ VI. and VII., relative to the journals or registers to be kept by you, applies no less to this part of your Expedition ; and we take occasion to observe, that, as we are possessed of little or no knowledge concerning the natural productions of the East coast of Greenland, it will be incumbent on you here, even more than elsewhere, to make out as full a catalogue as possible of the same, wherein you will be careful to indicate such as are likewise to be found on the West coast, as well as also to make drawings, as aforesaid.

X. During the Expedition to the East coast, your attention will be especially directed to the native Greenlanders you may meet with. You will, in particular, be careful to observe, if the people inhabiting the said coast differ from those of the West in form, stature, complexion, dialect, and manners ; if they inhabit

different dwellings, make use of different implements, &c. You
will make diligent inquiry, if they have among them any tradition
of their country having formerly been inhabited by another race of
men, and if any remains of their habitations, any Runic inscriptions,
or other traces of them, are to be found, of which vestiges, should
you meet with any, you will be careful to insert due notice, and,
where possible, drawings, in your journal.

	A. W. Moltke,	J. W. Hornemann,
Copenhagen,	Gede,	Zahrtmann.
Feb. 21, 1828.		

Note.—The Instructions for the Interpreter attached to the Expedition contain
nothing that could interest the reader, for which reason they are here omitted.

INTRODUCTION.

THE object of the expedition which is the subject of the following pages, was to explore the East coast of Greenland, a country that, for several centuries, has excited the curiosity alike of learned and unlearned. This coast was believed to have been inhabited, of old, by a flourishing colony of Icelanders, of whom some traces, it was supposed, might be still discoverable, and between whom and the inhabitants of Iceland and Norway, as well as, though less frequently, those of England and Holland, a regular intercourse was kept up until towards the close of the fourteenth century, when it ceased, and a deep mystery settled over the colony and its fate.

Before, however, I proceed to relate the few interesting incidents of my voyage, I conceive it fitting briefly to recapitulate the early history of this ancient colony, the supposed causes of its destruction, and the various attempts that have been made with a view to its re-discovery from the earliest to the present times.

The first colonization of Greenland dates from the year 983, and is mentioned in our old chronicles as follows :—towards the beginning of the tenth century, an Icelander, or Norwegian, named Gunbiörn, son of Ulf Krake, having been driven by a storm to a considerable distance west of Iceland, discovered some skerries*, to which he gave his name, and subsequently an extensive country, with intelligence of which he returned to Iceland. Some time afterwards, one Erik Raude, or the Red, fell under cognizance of the Thornæs Ting in Iceland, and was sentenced to banishment for the crime of manslaughter. Fitting out a ship, he announced to his friends that he purposed going in quest of the land which Gunbiörn had discovered, and promised, if his search should prove successful, to return. He set sail, accordingly, from Sneefieldsjökel in Iceland towards the West, a course which brought him to the East coast of Greenland. He then proceeded to the south, along the shore, looking for some habitable spot, doubled, and sailed to the west of a promontory which he called Hvarf†, and came to an island named after him Eriksey (Erik's island), where he passed the first winter. He employed himself hereupon three years in exploring the coasts, at the

---

* By this nearly obsolete word I understand rocks but slightly elevated above the level of the sea, though capable of serving as places of temporary refuge. The Danish word is *Skiær.—Trans.*

† The word *Hvarf* means *a place of turning,* a circumstance sufficing of itself to prove that it was not on the East coast that Erik settled.

expiration of which time he returned to Iceland, and made so favourable a report of the newly-discovered land, which he called Greenland, that, on his return thither the year following, no fewer than twenty-five vessels freighted with colonists accompanied him, of which number, meanwhile, but half eventually reached their destination, the rest either putting back, or perishing in the ice.

After the lapse of fourteen years from the date of Erik Raude's first settlement in Greenland, his son Leif *hin hepne* (i. e. the happy) went to Norway, where, by command of king Olaf Tryggvason, he was instructed in the principles of the Christian religion, and whence, the year after, he was sent back to Greenland by that monarch, attended by a priest, who baptized Erik and all his followers. After this, a number of other Icelanders went to Greenland, and the country by degrees was settled, wherever habitable. Of the character and aspect of the land, the old accounts extant are very various, and even contradictory. The description of it given in the Kong-Skugg-Siö (the Royal Mirror) is meanwhile, in all likelihood, the most to be depended on, and corresponds closely with what we know to be fact with regard to the West coast of Greenland. It is there stated, that the greater part of the country is covered with ice, but a small portion of it along the shore being habitable, and that grain could not grow there to maturity, so that the majority of the inhabitants had never seen it, or knew what bread was; but that, on the other hand, the country abounded in good pasturage, and the people subsisted by raising cattle, and by the chase of the rein-deer, bear, walrus, and seal. The population was estimated at about a third of the amount assigned a bishopric. The navigation to it is described as attended with much peril, from the seas about it being constantly blocked up with ice, for which reason, those who purpose sailing thither from Iceland, are advised to shape a course to the S.W. and W., until they passed the said ice, which is more abundant, it is stated, in the direction of N. and N.E. from the land, than to the South or West*. From the old chorographies† that have come down to us, we know that the inhabited districts were called, respectively, the East and West Bygd, and the uninhabitable tracts between them Ubygds ‡. The distance between these Bygds is differently given, Biörn Johnsen states it to have been a six-days' journey in a row-boat, which may be estimated at about 200 geographical miles; Ivar Bardsen, twelve *Vikur Siouar*, or twelve (Icelandic nautical) miles,

---

* This likewise serves to prove that the ancient colony was seated on the *West* coast of Greenland; for had it been upon the East, mention would scarcely have been made of ice in the West.

† Biörn Johnsen's *Greenland Annals*, and another from the fourteenth century, ascribed to Ivar Bardsen, of which afterwards.

‡ The word "Bygd" signifies *an inhabited place*, "Ubygd" *one that is uninhabitable*, or, at least, *uninhabited.*

—about seventy-two geographical miles. In the West Bygd were four churches, and ninety (or, according to others, 110) farms ; in the East Bygd, one cathedral, eleven churches, 190 farms, two towns (Garda and Alba), three royal demesnes (Foss, Tiodhillstadr, and Brattahlid, where the *Lagmand*, or justiciary, resided), and three or four monasteries, in the grounds of one of which (the monastery of St. Thomas) is said to have been a spring of boiling water, which, by means of pipes, was conducted into all the chambers of the building, as well as to the gardens, making these last so fertile as to yield the most delightful fruits and flowers. It is, meanwhile, to be observed, that neither Alba nor the monastery of St. Thomas are spoken of in the old Icelandic writings,—a fact which justifies the inference, that they existed but in the fictions of the fourteenth century. This Bygd had, further, a south-western aspect, and its southernmost point was Herjolf's-naze, situate between Hvarf and Hvidsœrk, which probably were two promontories.

One of the first achievements of the Greenland colonists was the discovery of North America by Leif in the year 1001. The tracts of country there discovered were called Helluland, Mark-land, and Viinland; great uncertainty, however, prevails with regard to their situation, Viinland being, in fact, the only one of them concerning which we have any positive information, it being susceptible of proof that it formed part of the present territory of the United States*.

Leif's grandson, Sokke, having summoned his countrymen to-gether at a place called Brattahlid, and represented to them that regard to their own credit, as well as to religion, required that the country should be provided with a bishop of its own, his propo-sition met with unanimous assent, and in compliance with the general wish, a learned priest, named Arnold, was, in 1121, elected, and, by the archbishop of Lund, consecrated first bishop of Greenland. A number of distinguished individuals, Icelanders and Norwegians, accompanied him to his diocese. One of them, named Asbiörn, was driven by a storm to the uninhabited parts of the coast, and none knew what had become of him, until a Greenlander, by name Sigurd, came by accident to the spot, and found two ships,—one a total wreck, the other susceptible of repair, with a quantity of goods in it, and, hard by, a house filled with dead bodies. The latter vessel he caused to be repaired, and con-veyed it to the bishop, who made a present of it to the church, giving the goods to Sigurd. Some time after, one Aussur, a

* It is stated by one of the ancient writers, that there was a more equal division of day and night in Viinland than in Iceland or Greenland, the sun being above the horizon there, upon the shortest day, from *Dagmaal* to *Eikt*. Now, as we know that by *Dagmaal* was formerly meant half-past seven o'clock A.M., and by *Eikt* half-past four o'clock P.M., it follows that the length of the shortest day at Viinland was nine hours, which gives the latitude of 41°.

4 INTRODUCTION.

nephew of the unfortunate Asbiörn, came to Greenland, and demanded restitution of his uncle's property, which being refused him, he privily did such damage to the vessel as rendered it unfit for use, and departed to another place, where he prevailed upon the crews of two Norwegian ships that he fell in with to espouse his cause, and aid him to take vengeance for the wrongs he conceived himself to have sustained. Accompanied by his new allies, he returned accordingly to Gardar, the residence of the bishop, but was not long there before he was murdered by Einar, Sokke's son, on whom the bishop, in the mean while, had inflicted punishment, in consequence of his having suffered, contrary to his oath, the property of the church (the ship in question) to be injured. Aussur's partisans immediately avenged his death by slaying Einar, upon which a battle was fought between the Greenlanders and Norwegians, and many fell on either side. The aged Sokke, Einar's father, was desirous of prosecuting the feud, and attacking with his followers the Norwegian ships; he was, however, prevailed upon to enter into compromise with the slayers of his son,—he submitting to pay a mulct to Aussur's party, the number of their slain exceeding by one that of his own, and they agreeing to quit the country without delay, and never to return to it. The story presents a curious picture of the state of society in Greenland in those days.

Of the history of the Greenland colonies subsequently to this period we have no regular, continuous accounts*. The country was governed by Icelandic laws, and had its own bishops (Holberg numbers seventeen of them, from first to last) who were suffragans, at first of the archbishop of Lund, but subsequently of the archbishop of Trondhiem. It had, it would appear, no military force, nor any trade, except, perhaps, in the beginning, in bottoms of its own. It is, indeed, on record, that one Asmund Kastrandatzi came to Iceland, in 1189, in a vessel whose planks and timbers were fastened and lashed together with pegs and the sinews of animals,—that is to say, in a vessel built in Greenland. He perished, however, on his way back, the following year. In 1349, or, as others say, 1379, when Alf was bishop, a sudden descent was made on the West Bygd by the Esquimaux, or, as the Icelanders called them, Skrællings, the aborigines of the country, who, it is related, killed eighteen Greenlanders of the Icelandic race, and carried away two boys captive. As soon as intelligence of the event had reached the East Bygd, Ivar Bere, or Bardsen, who is believed to have officiated as lay-superintendent of the diocese, was sent with succours to the sister colony. He found, however, on arriving there, not a human being left, but merely a

* All the accounts extant concerning Greenland, with much new matter, will be found embodied in Professors Magnussen and Rafn's work, "The Historical Monuments of Greenland," now in the press.

few cattle, which he took on board of his vessels, and sailed home with; and with this concludes all that has been handed down to us relative to the West Bygd.

With regard to the other, or East Bygd, we know that intercourse with it was kept up until towards the close of the fourteenth century, though the colony may not have been visited regularly every year, which it is evident, indeed, it was not, from the instructions given to the bishop Hendrick, on proceeding thither in 1388, to deposit the proceeds of the royal taxes, collected in the years when no vessel from the mother-country came to Greenland, at a given place.

The last bishop, or *officialis*, was, according to Torfæus, Andreas (properly Endride Andreason). He received his appointment in the year 1406, but whether he ever went to Greenland, or not, has been a matter of great uncertainty, until very lately, when Professor Finn Magnussen discovered authentic proof of his having actually officiated there, three years afterwards, at a marriage, from which the professor himself, and several other learned Icelanders, deduce their pedigree. From this date, however, all intercourse with Greenland ceased, the cause of which was, probably, Queen Margaret and King Erik's having laid a prohibition on its trade, which was considered a royal monopoly, and the proceeds devoted to the maintenance of the royal household, and of their successors being prevented from prosecuting it themselves by the wars in which they were perpetually involved. There is meanwhile one document extant, which throws some light upon the subsequent fate of the abandoned colonists; a letter of Pope Nicholas the Fifth to the bishops of Skalholt and Holum, discovered by Professor Mallet, some few years since, in the Papal Archives. I am induced to transcribe it here, by reason as well of its being little known, notwithstanding its having frequently appeared in print, as of its importance to the matter here in hand. The etter is dated in 1448, and (as given by Paul Egede) runs thus :—

" In regard to my beloved children born in, and inhabiting the island of Greenland, which is said to be situate at the farthest limits of the Great Ocean, north of the kingdom of Norway, and in the see of Trondhiem, their pitiable complaints have reached our ears, and awakened our compassion, seeing that they have, for a period of near six hundred years[*], maintained, in firm and inviolate subjection to the authority and ordinances of the Apostolic Chair, the Christian faith established among them by the preaching of their renowned teacher King Olaf, as well as, actuated

[*] Were this correct, the inhabitants of Greenland must have been Christians as early as the year 848; but, in point of fact, Christianity was not introduced by King Olaf into Norway itself until towards the close of the tenth century. It is, meanwhile, remarkable enough that there is a papal bull extant, in which the Greenlanders are mentioned as having been Christians ever since the year 835. Its authenticity on this point, however, is questioned by many.

by a pious zeal for the interests of religion, erected many churches, and, among others, a cathedral, in that island, where religious service was diligently performed, until, about thirty years ago, some heathen foreigners from the neighbouring coasts came against them with a fleet, fell upon them furiously, laid waste the country and its holy buildings with fire and sword, sparing nothing, throughout the whole island of Greenland, but the small parishes, said to be situated a long way off, and which they were prevented from reaching by the mountains and precipices intervening, and carried away into captivity the wretched inhabitants of both sexes, particularly such of them as they considered to be strong of body, and able to endure the labours of perpetual slavery; and whereas, as their complaints inform us further, many of them have, in lapse of time, returned from said captivity, and having, here and there, restored the desolated places, are desirous of re-establishing the worship of God upon its ancient footing, but, by reason of the cala- mities suffered by them as aforesaid, have found it hitherto impos- sible to do so, they, so far from being able to provide for the maintenance of clerical and secular authorities, being themselves in want of the absolute necessaries of life, so that, during this whole period of thirty years, they have been without the consola- tion of a bishop's presence, and without the service of priests, save when, in their longing after divine worship, they have undertaken tedious journeys to the settlements which the fury of the barbarians had spared: whereas we have cognizance of all this, we do empower and command you, brethren, being, as we are informed, the bishops whose sees are nearest the said island, after consulting with your metropolitan, if the distance between you and him permit, to nominate and send to them some fit and proper person as their bishop."

It appears from this document, that a hostile fleet made a descent upon the colony about the year 1418, and that the in- vaders killed or carried off into captivity a number of the inha- bitants, and laid waste their buildings; but also, on the other hand, that some parishes escaped their fury, and that many of those made captive subsequently returned home. What became eventually of this remnant of the colony is to us a mystery; probably they were either fallen upon and exterminated, like their brethren of the West Bygd, by the Skrællings, or, as an ancient book expresses it,—"When their priests and bishops died, and were succeeded by no new ones, they lost what little knowledge they once possessed of God's word:"—that is, they became heathens, and adopted the manners and customs of the Esqui- maux; or, perhaps, they may have quitted the country when they perceived that none cared more to trade with them, for without trade it was impossible for them to exist there, as we learn from the Kong-Skugg-Siö, which says—"All that is necessary to the support and maintenance of the colony they are obliged to buy from other countries, both iron and tar, and the timber with which to build their houses."

The fleet of which the above missive of Pope Nicholas makes mention, is conjectured by Eggers to have been that of a warlike prince named Zichmni; but it is a very doubtful matter, if such a person as Zichmni ever existed, and, if he did, his history closed with the year 1394. I will venture, in lieu of this, to substitute another hypothesis. It seems to have been customary in England, whenever that country was ravaged by the pestilence called *the black death*, to carry off (for the purpose, probably, of supplying the loss of population) the inhabitants of those countries of the North that it had spared. Complaints against this procedure are known to have been made repeatedly in the reigns of Margaret and her successor; and, in the year 1433, a treaty was concluded between Denmark and England, wherein it was expressly stipulated, that " with regard to all those persons who have been carried away forcibly from Iceland, Finmark, Helgeland, and other places, and are still detained in his dominions, his Majesty of England shall take measures to the end that they may be set at liberty, receive payment for their services, and return to their homes, whereof proclamation shall be made throughout all England within a year and a day from the date of this instrument." Now, as the above letter of Pope Nicholas to the Icelandic bishops states that many of the individuals carried away from Greenland into captivity, had actually returned, it is a very natural inference that this may have happened in consequence of the very treaty here referred to, in which case the hostile fleet spoken of must have been an English one. What tends to confirm me in this opinion is, that Pope Eugenius the Fourth did, in this very year 1433, nominate one Bartholomew bishop of Greenland.

A long time now elapsed, during which Greenland would seem to have been totally forgotten. The attention of the celebrated Archbishop Walckendorff was, however, at length attracted to it. He collected all the ancient accounts concerning it, consulted the oldest of his contemporaries as to what they remembered to have heard about the trade to Greenland (for there then lived none who had been there themselves), drew up a chart for the use of mariners navigating those seas, and submitted to the government a proposition for the re-discovery of the lost colony, and the re-establishment of trade with it, offering to bear the expenses of the enterprise, on condition of enjoying a monopoly of the trade for ten years. It is not unlikely that his proposition would have been adopted, and the certainty been long ago arrived at,—that there never was, in fact, a colony settled on the East coast, had he not incurred the enmity of the then all-powerful Sigbrit. He fell, however, into disgrace, and died at Rome. It is principally on the information compiled by him that their opinion rests, who have placed, not only the East Bygd, but the West Bygd likewise, on the East coast of Greenland, an opinion entertained by Walckendorff himself, and which it was very natural that he and his contemporaries should entertain, as Davis' Straits were not as yet discovered, and as they had a very false idea of the configuration of the land, concerning which, in fact, they knew but little more than that it was the land nearest Iceland to the West, and that Erik Raude, when he discovered it, had sailed from Iceland in that direction.

Christian the Third repealed the law interdicting trade with Greenland, and despatched several ships in quest of it, but without success. During the reign of Frederick the Second, in the year 1578, one Mogens Heinson, or Henningson, was sent out with the same intent. He came in sight of the East coast of Greenland, but failing, though he held on for a considerable time, and had even the benefit of a favourable wind, to draw nearer to it, he was seized with a panic, and returned home, giving out that a magnet, hid in the depths of ocean, had hindered his further progress. He would have gone nearer the mark had he laid the blame on the current. Another expedition, despatched by the same monarch, is said to have actually reached its destination, but this is all we know concerning it.

It would have been strange had so patriotic a monarch as Christian the Fourth neglected to do his part towards the rediscovery of Greenland. He despatched, accordingly, in 1605, Admiral Godske Lindenow, in command of three ships, to perform this duty. One of these vessels had been intrusted to one James Hall, an Englishman, who, separating from his consorts on the way, steered for Davis' Straits, "South-west from Iceland," says Holberg, "like the Icelanders of old." Lindenow, on the contrary, steered for the East coast. When he drew near the land, the natives came on board his ships, and gave bear and seal-skins in exchange for articles of steel and iron. He did not, however, set foot on shore, but, after a delay of three days, weighed anchor and put to sea, carrying off with him two of the natives, a procedure which so enraged the rest, that they bombarded the vessel, as she sailed away, with stones and arrows. In what latitude it was that Lindenow thus reached the coast, we know not. Hall, in the mean while, had landed on the West coast, and seized there four of the natives, who, however, made so desperate a resistance, that he found it necessary to put one of them to death, in order to intimidate the rest, who thereupon quietly submitted to be conveyed on board. Their countrymen, meanwhile, assembled about the ship, apparently with the intent of preventing its departure. They were dispersed, however, by a discharge of musketry and cannon, and the ship sailed with the three captives. It is stated, and if true is a remarkable fact, that they bore no resemblance in manners, dress, or language, to those whom Lindenow brought home with him.

The following year Lindenow once more set out, with five ships under his command, taking with him the three natives whom Hall had kidnapped at Davis' Straits,—a circumstance from which we may infer that there seemed more likelihood of discovering traces of the lost colony in the vicinity of the country whence they came than where he himself had seized his prisoners. Lindenow, indeed, steered on this occasion straight for Davis' Straits, without attempting to make the East coast. Four of his vessels reached their destination ; but the natives showed signs of hostility, and seemed determined to prevent his landing, and he was not inhuman enough to make use of his cannon to their destruction. One only of his people obtained permission to go on shore. He had hoped by means of presents to conciliate the natives; but scarcely had he set foot on shore, when they rushed upon him, and cut him to pieces with their knives made of the horn of the narwhal. Lindenow, on this, returned to Denmark, without having accomplished the object of his mission.

Notwithstanding the failure of these attempts, the king was unwilling to relinquish the hope of re-discovering the colony, and commissioned, therefore, Carsten Rikardsen, in 1607, to make a third attempt. It is not known to which side of Greenland Rikardsen directed his course. Certain it is, however, that he reached it no where, the ice, which stretched many miles out to sea, effectually barring his approach.

The object of Jens Munk's expedition, in 1619, was, strictly, the discovery of a North-West Passage. He appears, however, to have touched at Greenland, and to have communicated with its natives ; for it is stated that, in the fervour of their gratitude, they fell on their knees to his crew, and kissed and embraced one of his sailors who had black hair and a flat nose like themselves,—a mode of expressing gratitude, however, which is by no means characteristic of the Greenlanders. The strait to which Munk, on this occasion, gave the name of Christian's Sound was probably that which divides the island of Sermesok from the mainland. His wintering at Hudson's Bay is described as terrible. His people were attacked by scurvy, and the entire crews of both his vessels (sixty-four in number) perished miserably, two only excepted, with whom he returned home the following year. Another expedition with which Munk was charged was not eventually carried into effect, as, after taking leave of the king, he suddenly fell ill, and died*. In 1636, the Chancellor Früs, having

---

* It is said that the king had, on this occasion, reproached him with his conduct on his former voyage, and, on his replying somewhat too boldly, struck him with his cane ; an indignity which Munk took so much to heart, that he actually died in consequence.

been informed that some English mariners had discovered gold in Greenland, sent two vessels thither for the purpose of ascertaining the truth of the report. They returned with some specimens of iron pyrites, thus verifying the proverb which asserts that " all is not gold that glisters."

The voyages of David Danel, in the reign of Frederick the Third, are of importance, not as throwing any light whatever on the site of the old colonies, but as furnishing some data relative to the East coast. They were made under the auspices of the intendant of finance Möller, who had obtained the exclusive privilege of fitting out expeditions in quest of the old colonies, and a monopoly of their trade, if found, for thirty years, a privilege, however, which, as it yielded him no profit, he relinquished at the expiration of three. The first of these voyages took place in 1652. Danel sailed on this occasion North about Iceland, and, on the 2nd of June, discovered a part of the East coast of Greenland, which he took to be the Herjolf's-naze mentioned in the old accounts of the East Bygd, and, the day after, in lat. 64° 50′, two islands, which he named the White Saddle (*Hvid-Sadlen*)*, and the Dismasted Ship. Up to the 15th he kept the East coast constantly in sight, distant from about eight to sixty miles; but as the ice prevented him from getting nearer to it, he determined on running into Davis' Straits, where, at several points, he met, and traded, with the natives. A promontory in lat. 67° received from him the name of Cape Queen Amelia, as another on the East coast, in lat. 65½°, had previously that of Cape King Frederick. On his way home Danel again attempted to reached the East coast. On the 23rd of July he discovered a fiord in about lat. 61°, and the ship's log states that "they would have run into it the next day, the sea along the shore being free of ice, had not the night closed in so suddenly†." Subsequently they came to within four miles' distance of the shore, but without being able to effect a landing.

The year following Danel set sail once more, and proceeded, in the first place, as far north as lat. 73°, in pursuit, probably, of the whale fishery. From thence he sailed West round Iceland, and came, at several points, in sight of the East coast of Greenland, but, on account of the ice, was unable to get near it. His last voyage, which took place in 1654, was only to Davis' Straits,

---

* In a MS. of the year 1688 which Professor Finn Magnussen has discovered in the Arne-Magnæan collection, occurs, among other views of the East coast, one of this island, which there is called *Huid's-adel*. The MS. treats exclusively of Greenland, and is the work of one Henry Schacht. It is not unlikely that, by this island, Danel may have meant the *Hvidsærk* of the ancients.

† There is some mystery about this entry in Danel's journal which we cannot penetrate ; for, first, it appears from the same log that the vessel, the day previous, was still a long way from the land ; and, secondly, there is no night in lat. 61° upon the 22d of June, or, at least, no darkness sufficient to have prevented her running in.

then called by our navigators *Fretum Daniæ*, as Cape Farewell was called Cape Prince Christian; and on this occasion he took away with him, on his return, three Greenland women, a circumstance still fresh in the recollection of the natives when the first missionaries came among them, seventy years afterwards.

Like his predecessors, Christian the Fifth despatched, in 1670, an expedition in quest of the East Bygd, an expedition of which, however, we know nothing more than its date, and the name of its commander, Otto Axelsen. It is probable that he likewise went to the *Fretum Daniæ*, for we find that a ship was fitted out four years afterwards, for the purpose of taking possession of the country there, and founding a colony. The ship, however, was captured by privateers, and the plan abandoned.

For many years after this, Greenland appears to have been totally forgotten. At length, the attention of Hans Egede, minister of Vaagen and Gimsöe in Norway, was directed to this subject, and from that moment dates a new era in the annals of Greenland. This remarkable man conceived the project of going himself to Greenland to seek for traces of the vanished colonies, and diffuse the light of religion among its natives. Regardless of ridicule and slander, he advanced steadily towards his object; and, after wasting eight years in vain endeavours to attain it by means of memorial and petition, he actually resigned his living, and went to Copenhagen, where he pleaded his cause so eloquently and effectually, that King Frederick the Fourth resolved on establishing a colony in Greenland, and appointed Egede its priest and missionary. On the 3rd of May, 1721, Egede sailed from Bergen, and, after a perilous voyage of eight weeks, arrived at an island off the West coast of Greenland, in lat. 64°. which he called Hope's Island, and where he planted the first colony,—that of Good Hope. His judicious conduct gained him speedily the confidence of the natives, and to promote their welfare became the end and aim of his endeavours, though he perceived at once that they could not be descendants of the Europeans, who, some three hundred years before, had inhabited the country. To discover traces of these, he determined on visiting the East coast, and actually set out with that intent upon the 9th of August, 1723, in two barges. As he had not been able, however, to provide himself with sufficient necessaries for such an expedition, he was obliged, on reaching the island of Sermesok, in lat. 60° 20′, to put back*. Between the 60th and 61st degrees of latitude, at a place called Kakortok, now in the district of Juliana's-hope, he discovered a remarkable ruin, furnishing, like many others subsequently found, conclusive evidence that

---

* The southernmost promontory of this island I have named, in honour of him, Cape Egede. The native Greenlanders call it Kangek, a name they apply to almost all high headlands.

the Icelanders had formerly been settled there. All these remains, however, were held to be vestiges of the West Bygd, which itself had, until then, been assigned a place on the East coast,—an error which served more than ever to confirm men in the belief that the more important East Bygd was to be looked for in that direction. The ships, accordingly, which, after this period, annually sailed to Greenland, often received orders to attempt a landing on the East coast. As none of them, however, succeeded in accomplishing this object, or even in approaching the shore, but within a very considerable distance, a new plan was devised for attaining it. A Major Paars, to wit, and a Captain Landorf, who were sent to Greenland in 1728, the former in quality of governor, the latter of commandant of a fort to be erected there, were ordered to ride across the country on horseback from the West coast to the East. As the country was found, however, to be covered with ice, intersected with chasms and precipices, they made, as may be supposed, but little progress. Egede remained in Greenland fourteen years, labouring with indefatigable zeal to enlighten its rude natives, and improve its trade. He then resigned his important functions into the hands of his son Paul Egede, and returned to Denmark to watch over its interests. To him is due the honour of Greenland's new colonization [*].

I have to make mention still of two other important expeditions, —those of Peter Olsen Vallöe, in 1752, and of Egede and Rothe in 1786 and 1787. Olsen set out from the colony of Frederick's-hope in a Greenland skin, or women's-boat, in company with four other Europeans. He sailed close along the coast towards the South, explored several of the fiords in the now district of Juliana's-hope, a part of the country then as yet unoccupied by Europeans, and has given a description of some of the many ruins to be there met with, dating from the time of the old Icelandic colonists. On the approach of winter he built himself a hut somewhere in the neighbourhood of the fiord of Agluitsok, and the next year continued his voyage past Cape Farewell, the southernmost point of Greenland. On the 6th of July he found himself off the East coast, but his progress now became much impeded by the ice, for which reason, as well as on account of his store of provisions being insufficient for another winter, and the

---

[*] There are, at present, on the West Coast of Greenland thirteen colonies, fifteen minor commercial, and ten missionary establishments, four of which (New Herrnhut, Lichtenfels, Lichtenau, and Friederichsthal) belong to the Moravians. The colonies are, in the Northern Inspectorate, Uppernavik, Omenak, Rittenbank, Jacob's-haven, Christian's-hope, Egede's-minde, and Good-haven ; in the Southern Inspectorate, Holsteinsborg, Sugar-loaf, Good-hope, Fisher-naze, Frederick's-hope, and Juliana's-hope. The European inhabitants amount to about 150, and the whole population is estimated at 6000 souls. The trade gives employment to five or six vessels, which visit the colonies annually.

refusal of his companions to proceed further, he put back upon the 8th of August, having got as far as a place called Nennese, in lat. 60° 28′. Olsen was thus the first European whom we know to have set foot on the southern shores of the East coast of Greenland; but, with regard to the main object in view, his expedition, after all, was productive of no results, for he did not penetrate as far North as where the Bygd was supposed to have been situate *.

The expeditions of Lövenörn, and of Egede and Rothe, are of such modern date (1786 and 1787) as to be still fresh in the recollection of all. I shall, therefore, but observe, with regard to them, that the last-mentioned was one of the boldest and most successful upon record, they having, on one occasion, got as near as within ten miles of the shore. Had it not chanced that the ice was more than usually abundant at the time, a landing would, in all likelihood, have been effected. For the rest, I must refer to the published accounts of these voyages†.

Not more successful than our Danish navigators, were the foreigners, Davis, Hudson, and others, who attempted the solution of this problem. Even Scoresby's voyage, which, some years ago, attracted so much notice, does not lie without the scope of this remark; for, although he did succeed in landing at several points of the East coast, he did so at a much higher latitude than where the ancient colonies were to be looked for, and at points where, it is probable, a landing might in most years be effected. In fact, long before his time, the portion of the East coast between 70° and 75° latitude had been visited by Danish, Dutch, and English whalers. His merit consists in having furnished an interesting account of this part of the coast, and a more authentic chart of it than any we before possessed, though he, unquestionably, is in error, where he asserts that, by keeping close in shore, one may sail along the whole East coast from lat. 70° to Cape Farewell. Danel's, Olsen's, and Egede and Rothe's expeditions, prove the fallacy of this opinion.

Nor is it only travellers and navigators that have failed in their attempts to ascertain the site of the East Bygd. The speculations of the various writers that have made it the subject of their inquiry, have been to the full as unsatisfactory. Walckendorff, as has before been noticed, assigned it to the East coast, on the strength of its being recorded, in the account of Erik Raude's voyage, that he sailed from Iceland *to the West* (a course which, of necessity, must have brought him to the East coast). But he took no notice of what the said account goes on to state, that

* The voyage of Peter Olsen was published by Otto Fabricius, and may be read in " Samleren," a Danish periodical, for the year 1787, Nos. 7—18.

† Account of Egede's Voyage. Copenhagen, 1788.—*Extrait de la Relation d'un Voyage pour la Découverte de Groenlande.* Paris, 1823.

Erik, having made the land, *coasted along it in the direction of South*, and *sailed West about the promontory of Hvarf.* These words, indeed, could not but be a mystery to Walckendorff and his contemporaries, who neither were acquainted with the true situation of Cape Farewell, nor knew that the land stretches away again from thence towards the North,—in other words, who were ignorant that there actually was a point at which the prosecution of Erik's voyage in the direction indicated, was possible. Sigvard Stephensen (1574) and Gudbrand Thorlaksen (1606), two learned Icelanders, held that the Bygd was situated on the West coast; later Icelandic authors, on the contrary, such as Arngrim, Johnsen, Thordr Thorlaksen, and Thormod Torfesen, espoused Walckendorff's hypothesis. Of the writers of our own day who have treated this matter, Eggers* (1793) has defended the opinion of Gudbrand, Wormskiold† (1814) that of the others; none of them, however, have succeeded in proving satisfactorily where the East Bygd lay, and the question has continued involved in as much mystery as in the time of Walckendorff,—nay, while some have persisted in the belief that traces of it must be discoverable on the East coast, others have doubted if an East Bygd ever existed at all‡.

Our gracious monarch, who, even when Crown Prince, had devoted some attention to this matter, participated in the interest felt for it by the nation at large, and as soon as the termination of the late disastrous war gave to our beloved country the promise of better days, his Majesty resolved on fitting out an expedition to the East coast of Greenland. A variety of circumstances, meanwhile, retarded the execution of this design until the year 1827, when the king appointed a commission, under the presidency of Count Moltke of Bregentved, to take into consideration the means best calculated to effect his purpose. A coasting voyage in Greenland boats, like that of Olsen formerly, was judged to be the most likely to lead to the results desired, and, at the recommendation of the commissioners, was decided on by his Majesty, who was graciously pleased to appoint me to the command of the expedition. Mr. Vahl, a

---

* Prize-Essay on the true site of the East Bygd, Copenhagen, 1793. Vide also *Transactions of the Agricultural Society*, Vol. IV.

† Vide *Transactions of the Scandinavian Literary Society* for 1814.

‡ The fact is, the old accounts that have come down to us are both contradictory, and not altogether unadulterated, so that little or no reliance can be placed on them; and of none of them is this more true than of Walckendorff's compilations, which embody sailing-directions and statements of distances, from Iceland to Greenland, put together on authority which is not even named (it being merely stated at one place that they are given as communicated orally by Ivar Bardsen), and published one hundred years after all communication with Greenland had ceased. To accounts like these, the *Landnama-book* would be much to be preferred, it having been completed in the thirteenth century, when the intercourse with Greenland was still in full activity, were it not that the different copies of this book are themselves at variance.

gentleman of indefatigable assiduity and known scientific acquire-
ments, who had already made several botanical excursions in
various parts of Europe, was attached to it in quality of naturalist,
as were likewise an individual in the employ of the Greenland
board as interpreter, and a sailor as cook. The voyage, it was
determined, should be made in two "women's-boats," manned by
natives, male and female; and the 69th degree of latitude was
fixed upon as the extreme northern limit of the expedition, unless,
before reaching it, I should happen to fall in with vestiges of
ancient colonization, in which case I was directed to turn back on
getting to the 67th, in order that I might have more time to
devote to their investigation. That my actual progress North fell
short of this limit will be seen in the sequel, but I trust it will be
likewise seen that my failing to reach it is attributable to no fault
of mine. When I undertook the honourable charge intrusted to
me, I did so with the determination of fulfilling it at whatever cost
or peril; nor have I reason to complain of the result;—I entertain,
in short, the hope that my expedition will not have been in vain,
though I well know there are those who still will not abandon the
opinion, that the ancient colony of the East Bygd, or its remains,
at any rate, is to be found on the East coast, where certainly I
failed to find it.

Captain Zahrtmann, Hydrographer to the Royal Navy, and
member of the commission appointed to superintend my expedition, supplied me with a suitable assortment of nautical
and other instruments, in part his private property, and with two
chronometers, one the property of the Admiralty, the other of
Count Moltke; as also, for the use of Mr. Vahl, with the usual
meteorological instruments, a barometer for the measurement of
heights, a microscope, &c. Of these instruments, all that I took
with me on my excursion to the East coast, were a chronometer,
a sextant, an artificial horizon, and a good azimuth compass, the
nature of the service rendering it advisable not to risk the larger
and more costly ones.

With regard to the map, the northern part of the West coast, all
that portion of it, namely, comprised between latitudes $68\frac{1}{2}°$ and $73°$,
is laid down as surveyed by myself in the years 1823 and 1824, and
that between $62°$ and Cape Farewell, as surveyed by me in 1831.
I cannot answer for the accuracy of this map in all its details, as it
was got up in a tenth part of the time necessary to a work of the
kind. Still, as I had opportunities of taking a number of good
observations of latitude, as well as, by means of my chronometer,
of longitude, and of determining trigonometrically a good many
points, I am confident that no very material errors will be found
in it, except, perhaps, in the interior of the different firths, and
along that portion of the coast lying between Sermelik and
Sevinganersoak, where I have not been in person. The longi-

tude of the colony of Juliana's-hope was deduced from the observation of the occultation of a fixed star, also observed by Professor Schumacher in Altona, who had the kindness to have the observation calculated under his own superintendence. The East coast, in like manner, as far as 65½° north latitude, is laid down as observed by myself. For all North of this point, I am indebted to Captain Scoresby. The rest of the coast of Greenland, from Frederick's-hope to Egede's-minde, has been made up chiefly from Giesecke's Journal, kept by him during his various journeys in that part of the country between the years 1807 and 1813; the geographical position of some of its main points being given as determined by Ginge, Ross, Pickersgill, Egede, and the old Dutch navigators. The whole was compiled and executed at the Royal Hydrographical Office.

VOYAGE TO GREENLAND.

1828.

On Sunday, the 30th of March, the brig Whale, belonging to the Greenland Board of Trade, in which it had been arranged that I should take passage for Greenland, was ready to put to sea ; but, on account of a thick fog, the pilot decided on not weighing anchor. At two o'clock the following day the weather cleared up, and a light breeze from the S.E. springing up, we got our anchor up, waved our friends one more farewell, and speedily lost sight of the spires of Copenhagen. Besides Mr. Vahl and myself, Dr. Pingel, who intended visiting Greenland for the purpose of making geological researches, but was not attached to the expedition, was on board. We anchored in the evening in the roads of Elsinore, in six fathom water. Shortly after, the guardship arrived, and took her station.

On the 1st of April we had calms, and light baffling breezes, which preventing our departure, I took the opportunity of making some experiments on the effect of the local attraction on the compass. By the binnacle compass the maximum of deviation was but 3° with the ship's head at East or West. On the starboard gangway it was easterly, with the ship's head on the several points of the compass from S.E., through S., to N.W., maximum at S.W. 8°; westerly, with the ship's head at the several points from N.W., through N., to S.E., at N.E. about 8°. On the larboard gangway it was found to be westerly, with the ship's head on the several points from S.W., through W., to N.E., maximum 5°, at N.W.; easterly, with the ship's head at the several points from N.E., through E., to S.W., maximum 5°, at S.E. On the starboard side there was no deviation, with the ship's head at S.E., or N.W.; on the larboard none, with her head at S.W., or N.E.

From the 2d to the 7th the weather was raw and cold, the thermometer at between 2° and 5° below the freezing-point, and the winds variable between W. and N.E., accompanied with snow and hail. The ship's bows were completely covered with ice, and icicles hung from the rigging as in the depth of winter.

On the morning of the 8th, as the weather promised to be fair, I went on shore for the purpose of taking an observation, by which to rectify our time-keepers, whose rates of going we found, by daily comparison, to have changed since they were brought on board. I have, indeed, remarked, that this is generally the case, in a greater or less degree, with all time-keepers, on being brought on

C

board ship from ashore, or the reverse. The change, however, seldom lasts longer than from six to eight days, after which they commonly resume their former rates. The barometer rose this evening considerably above the point it had been stationary at for some time past, and led us to hope that the westerly winds, so long prevalent, would be soon succeeded by an easterly breeze.

On the 9th, at three o'clock A.M., we weighed anchor, with a light breeze at E.S.E., and at six passed Cronberg, at the head of a fleet of one hundred sail, which, in the course of the last eight days, had collected in the roads of Elsinore. Towards evening it blew fresh from the E., and at midnight we saw the light of Anholt.

On the 10th, at half an hour after noon, being in lat. 57° 39', N., and long. 1° 24' W. of Copenhagen*, we were surprised by the occurrence of a singular accident, the card of the binnacle compass making, without apparent cause, several revolutions. At the distance of four feet and a half from the compass lay, upon a bench, a small azimuth compass; but this could not have been instrumental in producing the result adverted to, for, before it was placed there, I had ascertained that, even when brought within half that distance, it had not the least effect upon the binnacle compass. We repeated the experiment indeed afterwards, and found that it could be brought to within a foot and a half of the compass, without sensibly affecting it. Two *Jan van Genters*† flew past us to-day towards the east. It is, I believe, very seldom that any of these birds are met with in our seas. Off the Shetland and Orkney Islands they are found in great numbers, sometimes sleeping on the waves, so that they may be approached in a boat, and taken alive. At four, P.M., we saw the Skaw lighthouse, bearing S. 30° W., distant five miles and a half. Shortly after, as we were taking a last look at our native shores, now vanishing in the distance, a sudden flaw of wind threw the ship considerably over, and obliged us to take in our top-gallant and studding-sails. I encountered a similar, but much more violent squall, once before, in 1820, on my first voyage to Iceland, in company with my friends, Lieutenants Holsten, Rathsack, and Scholten. It was a fine warm day of July, and we were about sixty miles distant N.W. from Lambanaze, in Shetland, steering from the Faroe islands, with a light breeze at S. I was in the cabin, employed in looking over some observations, when suddenly the ship was thrown on her beam-ends, and a noise was heard that made us think the boom had been carried away. We sprang on deck immediately, and found both topmasts gone; but the weather was fair, and the sky cloudless, and the wind continued to blow from the same quarter as before. Dr. Thienemann and

---

* Copenhagen is in long. 12° 34' 53'' east of Greenwich, by Naut. Al. 1837, and in 12° 34' 57'', by General Schubert's account of his Chronometric Expedition round the Baltic.—*See Journ. Roy. Geog. Soc.* vol. vi.—ED.

† *Sula alba.* Solan goose, or gannet.—ED.

Mr. Gunther, two naturalists from Leipsic, who, like ourselves, were witnesses of this incident, make mention of it, in a work published by them some years after. They helped us to cut a couple of new topmasts (for we did it actually, for the most part, with knives,) out of some spare spars we chanced to have on board. On the morning of the 11th we descried the hills of Norway, but the weather being hazy we did not make out what part of the land it was, till we got sight of the beacon of Hellesöe and Lindersnaze, which last we passed shortly after noon. The wind freshened towards evening to a stiff breeze, veering, at the same time, to the South, and we scudded before it across the North Sea. At one, A.M., on the 13th, we altered our course and stood to the S.W., as the weather was so hazy that we could not expect to get sight of the Shetland lights, and as we had had no observation of latitude the day previous. At day-dawn we resumed our course, and shortly after saw land bearing N. ¼ W., which, according to our dead reckoning, ought to have been Fair Hill, but proved to be Sumborough Head. At nine, A.M., the lighthouse, said to be 290 feet above the level of the sea, bore N.N.E., distant six miles. Our dead reckoning placed us 25′ to the S. and 13′ to the W. of our true position. We passed in the afternoon an American brig, lying-to under a close-reefed main-topsail. She hailed us, and asked our longitude: but it is not likely that our answer was heard by those on board of her, as we did not pass very near. It is to be regretted, that civilized nations do not agree on adopting one common system of signals : its employment would be found, on many occasions, of essential service to navigators. The rapid fall of the barometer from 29·75, where it had been at noon, to 29·05, gave warning of an approaching gale. It came accordingly during the night, and the wind veering to W.N.W., obliged us to heave-to, with the ship's head at North.

On the 14th we had a close-reefed topsail gale, with heavy squalls from the W. Two small land-birds, not unlike the common wren, flew several times round us, and at last alighted on the deck. It often happens that land-birds are met with in this way, at a distance from the shore of 150 or 200 miles, and upwards. Bewildered in the fogs, that are here so frequent, and exhausted by hunger and fatigue, they alight on the ships they fall in with, and readily submit to be taken, rather than encounter the certain death that awaits them in the waves, when their weary wings refuse their office. On my voyage to Greenland, in 1823, we caught in this way, at 160 miles' distance from Shetland, a sparrow-hawk, which for three weeks made himself quite at ease in his captivity, and seemed very well satisfied with ship's fare. On our throwing him, however, one day a half-dead mallemoke*, he flew upon it, and devoured it

* *Procellaria glacialis.* The fulmar,—a species of petrel, about the size and colour of a common sea-gull. —ED.

c 2

with such voracity, that he died in about an hour afterwards. The weather clearing up towards evening, we saw a ship to leeward, distant about eight miles, which we took to be a whaler. The temperature this day was 53° Fahrenheit, being considerably higher than it had been hitherto.

On the 15th at day-break, a sail was seen astern, which we at first believed to be the same that we had taken for a whaler the night before: she proved, however, to be an American, steering W. by S. The mallemokes, those constant attendants on whalers, surrounded us to-day for the first time.

On the 16th we passed a brig, belonging, as we judged, to the Hudson's Bay Company. A large land-bird flew several times round and round the ship. Some of us took it to be an eagle, others an owl.

On the 17th, we being then near Alof Cramer's banks, the temperature of the sea was found to be 48° Fahrenheit, or 1° less than on the preceding and following days.

On the 18th we fell in with, and hailed the ship Navigation, belonging to the Greenland Board, and bound for the colony of Frederick's-hope. The fair wind that had favoured us till now, appeared at length inclined to leave us. Towards noon, clouds began to collect in the W. and W.N.W., and we shortly after got a breeze from that quarter that speedily brought us under close-reefed topsails.

On the 24th, between one and two, A.M., we saw a splendid northern light, stretching through the zenith from W. to E.

On the 25th we passed what is laid down in the charts under the name of the Sunken-land-van-Buss, a danger made mention of even in the latest English Sailing Directions, but which mariners may be now assured is altogether an imaginary one. It is, by the way, remarkable enough, that precisely where this Sunken-land-van-Buss is thus laid down, the ancient charts place Frisland, that mysterious land which geographers have been so puzzled where to look for, and which but very lately has been ascertained to be no other than the Faroe islands. This very erroneous location of Frisland serves, in my opinion, to prove, that Zeno* was far from having that intimate and accurate knowledge of our Northern seas, which many give him credit for. In the evening vast shoals of porpoises played about the ship. This is held by some seamen to be a sign of blowing weather, and in the present instance would actually seem to have been so, for the wind began to freshen immediately after, and increased during the night to such a gale, that we were obliged to heave to, under a close-reefed trysail and fore-staysail. The gale continued till the 5th of May, when, towards noon, it suddenly died away. Mr. Vahl having, on its cessation, let down his thermometrograph, found the temperature

* The Venetian navigator of the fourteenth century.

of the sea, at the depth of 110 fathoms, to be 5°·50, while that at the surface was 6°·3, and the atmosphere's 8°·6. In the afternoon the wind shifted to the S., and we made 132 miles in the next twenty-four hours. A brilliant northern light was seen in the night of the 6th, and was succeeded, like that of the 24th of April, by gales from N.W. and W.N.W. The barometer stood both days at thirty inches, though the weather was squally, and it rained and hailed alternately.

On the 7th we fell in, for the first time, with one of those stupendous icebergs, so often met with in Davis' Straits and Hudson's Bay, and which originate, as is well known, from the glaciers that cover the greater part of the interior of Greenland. These vast floating mountains are usually met with under the meridian of Cape Farewell, occasionally much further out in the Atlantic, though I am not aware that any have been fallen in with, since 1817, E. of the Hook. That year, indeed, some were seen in lat. 40°, long. 32° (from Greenwich). It was in the same year also, that such unusual phenomena presented themselves in regard to the ice between Spitzbergen and Greenland, a body of field-ice, several thousand square miles in extent, which usually occupies a space north of Iceland, having suddenly disappeared, which circumstance it was that led to the expeditions of Ross, Buchan, Parry, Franklin, and Beechey, it being imagined that the sea would now be found navigable all the way to the Pole. Davis' Straits and Baffin's Bay, however, were, just that year, so completely blocked up with ice, from the coast of Greenland to that of America, as to be, for a considerable length of time, impracticable for navigators. On the 8th we passed some small drift-wood, of a sort of reddish pine.

On the 11th, 12th, 13th, and 14th, we had another hard gale from N.W. and N., during the first two days of which the barometer stood very high. From the 15th to the 18th we had baffling winds from N.E. to W.N.W.; the weather unsettled and stormy. On the 19th we found, by a lunar observation, the ship's position to be 3° 32' to the east of the dead reckoning. The error is probably to be attributed to the hard westerly gales we had had to contend with since the 20th of April, as well as to the current, which, in the parallel of 57°—58°, undoubtedly sets to the east, though both north and south of this limit it runs the opposite way. The latitude, by dead reckoning, was found to be almost every day from 5 to 10 minutes south of the latitude by observation. On the 21st we hailed the ship Sophia, from Copenhagen, bound for the colony of Egede's-minde in Greenland.

On the 22d we saw land bearing E.N.E. by compass, distant forty miles by estimation. We stood in, and speedily knew it, by its black sharp pinnacles and ice-clad ravines, to be the island of Sermesok.

On the morning of the 23d, the signal for ice was given by the

man at the mast-head; and a stream of it was shortly after seen to the
N., a second to the N.W , and a third, stretching along the shore,
from Sermesok towards the N.   It is this sort of ice that the
native Greenlanders call *the Great Ice**, on account of its thickness, which is seldom less than twenty feet, and often more ; and
it is frequently so closely packed, particularly in the vicinity of
land, as to form a barrier totally impenetrable by ships.   This ice
is constantly being carried by the current from the Polar Sea, along
the East coast of Greenland, and it is it that has rendered abortive
the many attempts made, from time to time, to land on the East
coast.   It sometimes occupied the whole extent of ocean between
Iceland and Greenland, which appears to have been the case in
1787, as well as between Greenland and America ; it often forms a
belt round Statenhook, or Cape Farewell, reaching from 120 to
160 miles out to sea, and frequently extends along the South-west
coast of Greenland, or the district of Juliana's-hope, making it
necessary for ships bound thither to seek a more northerly port,
and there await its breaking-up.   Sometimes, however, the sea
along this coast is perfectly open, so that ships are able to run
direct from sea into port.   Such was the case, for instance, in
1826, and 1827.   Some persons have been inclined to think, that
what I have here adverted to, with regard to the ice on the West
coast, obtains no less upon the East; that is to say, that there are
seasons when this coast, too, is free from ice ; in fact, that it might
be reached in most years from seawards, if those engaged in the
attempt would but have patience to await the breaking-up of the
ice.   To this opinion, however, I cannot subscribe ; for, not to
mention that the experience of 200 years proves the reverse to be
the fact, it seems evident, that there must always be a greater
accumulation of ice on the East coast than in Davis' Straits; first
because a good deal of it, on its way thither, (to Davis' Straits,)
dissolves and disappears; and next, because the westerly current is
constantly conveying more and more ice to the East coast, while
on the West, where the current sets *along* the shore, a very gentle
off-shore breeze suffices to remove it.

The vessels engaged in the Greenland trade are not calculated to
navigate icy seas, not being built, as whalers are, so as to be able
to endure a considerable pressure of ice.   They have, therefore,
when they fall in with it, no choice but to avoid it as well as they
can.   Captain Gram, who commanded the brig in which we sailed,
determined now, accordingly, on altering his course, and standing
to the S.W., by which means, after sailing a few hours through
" open ice," we got once more into " clear water."   An unusual
appearance of the sea attracted our attention in the afternoon.   We
observed, here and there upon its surface, spots of various sizes,
and even some well-defined currents, as it were, of a dirty yellowish-

* Heavy drift ice.

green, or sometimes straw colour. Some on board were of opinion, that this discoloration of the water was caused by the ice we were sailing through, and so powerful a hold did this idea take of their imagination, that they maintained the water, so discoloured, to be fresh, an opinion, whose fallacy, however, was speedily exposed, on appeal being made to the sense of taste, unbiassed by that of sight. In a drop of this water, seen through the microscope, some small yellowish, transparent animalcules were perceived; but the appearance of the water, adverted to, cannot be attributed to their presence, for they were found no less in the ordinary blueish-green sea-water.

On the 24th we once more changed our course and stood to the N.E., and passed in the course of the day some twenty icebergs, one of which resembled the ruins of an old gothic castle. It was the largest we had yet fallen in with; its height above water being estimated at 90, and its length at 500 feet. In the evening we came to a new stream of ice, which obliged us to stretch away to the west, and keep this course during the night. The whole of the next day we sailed through " open ice " along the edge of a pack. A vast number of seals (*Phoca cristata*) lay quietly on the floes, quite devoid, as it appeared, of fear, though they were observed to keep a sharp look-out for the polar bear, which, next to the Greenlander, is undoubtedly their most formidable enemy. These seals are, by the way, courageous animals. One of them, having received directly in the head the contents of a musquet fired at him from on board, sprang up, and seemed disposed to attack us; nor did he make his retreat before a second, and even third shot, was fired at him. We picked up to-day a large fragment of the root of a sort of white pine.

On the 26th we had a light breeze from S.E., and, what is very unusual in Davis' Straits with wind from that quarter, (it commonly accompanying only N. and S.W. winds,) a fog. No ice, except a few solitary hummocks, was now in sight; but breakers were distinctly heard to windward. Even since morning we had been sensible of a gentle swell from the North, which gradually increased, and led us to surmise that we should be shortly clear of the ice, an expectation fully verified by the event, for when it cleared up in the afternoon, we found ourselves in " open water." The temperature of the sea had been observed regularly three times a-day, ever since our departure from Elsinore. It was found to be in the Cattegat, from 35° to 38°; in the Skaggerak, from 37° to 40°; in the North Sea, from 44° to 45°·6; and in the Atlantic from 50° to 41°·5, Fahr., exactly as in 1823 and 1824. During the last few days, in the mouth of Davis' Straits, it was found to be from 41° to 39°, though we were in the vicinity of ice. I inferred, from this circumstance, that there must be a current here from the south, as I had never before found the temperature of the sea to be

above 36° in the vicinity of ice ; and this inference was confirmed
in the afternoon, it being then found to be but 34°·5, the brig
having in the mean time got to the northward of the ice.

In the forenoon of the 27th we got sight of land, which we took
to be Nunarsoit, (Davis' Cape Desolation,) a large island remarkable
for its rugged and lofty mountains, and which forms part of the
tract of the country taken by Eggers to be the Ubygds of the
ancients, situated between the East and West Bygds. The current
was found, by observation, to have set us, during the last two days,
twenty-one miles to the north, being at the rate of about half a mile
an hour*. At five, P.M., we made Omenak, a somewhat lofty round-
topped island, and shortly after Little Vardöe, off Frederick's-hope.
The superintendent of the colony, Mr. Matthiesen, who was attached
to the expedition in quality of interpreter, came on board with
the pilot, who brought the brig to anchor in the harbour.

The colony of Frederick's-hope was founded in the year 1742
by Jacob Severin, a personage well known in the commercial and
missionary history of Greenland. It is situated on a peninsula, in
lat. 62°, and long. 50° West of Greenwich. The harbour is a good
one, and capable of accommodating several vessels; but there
are some sunken rocks at its entrance, over which, when there is
any ice abroad, the sea does not break, and which are consequently
so much the more dangerous. The aspect of the place very much
resembles that of the harbours on the West coast of Norway, the
only difference being that the hills are of a darker hue, and present
still fewer signs of vegetation. It was here that Otto Fabricius lived
as missionary. I was shown the very room, or rather the dark
closet, where he turned to so good account the years of his
residence in this country, and where he collected, during the winter
months, the materials for his Fauna, his Lexicon, and other works,
destined to immortalize his name, while he passed the summers in
roaming the country with the native Greenlanders, having learned
to manage a kajak, and strike a seal, with a dexterity which no other
European, probably, before or since his time, has ever attained.

Some miles north of Frederick's-hope lies what the Dutch call
the Witte-blink, a lofty, precipitous coast or cliff of ice, formed by
the land-ice, or glaciers, extending to the very water's edge,
where it accumulates, and hiding from sight the whole actual shore,
except here and there some inconsiderable naze†.

---

* It is this current that carries the timber of Siberia down between Spitzbergen
and the East coast of Greenland, to Cape Farewell, its southern extremity, whence
it takes a north-westerly direction along the Greenland shore, until it meets the
southerly current from Baffin's Bay, at Queen Anne's Cape, near the Arctic circle.
The drift timber is frequently cast ashore as high as Holsteinborg, but never to the
northward of that place. The breadth of the current at Cape Farewell may be
considered to extend about one hundred miles from the land, gradually diminishing
its distance off the coast, until it is entirely lost at Queen Anne's Cape.—J. C. Ross.

† To such cliffs, or barriers of ice, I shall in the sequel give the name of ice-
blink, or simply blink. The reflection of ice in the atmosphere, which is usually

VOYAGE IN A BOAT TO JULIANA'S-HOPE, DETENTION THERE, AND AT NENNORTALIK.

1828—29.

HAVING made some observations to determine the deviation of the compass, which was found to be 56° 25', and the intensity of the magnetic force, I left Frederick's-hope, on the morning of the 5th June, in a Greenland boat, for Juliana's-hope, from whence my projected expedition was, in the Spring of 1829, to take its beginning, accompanied by Dr. Pingel and Mr. Vahl. We passed the firths of Qvannek and Narksalik, off which lie a multitude of islands, some of considerable size. Narksalik is one of the firths that *calve*, that is to say, where the land-ice detaches itself from the shore in large masses, and is projected with great impetus into the sea, by the pressure of the ice above. In the evening of the 6th of June we encountered a violent snow-storm, which obliged us to put in shore, where we were agreeably surprised to find an abandoned Greenland hut, that promised us better shelter than the very indifferent tent we had been supplied with at the colony. This hut, our guide informed us, had been the scene, the Winter previous, of a melancholy incident. A Greenlander, whose residence it was, had seized his gun, with the intention of shooting a fox that had made its appearance outside his window; but, as he was in the act of cocking it, the gun went off, and its contents were lodged in the body of his only son, a young man grown, who died in consequence. The unhappy family immediately removed to another place, to avoid the sight of objects that must perpetually have reminded them of their calamity.

We resumed our voyage on the morning of the 8th, and rowed through the so-called Narrow Sound, where there is a harbour which, however, cannot safely be run into without a pilot, as well on account of the absence of good land-marks, as of some dangerous skerries lying off its mouth. The entrance into this sound is in about lat. 61° 34', and long. 49° 18'. A little further south rises the lofty mountain to which the mariners frequenting these seas have given the name of "Tinding," (the *Peak* or *Pinnacle*,) and which is from 1400 to 1600 feet above the level of the sea. From hence the firth of Sermeliarsuk stretches to the E., or E.N.E. It, likewise, is one of the firths that calve, and is especially characterized by the circumstance that all the icebergs proceeding from it are of a beautiful semi-transparent blueish colour. The

designated by that name, I shall, for distinction's sake, call *sky-blink*. By *glaciers*, I mean the ice covering the land, even when reaching to the water's edge, *except* where it terminates in lofty precipitous cliffs. *Icebergs* are the vast and lofty masses, or mountains of ice, found floating in the ocean, and which proceed from the ice-blinks.

large islands of Sermesok, Omenak, Storöe, that is, Great Island, Sennerut, Arsut, and Dadloodit, which last is, by the Europeans, called Hvidsærk*, are all of them lofty, and easy to be recognised, particularly Omenak, whose top resembles a high, leaning tower. Within these islands winds the firth of Arsut, on the northern side of which the mountain Kunnak lifts its ice-clad summit to the clouds. It is, beyond question, the highest mountain, Hart's-horn, (*Hiörtetakken*) near Good-hope, excepted, on the West coast of Greenland. I have calculated its height from several points, and found it to be 4,300 to 4,500 feet above the level of the sea. In the firth of Arsut we fell in with a large concourse of people, engaged in the angmaksak fishery (capelin of the Newfoundland fishery). The Greenlanders catch these fish in vast numbers. They are scooped up in small pails, or buckets, dried in the sun, and put by for winter consumption. The hills about the firth of Arsut are supposed to contain tin and lead-ore; and Giesecke found there the formerly rare mineral, cryolite, which, when pulverized, the Greenlanders mix with their snuff, as they likewise do quartz, to make it go the further. This firth divides into two arms, or branches. Some good meadows are to be found here and there about it, which did not escape the notice of the old Icelandic colonists, as is evident from the ruins of their dwellings still extant, it is said, at three different places on its shores. I myself have seen but some inconsiderable ruins close to the foot of the mountain Kunnak, and these were in so dilapidated a condition, that the only circumstance that satisfied me of their not having been mere Greenland huts, was their situation†. The latitude of this place, the seat, at present, of a commercial establishment, called Arsut's Endeavour, (*Arsut's-forsög*,) is 61° 10', and its longitude 48° 25'. About two miles west of this station lies a small island, called Kajartalik, with a harbour, which, however, cannot with safety be run into but in good weather, and with the aid of experienced pilots. On the South-west coast of Dadloodit, likewise, there is said to be a harbour or two, as well as among the small, low Innusutut Islands, east of Great Island, (*Stor-öe*,) none of which, however, I had an opportunity of exploring. I was informed that none of them could be entered with southerly winds.

At Kakortok, situate on the southern side of Sennerut, we were obliged by high winds to-run in shore. This place was visited some fifty years ago, by Arctander and Bruhn, to whom we are indebted for the earliest detailed accounts of the ruins in the

---

* Though scarcely, I should suppose, from their taking it to be the Hvidsærk of the ancients.

† This firth, according to Eggers, falls within the limits of the Ubygds. If Eggers has correctly translated the account of *Erik hin Raude's* voyage, we must infer, that, besides the East and West Bygds, there was a third, or Middle Bygd, by which Middle Bygd we are probably to understand Arsut and its environs.

district of Juliana's-hope. The former states that he discovered at Kakortok, on the top of a small eminence, a fresh-water mountain-lake, containing cod and halibut, and whose waters rose and fell. I conceive, however, he must be in error, for not only have I failed to find this mountain-lake, though frequently upon the spot, but the native Greenlanders themselves are wholly ignorant of its existence. The latitude of Kakortok, by observation is 61°; its longitude, by chronometer, 47° 55′.

In the height between Sennerut and the isthmus of Itihheitsvak, which constitutes the boundary between the districts of Juliana's-hope and Frederick's-hope, the mainland is almost everywhere covered with glaciers, which, at some places, extend to the water's edge. South of Itihheitsvak lies the large island of Nunarsoit, separated from the mainland by the sound of Torsukatek, through which the regular trader to Juliana's-hope commonly passes, sailing from thence to the colony, within the barrier of skerries, that line the coast. On both sides of this channel may be found good harbours. On the present occasion we fell in, in one of these, Aurora Harbour, with the vessel we had come in from Denmark, and learned the loss upon the coast of the ship freighted by the society of missionaries, for the purpose of conveying the materials of a church to Juliana's-hope.

Aurora Harbour, situate at the eastern extremity of Torsukatek, is a cove running into the mainland, in the direction of W.N.W., and affords good shelter to inward-bound vessels, when the wind falls southerly. Its depth of water is from seven to eight fathom, and its anchorage good. The harbour is sufficiently large to allow of a ship's riding at a single anchor; though should it be preferred, she can be secured by hawsers to the shore. Off its entrance, and about mid-channel, lies a sunken rock, to avoid which it is necessary, on running in, to hug the point of land that shuts in the harbour towards the south.

From Nunarsoit the mainland trends due east to a distance of from fifty to sixty miles, and then inclines again to S.S.E. and S.E. towards Cape Farewell, forming a large bay, sown, as it were, with innumerable rocks and islands. There is no doubt that a ship might find a passage among most of them: but there is no lack of shoals and sunken rocks, rendering any attempt to thread this labyrinth a dangerous experiment for those not familiar with its intricacies. The course usually followed is from Torsukatek, through the channel of Kikkerteitsiak, the inner Karmæt channel, south about Auertamiut, and through Ikarisarsuk, the sound between Irsarut and Kingitok. The ice, however, makes it often impossible for ships to pass this way; and as the pilots themselves have but a very imperfect knowledge of the other passages, the utmost vigilance is always requisite on the part of the ship-master. Along the coast are several lofty mountains that serve the purpose

28   VOYAGE TO GREENLAND.

of sea-marks, being easily recognised a long way off, among which
Narksak, Kidlaueit, or the Coarse-toothed Comb, and Akuliarisor-
soak, are from 3,500 to 4,000 feet high.

We arrived on the 16th at Juliana's-hope, where we were
received in the most kind and hospitable manner by Mr. Wolff,
superintendent of the colony, and the missionary, Mr. Esmann.

This colony, situated in lat. 60° 42′ 54″, and long. 46° 0′ 44″,
was founded in the year 1775. The Greenlanders, it is said, had
long before been heard to speak in high terms of the country in the
vicinity of Statenhook, and various persons had advised the establishment of a colony in that neighbourhood : but the trade to
Frederick's-hope had been attended with the loss of so many
vessels, and given so much trouble in various ways, that the
government hesitated to found another settlement further to the
South, where the ice is usually still more abundant, and composed
of larger masses. At length, however, one Anders Olsen, a
merchant, received orders to explore the coast as far as Statenhook,
and the result of his expedition was the founding of Juliana's-hope,
which in the sequel became, in respect of its proceeds, one of the
most valuable of our settlements in Greenland, and whose population now amounts to a third of that of the whole country. Olsen,
indeed, could scarcely have selected a better site for his new
settlement. It lies in the centre of the district bearing its name,
and is possessed of a good harbour, a convenient wharf, an inland
lake near by, abounding in fish, and out of which flows a salmon-
stream, that takes its course among the very houses of the settlement, and sufficient pasturage in the summer for a number of
cattle. Here, on an arm of the firth of Igaliko, at a spot whose
luxuriant vegetation gave a promise of success to this branch of
husbandry, did this adventurous man, in his old age, take up his
residence. In the midst of stupendous ruins, remains of what had
been the habitations of the old Icelandic colonists, he built himself
his home, and here his descendants still abide, subsisting by raising
cattle, by the seal, and other fishery, and by the chase*.

As it had been settled that the boats to be employed, on my
impending expedition, should be built at this place, I made immediate inquiry about workmen for that purpose, but was informed
by Mr. Wolff that no good ones could be got upon the spot ; for
it is by no means every Greenlander that understands this business.
Messages were, therefore, sent for some of those in best repute,
and on their arrival, a few days afterwards, the work was taken in

* The cultivation of the potato would, in all likelihood, be successful at this
place. It were, at any rate, worth while making the experiment. Mr. Esmann,
the missionary, has, for three years past, succeeded in raising them at Juliana's-
hope. In 1831 he planted some in the garden of a merchant, where the soil
seemed favourable to their growth; and when I left the country, in the month of
September, they gave promise of a good crop, notwithstanding that the summer
had been exceedingly raw and cold.

hand. The Greenlander, in building his boat, makes use neither of rule, line, nor compass. A long-handled knife and an adze are his tools, his eye his rule : and one has but to give the length of the boat, to enable him to manage all the rest.

As but few have any correct idea of the mode of building a Greenland skin-boat, or, as it is likewise called, because rowed by women, women's-boat, it may not be amiss to give a brief description of it here. The bottom is flat, and consists of the keel, and what perhaps may be designated floor-head keels, which, by lashings and treenails, are made fast to the stem and stern-post. To the keel and floor-head keels the floor-timbers are secured by thongs, made of the sinews of the seal. On the top of the stem and stern-post, which rise almost perpendicularly, and must be of good timber, two pieces of plank, or other strong wood, are made fast, the sides of which are rabbeted, so that the laths fit into the groove, and, being there secured by lashings, form the boat's rail. Between the laths and the floor-head keels are placed the futtocks, two to each floor-timber. A rib serves as a support to the thwarts, or benches, being itself rabbeted into the stem and stern-post, and further secured by being lashed fast, as well to these as to the thwarts. Outside the futtocks is placed another rib, for the purpose of keeping the skin, with which the boat is covered, from chafing. What serves chiefly to give this sort of boat its proper shape, as well as strength, are the thwarts, the ends of which are hollowed out, so as to grasp the futtock, while they, at the same time, rest upon the rib, to which they are securely lashed. In lieu of an outer sheathing of planks, or boards, a hide is used, composed of the skins of from sixteen to twenty large seals, the hair being previously taken off, and the skin stretched and saturated with blubber, and, finally, well dried ; after which operation it is as light as a drum*. Neither nails nor spikes are made use of in the construction of these frail boats, whose strength consists wholly in their elasticity. The oars employed in rowing them are short, and have a broad blade, which, at the end and edges, is shod with bone, or some hard wood, to enable them to bear the better the concussion of ice. On the stem is placed a mast, on which the Greenlander hoists a skin by way of sail, or, if he be rich enough to own such a commodity, a piece of woollen stuff or linen ; it is, however, only when the wind is free, that any use can be made of it. The wood employed in building the ordinary Greenland-boat is drift-wood ; that is to say, timber floated down the rivers from the forests of Siberia, and carried by currents across the ocean, to the shores of Iceland and Greenland. The usual length of this description of Greenland-boat is from twenty-two to twenty-four feet, and its breadth five or six, and it is so light that a couple of hands can carry one of

---

* The sort of seal's skin preferred for that purpose, is that of the Atarsoak, or *Phoca Groenl.*

them with ease. Those built for the expedition measured, from
stem to stern, thirty-eight feet and a half, by somewhat more
than seven feet, where broadest; and in height, two feet and
one-third.

No sort of boat is, probably, better adapted to the navigation of
these icy seas than this umiak of the Greenlanders. It is not
difficult to row; rooms a considerable cargo; may with ease be
hauled ashore, or on the floes of ice, by three or four men; and,
though indeed more exposed than other boats to the risks of
springing leaks, is capable, whenever this happens, of being easily
repaired by the simple contrivance of thrusting a bit of blubber
into the hole, until an opportunity arrive of sewing on a patch of
skin over it. This resource, however, is only available when
there is little or no cargo in the boat: in cases where the boat has
a full lading it must often be impossible to discover and stop the
leak in time to save her from filling. To guard against such
accidents, accordingly, the Greenlanders, when navigating through
new ice, or brash ice, usually hang a skin out at the bows. As
this, however, impedes the progress of their boats, I adopted, in
lieu of it, a couple of ice-boards, so made as to be fixed, when
required, into the water-way, and which, forming a sharp angle
before the bows, were found to answer fully the purpose for which
they were intended. These flat-bottomed boats cannot live, of
course, in a stiff breeze, or heavy swell. They capsize easily, and
a moderate sea is capable of breaking them to pieces. A boat, with
a cargo on board, rowed by four or five women, can, in calm
weather and smooth water, accomplish a distance of thirty miles,
or somewhat more, in a day. If, however, the voyage is to be one
of several days' duration, one cannot calculate on more than from
twenty to twenty-four miles on an average daily, and every fifth
day must, moreover, be a day of rest, in order that the boat's skin,
saturated by the sea, may dry. In this description of boat the
Greenlanders perform all their voyages, taking with them occasionally all their goods and chattels: they even take them with
them sometimes on their expeditions over-land, being frequently
obliged, in the chase of the rein-deer, to cross the lakes which, here
and there, are met with in the interior.

The kajak is a description of boat different from the above, and
only used by men. It is from twelve to fourteen feet long, from
one foot and one-third to one foot and a half broad, sharp at both
ends, and covered entirely with skin, there being but a small round
opening left a-mid-ships, where the Greenlander takes his seat.
Before him are placed his implements of fishery and of the chase,
his shaft for killing birds or seals, and his harpoon with its line;
behind him is the kajak bladder, and the spear with which he
gives the seal its *coup-de-grace*. In this small bark, which is so
light that a person without experience in its management is sure

to upset with it in the most trifling swell, the Greenlander defies the storm, and gives battle to the polar bear, and to the monsters of the deep.

On the 3d of July Mr. de Fries, one of the missionary establishment at Friederichsthal*, arrived at Juliana's-hope, accompanied by one Ernenek, a Greenlander of the East coast, who came thither for the purpose of traffic. The arrival of this man was to me especially a joyful incident, as I hoped to collect from him some authentic information concerning the geography of the East coast, and still more because I hoped to persuade him to accompany me upon my expedition to that unknown region; for I feared that I should find the natives of the West coast unwilling to attend me very far. These people have, all of them, more or less, a dread of the East coast, which they imagine to be inhabited by a savage and cruel race, that often suffer famine, and, whenever so situated, butcher and eat one another. The further we go to the North, the more firmly do we find this notion rooted in the people's minds. The Greenlanders about the Bay of Disco habitually call the Eastlanders cannibals, and apprehend that they will, one day or the other, cross the country and eat them up. About Nennortalik† and Friederichsthal, on the other hand, this superstitious fear assumes a milder form, for the people there are better acquainted with the Eastlanders, many of them being even in the habit of going a short way up the East coast to traffic with its natives, and to catch seals. They are, indeed, not ignorant that the Eastlanders have sometimes had recourse to the horrible and revolting act adverted to, but they know, too, that they have never done it, but when impelled to it by famine‡.

Ernenek may have been at this time from thirty-six to forty years old. He had the long, lank, black hair, and the black eyes of his race, but nothing else in his exterior characteristic of the Esquimaux. He was about six feet high, and strongly built: and though this was the first time that he had set eyes on Europeans, and saw himself surrounded by a number of inquisitive beings whose appearance must have had in it enough to excite his amazement, his manner was free from all restraint. With the aid of Mr. Motzfeldt§, the only European on the spot that could make

* The most southerly situation in Greenland now inhabited by Europeans.

† A commercial settlement south of Juliana's-hope.

‡ Besides feeling this dread for the natives of the East coast, the Greenlanders represent a journey thither as perilous in the extreme, making mention particularly, as one of its chief dangers, of a large blink, off which the ice is constantly being forced upwards from the bottom of the sea. One bold and active fellow, whom I was desirous of taking with me, as he understood Danish, objected to my proposal solely on account of this perilous blink, observing, "You may be able to pay me for my services, but you can't pay me for my life!"

§ Mr. Motzfeldt is equally familiar with the Danish and Greenland languages, is intimately acquainted with the manners and customs of the Greenlanders, and understands to perfection how to treat and manage these children of nature. He

himself intelligible to him, and who was kind enough, on that
account, to take upon himself the office of interpreter, I gave him
to know that I purposed making a voyage, the next year, to the
East coast, and proposed that he should go with me in quality of a
guide.   He seemed at first to think that I was jesting with him ;
but on my repeating the proposal, and following it up with some
trifling presents, besides acquainting him that he should be paid
for his trouble, he promised to meet me in the neighbourhood of
Statenhook, and to accompany me from thence to Narksak or
Narksarmiut, where, for the time being, he resided.   To spend the
winter on the West coast, as I wanted him to do, he would not
promise, he being, as it seemed, subject to the authority of his
wife's father, a man named Sidlit, who, with the rest of his family,
now waited his return at Nennortalik.   Thus situated, and as it
was a matter of some moment to me not to lose sight of Ernenek
till the Spring, and then to get him along with me to the East
coast, I determined to go with him to Nennortalik, and secure the
concurrence of his two wives to my plan, it being very clear that
its good or ill success would depend chiefly upon their decision.

Mr. Vahl and I, accordingly, set out for Nennortalik the next
morning, attended by Ernenek and a number of Greenlanders
from the southern part of the country, who had come to Juliana's-
hope to inquire what goods the ship had brought from Europe.   In
the neighbourhood of Uppernaviarsuk, about a mile to the east
of the colony, and at Kinalik, we examined some ancient ruins
not mentioned by Arctander; but, like almost all the rest, they
were found to be so completely dilapidated, as to render it impossible to ascertain even their dimensions, the walls having fallen
in, and being overgrown with dwarf-willow*, crowberry†, and
whortleberry‡ bushes.   One of those at Kinalik seemed, however,
to be the remains of a spacious building, probably about forty paces
long, by some twenty broad.   Off the firth of Agluitsok lie a
number of somewhat lofty islands, two of which are called by the
native Greenlanders Uiarartorbik, or the Quarry Islands, a name
which seems to indicate them as a place whence stones for building
were formerly procured.   We arrived at Lichtenau, one of the
settlements of the Moravian missionaries, at about five, P.M.   The
brethren of the establishment, at the head of whom is Mr. Müller,

rows his kajak with the skill of a native, is an expert hunter and catcher of seals,
and is gifted with a talent of observation by no means ordinary.   This combination
of qualities, united to his own wish of visiting the East coast, pointed him out as an
individual peculiarly well fitted to accompany the expedition in quality of interpreter,
and I, accordingly, made application for him, to Captain Holböll, who readily
granted him an exemption from his duties, in the service of the Greenland Board
of Trade.   Yet he did not after all go with us, being prevented by causes which
I never yet have heard distinctly explained.

* *Salix glauca* and *herbacea*.   † *Empetrum nigrum*.
‡ *Vaccinium pubescens*.   Flora Dan.

received us with hospitality, and showed us whatever was worthy of notice in the neighbourhood; and among other things a rock, on the top of which are cut the names of Anders Olsen, and his wife, and that of the first missionary of the place. Lichtenau is pleasantly situated on the northern bank of the firth of Agluitsok, in lat. 60° 31½′, and long. 45° 30′. Its church and houses are built of stone, in a style of architecture far superior to that of the wooden edifices usually met with in this country. The firth of Agluitsok has three arms, Sioralik, Amitoarsuk, and Kallamiut. In its vicinity are to be found a great many ruins of what were once dwellings of the old colonists. Arctander makes mention of about fifty, and the native Greenlanders tell of many more of which he had no knowledge. Some of these occupy sites where there are no fields nor meadows near, a circumstance justifying, apparently, the inference, that not all the ancient colonists subsisted by raising cattle, but that the seal, and other fishery, constituted the main employment of a large proportion of them*. If, at least, we may judge of the Greenland meadow-lands of that day, from what we now know of them, we cannot suppose that any very considerable number could have managed to gain a livelihood by raising cattle, as it is no easy matter to find a sufficiency of winter fodder for the few that are now raised in the country, it being necessary sometimes to fetch it by boats, from a distance of twenty miles commonly from the site of a Greenland encampment, for there the soil, fatted with blubber and seals' blood, produces grass in abundance, while everywhere else it is almost overgrown with thickets, so as only to be convertible to meadow-land, at the expense of much toil and labour.

On the morning of the 6th we resumed our voyage, followed by upwards of thirty kajaks. As they went along, the Greenlanders amused themselves with throwing their darts at pieces of ice, or sea-weed, or whatever else they saw upon the surface of the sea; and I could not but admire the dexterity with which they manage the weapon. I have frequently seen a number of them strike, at one and the same moment, an object from forty to fifty feet distant ; nay, a bird on the wing, if it come but within range, seldom escapes.

As the ice was open, and the weather fair, we rowed outside the large island of Sermesok, the same that is in Greenland called Cape Farewell, which name, however, is most incorrectly given to it, as this cape, according to all the charts, lies from thirty-two to thirty-six miles further south than the southern extremity of Sermesok†. The mountains of this island, particularly those on its

---

* That the chase of the larger aquatic animals did actually form an important branch of their industry, is evident from the Pope's having once received a tribute of 127 lispounds of walrus-teeth.

† Cape Farewell, by Captain Graah's observations, is in lat. 59° 49′ N., long. 43° 34′ W., of Greenwich.—ED.

east side, are very lofty, and for the most part covered with perpetual ice, a few sharp, naked peaks rising above it, and looking like the towers and spires of some old castle. The highest of these mountains has never yet been scaled by any native Greenlander; but it is said that Giesecke, who held an appointment here under the crown for several years, performed that feat, and cut his name on a rock at its summit. Ruins of old houses have been discovered on this island, as well as at Nennortalik, but they are now in so dilapidated a state as to be scarcely distinguishable.

On reaching Nennortalik, I was informed by Mr. Aröe, the superintendent of the commercial establishment at that place, that Sidlit and two of his wives (for he had three in all*,) had left it the day before ; his third wife, however, Ernenek's mother-in-law, and both of Ernenek's own wives, were there. I had them sent for to me the next morning; made inquiries of them touching the East coast, and received the same answers that Ernenek had previously given. After having shared out some bread among these poor people, I once more proposed to Ernenek to attend me thither in the ensuing Spring, promising him, besides other payment, a rifle, which he long had had his eye on, and seemed to covet greatly. This proved a powerful temptation. He began consulting with his wives, while I seized the opportunity of producing some beads, looking-glasses, and other trifles, the sight of which speedily removed whatever scruples these fair ladies may have previously entertained. They not only promised, in a word, to go with me to the East coast in the Spring, but even to winter at Nennortalik, stipulating only for permission to go back, in the first place, to Narksak, in order to fetch their goods and chattels.

On the 9th we took our departure once more from Nennortalik, and a favourable wind brought us shortly after noon to Friederichsthal, the southernmost establishment of the Moravians. Friederichsthal was founded in the year 1824. It is, without exception, the handsomest settlement in all Greenland, and does its architect, the missionary de Fries, much honour. The head of the mission at this place is Mr. Kleinschmidt, a venerable old man, who, for nearly forty years, has devoted himself to the instruction and improvement of the Greenlanders ; a pious labour, in which, as he is perfectly familiar with their language, it may be conceived he has not been unsuccessful. Notwithstanding that the establishment over which he now presides is of so modern a date, it counts no fewer than 400 among its members ; and it is gratifying to know, that more and more flock to it yearly from the east coast, to enjoy the benefit of Mr. Kleinschmidt's instruction, who lives here among the Greenlanders as a father among his children. I found the latitude of Friederichsthal to be 60° 0′ 10″, and its longitude 44° 37′.

* Two of them were mother and daughter.

Precisely on the spot where the buildings of the mission now stand, stood anciently some Icelandic edifices; and here it is that Eggers places the most easterly of the Bygds, Skagefiord. In digging up the soil hereabouts, several small pieces of pot-stone have been found, variously shaped, and perforated at one or more places, some of them having, moreover, a mark upon them like a cross. One cannot be sure, however, that these fragments are relics of the old Icelandic colonists, as similar ones have been discovered (I myself have found some,) in old Greenland earth-huts.

The mountains about Friederichsthal have a wild and imposing aspect, owing to their great height, their sharp, irregular pinnacles, and the immense masses of ice that perpetually cover them. In the neighbourhood there are spacious fields, and the soil is favourable to the growth of all sorts of culinary vegetables, not-withstanding the near vicinity of the Atlantic filled up with ice, and the frequent and terrible storms from S.E., that threaten even the most solid edifices with destruction, and have made it necessary to remove the houses of the settlement from the site they at first had occupied.

On the morning of the 11th Ernenek came to me, and informed me, that he was now about to take his departure. It had been my intention to go to Narksak with him, in order to make sure of his return; but as he now announced it to be his intention to make some stay there, for the purpose of catching seals, and as he repeated his promise of returning to Nennortalik before the winter set in, I abandoned the design, presenting him, at parting, with a couple of spear-heads*. As soon as he was gone, Mr. Vahl and I likewise left Friederichsthal. On our way back we visited the hot springs at Ounartok. The western side of this island, which lies at the mouth of a firth of the same name, is lofty, rugged, and almost totally naked, while the opposite side is low, and clothed with the most luxuriant vegetation. It is on this side that the springs are situated, lying, all three of them, close by one another, at the N.E. corner of the island. Of these springs, the one nearest the sea is altogether insignificant: the temperature of its waters was found to be 26°; the second, a few paces from it, forms a lake of about forty-eight feet in circuit, and the temperature of its waters was 27°; the third is still larger, being about seventy feet in circuit, and its waters from 32° to 33½°, all of Réaumur. The depth of these pools nowhere exceeds a foot, and their bottom is composed of a soft blueish-gray clay, through which the warm water bubbled up at several places. The two large ones the Greenlanders have dammed in with stone, and make use of as

---

* They are of iron, and are provided with several barbs. The Greenlanders make use of them in the chase of both birds and seals.

bathing-places. Near the middle one, Arctander found, in 1777, the remains of a small building, which he took to be from the time of the old colonists, and whose walls were then one foot and a half high. Every vestige of them has, however, vanished, and their place is occupied by the ruins of an old Greenland hut. The water of these springs deposits a siliceous or calcareous sediment, like Geiser and Strokr in Iceland. The Greenlanders state that it is much hotter in winter than in summer ; but this opinion may proceed from the circumstance of the atmospheric air being then much colder, and the contrast between its temperature and that of the water much more perceptible, of course, than in summer.

On my arrival at the colony, on the morning of the 15th of July, I found my women's-boats so far advanced, that I was obliged to apply for the services of three carpenters belonging to it, in order to have some work done to which the natives were incompetent, and Mr. Wolff was kind enough to lend me them, though some business of his own was put a stop to in consequence. The work in question was the making of some flooring and spars, together with a few cases to contain our provisions, instruments, &c. The flooring commonly used consists of entire boards, reaching from stem to stern ; but they have the disadvantage of being not easily removable, insomuch that, in order to bale the boat or get at a leak, one is obliged, in the first place, to take out the whole cargo, which is in many instances impracticable. I caused, therefore, the flooring of my boats, on this occasion, to be made of short pieces so put together, that one or more of them could be removed with ease, whenever circumstances might make it necessary. As for provision-cases, I considered them absolutely indispensable, as without them we could neither take a sufficiency of stores on board, nor keep what we might take with us in good order.

While the carpenters were busy at this job, a number of women were employed in preparing some water-proof skins*, of which we stood in need of a considerable quantity, to serve for provision-bags, coverings for boxes, and, above all, outer clothes for our rowers ; for I knew by experience how unwilling the Greenland women are to row in rainy weather, a circumstance which, indeed, is not to be wondered at, when it is considered that they usually carry their whole wardrobe on their backs, and that their dress, besides, affords them but indifferent protection against the inclemency of the weather, being, in fact, as ill-adapted to the climate and their mode of life, as it well could be†. To this disgusting

---

* The hide of the seal, stripped of the hair.

† Fashion and vanity have, even here, done their best to make the dress of the women more unsuitable to the climate than it originally was. Formerly their sealskin jackets reached a good way down over the hips, thus covering the whole body. Since shifts, however, came into use, they have been so much curtailed, as to reach now only to the waist: the linen of the ladies would not else be visible.

process* a number of old women lent their teeth, while some more dainty nymphs employed themselves in the more delicate work of sewing our sails, of which I had two made for each boat, and also in making up our flags.

Report had reached us that on an island, named Akkia, lying directly opposite the colony, a remarkable cavern was to be seen, which no European as yet had visited. This determined me at once to make an excursion thither, in company with Dr. Pingel and Mr. Vahl. We set out, accordingly, and, after a somewhat fatiguing journey of three hours, reached the spot. The entrance of the cave we found to be so narrow that we were almost literally obliged to creep in. The cave, however, soon widened, and a black abyss appeared to yawn before us. For some moments we stood still, reflecting if it really was worth while to venture into such a place; for the stones we trod on in our descent were partly loose, and the light of our lanterns was altogether insufficient to enable us to judge how deep the cavern was, difficulties that were enhanced still more by the unwillingness of our Greenland guide to show us the way. Curiosity, however, got the better of all our scruples; with a rope about my waist, a small compass in my pocket, a thermometer in one hand, and a lantern in the other, I let myself be lowered down, and was followed by Mr. Vahl. Guided by the feeble light of our lanterns we advanced slowly, one moment stumbling over a bank of sand, the next over a little hill of stones, fallen from the vault above, and reached at length a sort of arched gateway, that was defended, as it were, by a natural rampart of stone, beyond which the cave again widened, altering its direction, at the same time, from E., the course we hitherto had followed, to E. by N., by the compass. Having penetrated in this way to the bottom of the cave, we found there a lake, of whose dimensions however, I can say but this, that they are by no means inconsiderable, since some stones that I threw across it with all the strength I was possessed of, were heard to fall into the water, without previously striking and rebounding from the sides of the cave. The water of this lake was perfectly tasteless, and its temperature $+2\frac{1}{3}°$, while that of the atmosphere in the interior of the cave was $-5°$ Réaum. Whether it owes its existence to some subterranean source, or is but an accumulation of water that has oozed through the crevices and fissures in the rocky vault above, it would probably be no easy matter to determine. After staying half an hour at this place, we set out on our return, measuring, as we went, the length of the cave, which was found to be, from the entrance to the lake, 209 feet, by 32 in breadth, where broadest, and about 70 in height. I neglected to note the temperature of the air within the mouth of

---

* The skin is first soaked in urine till perfectly saturated, and the hair, which is thereby loosened, is scraped, or torn off afterwards by the teeth.

the cave; on the outside of it, in the shade, it was $+12\frac{3}{4}°$. Should any future travellers be tempted to visit this cave, I would advise them to provide themselves, before entering it, with a couple of good torches, and to let themselves be lowered down by means of a rope about the waist, lest the torches should not give sufficient light to enable them to see the inequalities of the ground to some distance within the entrance. Standing at the mouth of this cave one commands a splendid view of the ice-clad ocean, and the islands to the South, as far as the towering, snow-topped Sermesok. Still another, but smaller cave, is said to be at Akia, containing, if we may believe the Greenlanders, some ancient graves, out of dread of which none of them dare enter it. The Greenlanders are of opinion that the two caves are connected. On our way back one of our party took it into his head to bathe in one of the many mountain-lakes about this island, and would have paid for his imprudence with his life, had not the rest of us fortunately remained near by, and lent him a helping hand. It is this island Eggers took to be the Langey mentioned in the old chorographies, where there is said to have been eight farms. Three heaps of greatly-dilapidated ruins have been found upon it, one of which I myself have seen. By the European colonists it is called Mathæus's, or Mathias's island.

Near the colony may be seen a fine ruin that has all the appearance of having been, in its better days, a church, and which, on this account, is usually called Kakortok Church, Kakortok being the name of the place where it stands. This ruin Dr. Pingel had determined to explore, justly conceiving that the best way of throwing light upon the much-contested question of the site of the East and West Bygds, was carefully to examine some of the principal ruins in this district; for it seemed highly probable that stones might be discovered with inscriptions on them, which, when collated with the accounts, written and oral, that have been handed down to us, might at once dispel all doubt upon this subject; and none of these ruins seemed so likely to reward the pains that, with this view, might be bestowed on them, as the church in question, which stands a noble monument of the once-flourishing condition of the old colonists. As, however, unforeseen circumstances rendered it impossible for Dr. Pingel to carry his project into effect, I determined to take on myself the charge of its execution; and Captain Gram, who happened at the time to be detained at Juliana's-hope by contrary winds, kindly lent me the aid of his people for this purpose.

Accompanied by Mr. Vahl, Captain Gram, Mr. Matthiesen, and Mr. Motzfeldt, I set out, accordingly, on the 21st of July, for the ruin, which is situated on an arm of the firth of Igaliko, about ten miles from Juliana's-hope. It stands on a not very wide, but somewhat deep plain, rising gradually, as it recedes in a slanting direction from the sea, and covered sparingly with grass, intermingled with thickets and moss. On the north this field is bounded by a perpendicular wall of rock, forty feet high, behind which the mountains of Yviengiset, Kirkefield, and Redekam, rise to from 3000 to 4000 feet above the level of the sea. The church is built in a style at once simple and elegant, of large blocks of stone, hewn, doubtless, out of the perpendicular rocks just mentioned, the quality of the stone in them and in the walls being identically the same. Each block has evidently been adjusted and fitted in its place with care, but there is no indication on the outer wall of any sort of cement having been employed. On the inner side, however, far in between the stones, were found a few very small pieces of a hard white substance, which, there can be no doubt, was mortar. Mr. Vahl, who is a skilful chemist, collected a little of it, for the purpose of closer investigation at his leisure. He lost it, however, subsequently, and we could find no more. Arctander states, that he found some clay in the interstices of the stones; there is, however, no vestige of anything of the sort at present.

In the side of the church facing the south, and the sea, and which evidently was its front, there are four windows and two doors, of which last the one to the east is one foot and a half lower than the other. It was, probably, the private entrance of the minister of the church, the other being that of the congregation. This disparity in height does not, however, offend the eye, as the cornices of both doors are on a level, so that, in fact, it is not observable except on actually entering. The obliquity of the ground on which the church stands is, probably, the cause of its wall having begun to lean; as it is, it will scarcely be able to resist for another half century the fury of the winds. On the northern side of the building but one window is to be seen, the part of the wall where another one, corresponding with it, must have been placed, having fallen in. The main entrance was on its western side; above it is a large window, and at precisely the same height in the wall opposite, there is another one, arched in a very artist-like manner. Within the church attention is arrested by some small rectangular niches in the walls, intended, perhaps, for the reception of tablets inscribed with texts of Scripture, or, it may be, of small images of the saints, carved in wood or bone. That the chalices and other holy vessels of the church were kept in them, appears improbable, as these, in all likelihood, must have had a place assigned them near the altar, which in this, as in all other churches, must have stood at its eastern end, immediately opposite the main entrance, whereas the niches here adverted to are situated, three of them in the northern, and four in the southern wall: besides, similar niches are to be seen on the outer wall facing the north. I may mention further, as not undeserving of especial notice, a stone, forming part of the inner wall to the north, on which are distinctly seen, if I remember rightly, twenty-four or twenty-six parallel lines evidently traced upon it by human hands. At one place an inscription appears to have been begun. The whole, however, is in so dilapidated a state, that what I took to be the beginning of an inscription, may, after all, be nothing more than the commencement of the stone's superficial disintegration.

This remarkable edifice, which, on the whole, displayed as much architectural skill as taste, is fifty-one feet long, by twenty-five feet broad; its northern and southern walls are upwards of four feet thick, and their height where lowest seven feet, where highest thirteen feet. The end-walls are nearly five feet thick, and the height of the eastern, eighteen feet three inches (in 1777 it was twenty-two feet), and of the western almost sixteen feet. The main entrance is three feet and a half broad, by six feet and a half high: over it is a large stone twelve feet long, twenty-five inches broad, and from seven to eight inches high. The small niches are twenty-three inches long, seventeen inches deep, and fourteen inches high. The arched window, measured outside, is three feet nine inches, and two feet one inch and a half broad; measured inside five feet four inches high, and four feet four inches broad; the window opposite, in the western wall, outside, three feet and one inch and a half high; and the four in the principal front, as well as the one in the northern wall, measured outside two feet, eleven inches high, and one foot four inches broad; inside, four feet four inches high, and four feet two inches broad.

Around the whole building, and at a distance from it of from fifty to sixty feet, there seems to have been a stone wall. It is but here and there, however, that remains of it are now observable. In all likelihood it served as an enclosure to the church-yard.

As soon as we reached the spot, we commenced our operations, by digging up the ground included within the four walls of the church a task that employed twenty-one men twelve hours; some using spades, some shovels, &c., while others who could find no implement with which to work, employed themselves in removing out of the area of the church the loose stones that were dug up, The work went on cheerfully, for every one engaged in it entertained the hope that fortune would throw something in his way; those that did not care for Runic inscriptions, or scraps of monkish Latin, trusting, at least, to find a lump of gold or silver. All were, however, alike destined to be disappointed, for nothing worth notice was discovered, notwithstanding that the whole space within the walls was dug up to a depth of two feet and a half, and the part of it nearest the east and west walls to a depth of three feet, and notwithstanding that every stone turned up was, previously to its removal, carefully cleansed and examined. The whole result, indeed, of our search, was the discovery of a few fragments of bones, which were taken to be human bones, (some of our party would have them to be the bishop's,) some bits of coal, which seemed to indicate that the church had been destroyed by fire, and a small piece of red jasper, which possibly may have been a fragment of a baptismal font.   The Greenlanders, meanwhile, averred, that the bones were those of seals, and the bits of coal the remains of the fires their countrymen sometimes kindled here, without regard to the sanctity of the spot, for the purpose of cooking by them the flesh of those animals ; and their statement did certainly receive confirmation in the circumstance that traces of such fires were, in fact, easily discernible.   In the course of our excavation we found, everywhere, at the depth of a foot and a half, a thin stratum of white clay, mixed with sand.   That a mound of stones was thrown up by us, on this occasion, reaching from the eastern entrance quite across the area of the church, I think it necessary to note, for the information of future investigators of these ruins.   Vestiges were noticed by us of two former explorations, one of which is known to have been made by Hans Egede, who, like ourselves, found some bones and coal, as well as some fragments of pottery.   As he took no especial notice of the latter, it is to be inferred, that they were not regarded by him as relics of the old Icelandic colonists, but as fragments of vessels made use of by the Dutch, who, in Egede's time, drove a brisk trade with the Greenlanders.   We discovered, on the present occasion, no such remains of pottery, but, in their place, some fragments of vessels from the porcelain manufactory at Copenhagen.

Strange it is, that we discovered no vestiges whatever of a floor among these ruins.   In an edifice, on which so much care and pains have been bestowed as evidently were bestowed on this, one could not but look to find a floor of large and handsome flags.   Nothing of the kind, however, was discovered.   Earth and stones of all shapes and sizes lay jumbled confusedly together as far down as we dug.   Perhaps the cause of this may be, that the church of Kakortok was never completed; and if this conjecture be correct, we find in it at once the solution of another difficulty already referred to, the absence of everything like an inscription, though some of the stones about the building, the large one, for example, over the main entrance, seem to have been well adapted to, or rather expressly intended for, that purpose.   The comparatively perfect state of preservation which distinguishes this church from the many other ruins in the district of Juliana's-hope, would seem, at any rate, to indicate, that it is one of the buildings latest erected by the old colonists, perhaps the very latest ; and, possibly, one of those referred to in the letter of Pope Nicholas V., as having been built by those unfortunates who had been carried into captivity by the barbarians, but had afterwards been liberated and returned home.

There is, in fact, a tradition still current among the native Greenlanders, which, if any faith may be attached to it, establishes the point, that it was precisely in this vicinity that the old colonists made their last stand. "A long time," or, as Arctander expresses it, in the words of his Greenland informers, "many winters after the Icelanders had been exterminated everywhere else throughout Greenland, the northern arm of the firth of Igaliko was still inhabited by a body of them, who owned subjection to an old man of large frame, and more than ordinary strength, from whom the firth itself has derived its Greenland appellation of Igaliko. This Igaliko, at the date referred to in the legend, was the father of several grown-up sons, and of one as yet a boy. Eminent as he was among his countrymen, over whom he exercised the authority of a chief, the enmity of the natives was particularly directed against him, and various had been the attempts made by them to destroy him with his whole family; but they had not only failed, in every instance, of accomplishing their purpose, but paid for their temerity with the lives of many of their fellows. Being, however, determined on utterly exterminating this last remnant of the European occupants of their country, they devised, at length, a new expedient, which proved successful. During the Summer months the wind blows, almost invariably, from the sea into the firths along the coast, and, among the rest, of course, into the firth of Igaliko; and of this the Greenlanders availed themselves to accomplish their murderous design. They manned some women's-boats with a party clad in white furs, and who were directed to couch down in the boats, in such a manner as to be invisible to those on shore. These men were provided with arrows, harpoons, lances, dried moss with bits of blubber intermixed with it, and other combustibles; and, thus prepared, let themselves, one evening, drift before the wind into the firth. The Icelanders saw the flotilla as it approached, but, disguised as the boats and their crews were, they took them to be merely pieces of floating ice, and gave themselves no concern about them. The boats, meanwhile, about midnight, reached the shore, and the Greenlanders disembarking proceeded to the dwellings of the Icelanders, which they set on fire. The inmates of them, roused from their slumbers, attempted to escape. The Greenlanders, however, had stationed themselves at the doors, and massacred them as they came out; and thus perished every soul of them, with the exception of Igaliko and his youngest son; for, seeing the fate of his companions, that aged chieftain lifted the youth up in his arms, and, notwithstanding his own advanced years, and the load he bore, baffled the efforts made to prevent his flight, and escaped with him to the hills. Of his subsequent fate the Greenlanders know nothing, for neither he nor his son were ever heard of more."

Besides the church of Kakortok, several other ruins are to be found in the neighbourhood, of which Arctander has given an account. The most remarkable of them is situated at the distance of from 200 to 300 paces east of the church; its wall, which is of rough hewn stone, is circular, and from two to five feet high, and its area from twenty-two to twenty-four paces in diameter.

On the 21st of August both my women's-boats were ready. Our stores were thereupon packed in the cases I had had made for them, and everything appertaining to my intended expedition despatched to Nennortalik, which place I had fixed on for my winter quarters, as well because it is somewhat nearer the East coast than Juliana's-hope, as because the greater number of my boats' crews were from that island. The boats were placed on a frame resting upon props, from four to five feet high, erected for the purpose, and there lashed fast, in the usual way, bottom up.

The following day I set out, accompanied by Dr. Pingel, (who had now completed his geological researches in this neighbourhood, and made up his mind to winter at the colony of Frederick's-hope,) with the view of commencing my survey of the district of Juliana's-hope. Some miles north of the settlement, the firth of Tunnudliorbik, remarkable for its many ruins, of which Olsen and Arctander have given a detailed account, stretches to the N.W. From this point the land trends due west, being covered almost everywhere with ice, reaching to the very margin of the cliffs that form its coast. There is but little under-land* along this portion of the coast, and no ruins whatever, a circumstance confirming the opinion of Eggers, who holds, that the East Bygd was situated in the district of Juliana's-hope; for it is observed in Ivar Bardsen's chorography, after all the firths, ending with Erik's firth, which Eggers takes to be identical with Tunnudliorbik, have been enumerated, "from hence," it is said, "the course lies westward to the island," an expression which would seem to intimate, that the main-land trends to the west from Erik's-firth, and was neither inhabited, nor habitable. At the same time, I must not neglect mentioning what some Greenlanders have told me, that a few inconsiderable ruins of Icelandic houses are to be seen on the banks of the firth of Immartinek, a firth yet unexplored by the modern colonists†. At Artsut, where we arrived on the 26th, I found the variation of the compass to be 53° 14'. A splendid northern light displayed itself the following evening. It produced no sensible effect on a magnet suspended by a silken fibre. Its colours, particularly the red and green, were vivid in the extreme, and it shone at times with such brilliancy as completely to eclipse stars of the fourth magnitude.

On the 28th, at six o'clock, A.M., I left Artsut, having taken leave of Dr. Pingel, who purposed proceeding the same day on his

* By "under-land," here and elsewhere, is meant the low, flat shore between the sea and the cliffs.—*Trans.*

† This firth, as well as the whole extent of the coast from Tunnudliorbik to Nunarsoit, is laid down in the chart only as computed.

way northward. At Itiblieitsiak, where I arrived in the evening, I fell in with a large company of Greenlanders, busied with pitching their tents, and learned that they had just returned from hunting the rein-deer at Good Hope, where multitudes of Greenlanders spend the summer, much to their own detriment and that of trade, since the seal-fishery, by far the most important occupation of the two, is thereby neglected. This hunting the rein-deer, meanwhile, amuses them, and yields them, while it lasts, enough to live on; and the Greenlander, who seldom thinks of providing for the future, cares for no more. Multitudes of reindeer are, accordingly, shot, or harpooned, by the kajakkers, in the large fresh-water lakes of the interior, whither the poor persecuted animals fly for shelter. Their hides and horns are carefully preserved by their destroyers, the former for making tents and clothes, the latter for making ornaments to their kajaks, and hunting-tackle for themselves; and if they were but as careful to preserve its well-flavoured flesh, the chase of the rein-deer might become, as I conceive, a valuable branch of industry. This, however, they are not, the greatest quantity of it being, on the contrary, left among the hills to be the prey of ravens, or the solitary bear, whom its odour may attract to the spot. The Danes settled in this country generally agree in reporting, that the greatest irregularities are indulged in by the Greenlanders during the continuance of this hunt, and that their moral character suffers greatly in consequence. I know not, for my part, how far this may be true; but certain it is, that it has been a constant pursuit of theirs from the date of their first occupation of the country, and that their moral character is a good deal more estimable than that of most nations calling themselves civilized. It is, moreover, a source to them of true enjoyment, and, as such, should not be denied these poor people, who, during the rest of the year, experience the most bitter hardships in obtaining the mere necessaries of life. The rein-deer are most abundant in the vicinity of Good Hope, the Sugar-loaf, and Holsteinsborg*, and many thousands of them are killed there annually. It is a pity that the Greenlanders, in the pursuit of them, do not spare even the young animals, of which, on the contrary, such numbers have been destroyed, particularly of late years, that there is reason to apprehend their utter extermination. One means of preventing this evil might be not to suffer Greenlanders to get rifles, the possession of which is, after all, in my opinion, of no great importance to them, except

* This is an important place to our whalers, as it is a good harbour, and, from the great rise and fall of tide, affords every facility for [repairing any of them that may have sustained injury from the ice; but it is laid down, even on Graah's chart (for he had no good opportunity of determining its position), too far to the south and west. Its true position is in lat. 66° 55′ 32″ N., long. 53° 34′ 28″ W., Dip. 82° 45′ N., Var. 67° 19′ W., as determined by me in H. M. S. *Cove*, in 1836. I have also made a survey of the harbour, for the use of whalers.—J. C. Ross.

here and there for the purpose of shooting seals. Rein-deer were formerly found, likewise, in the district of Juliana's-hope. A length of time, however, elapsed during which none were seen within its limits, until about two or three years since, when one made its appearance, and traces of several more were observed in the vicinity of Narksak, at Tunnudliorbik.

On the 14th of October, in company with Mr. Vahl, who, ever since our arrival in Greenland, had been actively engaged in botanical excursions among the mountains, and had already made a rich collection of plants, many of them rare, I set out for Nennortalik, where, in consequence of the European house at that place being too small for our accommodation, we took up our quarters, together with our Eastlander Ernenek, who, according to his promise, had arrived a few days before, in a·Greenland earth-hut. These huts are not, as many have imagined them to be, subterranean caves, but have regular walls, from six to eight feet high, built of earth and stone. From centre to centre of the two end-walls is laid a beam of heavy drift-timber, which, at one or more places, is supported by props. Across this, and with their ends resting on the two side-walls, are laid smaller beams, and over these again still smaller ones, crossing one another in various directions. Upon the frame-work thus constructed, and which is put together without spikes, nails, lashings, or fastenings of any sort, is then thrown a quantity of juniper-bush, and, over this, a layer of sods, next a layer of earth, and, finally, to complete the roof, some old boat and tent-skins. The windows are placed on the sunny side, which usually faces the sea, and are glazed, if I may use the expression, with the skin of the intestine of the seal, or the beluga, (*Delphinus albicans,*) which, though too opaque to permit of one's seeing through it, admits sufficient light for ordinary purposes. The entrance, which, likewise, is always on the sunny side of the house, is a passage of from twenty to thirty paces long; at one place straight, at another somewhat crooked, and so low, that in making one's way along it, one rather creeps than walks; the whole being arranged in this way with the view of excluding the cold the more effectually. Within, the walls are lined with broom, and hung with skins, and the floor paved with flat stones. For the rest, the interior arrangement of these houses is exceedingly simple. Along the walls, on every side, benches are erected. The one opposite the door and windows is about six feet deep, and is divided by skins into compartments that remind one of the stalls in a stable. Each family takes possession of one of them ; another is set apart for the unmarried women, and the unmarried men take up their quarters on the *brixes,* or benches, along the sides and front. Opposite each stall is a small elevated floor of stone, upon which a lamp is placed, (sometimes two or three,) made of pot-stone, (*lapis ollaris,*) and over it is suspended a kettle of the same material, in which, towards evening, when the men are expected home from sea, and the principal meal of the day is to be made, the flesh of seals, belugas, walrusses, bears, birds, or fish, whatever, in short, the larder can furnish, is cooked. When the Greenlanders have blubber in abundance, and all their lamps are lit, there is a heat within these houses, of which none who have not experienced it can form an idea. The Greenlanders, who sit naked on their brixes, though at the moment there may be, out of doors, a cold of from 20° to 30°, suffer no inconvenience from it; but the European who will not imitate their example, frequently becomes so faint, in consequence, that he is obliged to hurry out into the open air. The dimensions of these Greenland houses vary with the number of families that dwell in them together, and this sometimes amounts to seven or eight. In such case the house is made about sixty feet long, by twelve or fourteen broad. The building of the house falls within the province of the women. All that the men have to do, is to furnish the timber necessary for the purpose, and to shape the boards for the brixes.

Some Greenlanders, whom I had engaged to attend me on my expedition to the East coast, had informed me, that the sea east of Friederichsthal would not be navigable before the end of May, or the beginning of June, stating that till then it would be frozen over, and that for many miles along the coast, not a single harbour or landing-place was to be found. As this, if true, was little in accordance with the hope I entertained of being able to set out early in the spring, I determined, notwithstanding that the season was so far advanced, at once to make a short excursion to the east, in order to obtain by personal observation a more correct knowledge than I could glean from the incoherent reports of others, of the state of things, and be the better able to determine the time of my departure in the spring ; the rather because I entertained a strong suspicion that nothing but an unwillingness, on the part of those concerned, to stir until the milder season of summer might set in, had dictated that report. Being myself unacquainted with the Greenland language, I prevailed on Mr. de Fries, of Friederichsthal, to accompany us. We rowed through Torsukatek, between the island of Sedlevik and the mainland, and came to Illoa, a firth which, according to the hypothesis of Eggers, is the Œllumlængri of the ancients. Ivar Bardsen's description of that firth corresponds, indeed, upon the whole, with Illoa, except where he states that " it is so long (runs so far into the land,) that none know where it terminates." However, it is very possible, that where the vast ice-blink, now occupying the bottom of the firth of Illoa, and stretching from thence quite across the country into the sea on the East coast, now stands, there may have been, some 400 or 500 years back, a prolongation of the firth, and, perhaps, at a still more remote date, a sound. The supposition has the opinion of the native Greenlanders in its support; and that such changes in the face of the country do actually sometimes happen, in this part of the world, we have a decisive proof at a spot north of Frederick's-hope, a firth of about forty miles in length, with a number of old Greenland dwellings on its shores, which, however, are now inaccessible, except by land, enormous icebergs having long since blocked up its mouth. It is highly probable, that, in the course of a few centuries, every vestige of the firth will have disappeared, and a vast ice-blink occupy its site, insomuch that our descriptions of it may be all that will be left to testify the fact of its existence. With the aid of a fresh breeze we passed, shortly after noon, the spot that formed the extreme limit of Giesecke's progress to the east, about twenty years ago. It was pointed out to me by one of my boat-women, who accompanied him on that occasion. About four miles from hence begins a sound, running almost in a straight line, in the direction of E.S.E., between the mainland and a large island, to which I gave the name of Christian the Fourth's Island, as it was, probably, somewhere hereabouts that one of the expeditions fitted out under the auspices of that monarch reached the East coast. The sound itself I named after his royal highness Prince Christian Frederick. It is from thirty-two to thirty-six miles long, by two in width, where widest, though at many places it is not more than half so broad, and at some not more than from 200 to 300 fathoms. At the mouth of it, on the side of the mainland, is a large ice-blink, and the water there is so shoal that ships coming from the west cannot enter the sound, a circumstance seeming to lead fairly to the inference, that the Biargafiord, mentioned in the old chorographies, was somewhere in this vicinity, notwithstanding that it is said to have been west of Œllumlængri. It is stated, to wit, in Ivar Barsden, " Far to the east of Skagafiord, (according to Eggers, Narksarmiut, or the firth at Friederichsthal,) is a firth, on which no settlements have been made, called Biargafiord. At the entrance into it stretches out a long reef, making it impossible for large vessels to run into it unless with a strong tide in their favour ; and when such a tide does set in, there are seen multitudes of whales, &c., &c." It is evident from this description, that the ice-blink must have blocked up this firth*. The depth of water in Prince Christian's Sound is, doubtless, very considerable, as the land on either side of it is bold and precipitous, insomuch that there is seldom, anywhere along it, beach enough to allow of a boat being hauled up. That no sign

---

* About this Biargafiord it is further said ; " In the said firth there is a large hole, called Whales'-hole, and into it, when the tide runs out, all the whales retreat." What is meant precisely by the word which I have here rendered by *Hole*, it is not easy, perhaps, to determine. I have taken it to mean a hollow at the bottom, where a quantity of water remained when the tide ran out, thus forming, as it were, a sort of salt-water lake.

whatever of vegetation was observable upon these walls of rock, it
is almost superfluous to state.   Not a blade of grass, nay, at many
places, not even a bit of moss, to be seen about them.   Nor did
the animal kingdom, in this desolate region, exhibit more signs of
life than the vegetable.   The water-fowl that, off Illoa, had been
flying about us in flocks of thousands, had disappeared, as well as
the seals and other marine animals ; and a solitary raven that, in
the evening, flew croaking over our heads, was the only living thing
we saw: with this exception, the solemn stillness that reigned
around us was unbroken but by an occasional report, caused by
the calving of the ice-blink, or the bubbling sound proceeding from
the rapid current.   Just before night-fall we were fortunate enough
to reach one of the few spots along this sound where it is possible
to haul a boat on shore; and scarcely had we effected this with
ours, when it set in to blow a violent gale from the North.

The following morning, the wind having somewhat lulled, we
made all haste to get under way, in the hope of reaching before the
close of the day the eastern extremity of the sound.   The wind,
however, freshened again, and increased at length to such a gale
that we had reason to esteem ourselves fortunate enough in finding,
after a run of three hours under bare poles, (meaning by this, a
pair of upraised oars,) another landing-place at Ujararsoit, on the
northern side of the sound.   From this point the mainland seemed
to assume a new aspect, the heights about it, though still very lofty,
being less rugged and abrupt, and the under-land being overgrown
with dwarf juniper, and other bushes.   Close by our tents were a
couple of ice-blinks, but in so frail a condition, that I dared not
venture on mounting them.   In the evening a beautiful aurora
borealis displayed itself in the shape of a bow stretching through
the zenith from East to West.   It produced no perceptible effect
on the magnetic needle.

I ascended, on the 27th, a lofty eminence, commanding an
extensive view of the ice-clad ocean that washes the eastern
shores of Greenland.   I observed, and the circumstance is not
undeserving of notice, that at the top it blew a stiff breeze from
the East, while half-way down there was a dead calm, and at the
bottom it blew a storm from N.W.   The latitude of Ujararsoit
was found to be 60° 10′.   It had previously been my purpose to
penetrate, on this occasion, to the extremity of the sound ; in
consequence, however, of the continuance of boisterous weather,
I was induced to abandon my design, and make up my mind to
return as soon as an opportunity might offer.   My Greenland women,
who had no mind to go further from home at this season of the
year, dreading the thought of passing the Winter in these regions, a
thing for which we were, indeed, quite unprepared, were so rejoiced
on my announcement of this resolution, that they spent the whole
night in singing and dancing about a large bonfire made in the

fields, jesting and laughing with our guide Ernenek, or little Ernenek, (Erneningoak,) as they ironically called him. I may here notice, by the way, that the Greenlanders are not only very much addicted to giving nick-names, but display much ingenuity in their invention and application. Any peculiarity, however trifling, in speech or manner, a good action, or a 'bad one, affords sufficient pretext for them to fix upon the individual who displays the one, or commits the other, an epithet either honourable or opprobrious, and which from thenceforth becomes, in fact, his name ; a custom that often places a man in the disagreeable predicament of being at a loss how to call himself; pride in the one case, and modesty in the other, restraining him from using the designation thus applied to him. Even the Europeans are not exempted from the operation of this custom ; the natives, on the contrary, being rejoiced whenever an occasion offers for the exercise of their wit at their expense. They gave thus to Mr. Vahl the name of " Piniartorsoak," i. e., *the diligent earner,* not because he exhibited any great skill at catching seals, (which the word literally signifies,) but because they observed him to be constantly in chase of gnats and flies, intended to be added to his collection of insects.

The appearance of the atmosphere, in the morning of the 30th, gave warning of an approaching change of weather. We, accordingly, took our departure from Ujararsoit, notwithstanding the wind still blew from the North. Before we had rowed the distance of four miles, it died away, and was soon succeeded by a breeze from the S.E., which enabled us, to the great joy of our Greenland boat-women, to take in our oars, and hoist sail. A multitude of small icebergs surrounded us, and it was exceedingly interesting to observe the effect produced on them, by the rapid and very irregular currents running in Prince Christian's Sound. They seemed to me like so many sail steering different courses, and crossing one another in various directions. Two of them, the distance between which did not exceed 100 fathoms, shot past us, one on either side, with very different degrees of velocity, while the boat in which I was apparently made no way at all, notwithstanding it was blowing a fresh top-gallant breeze. Towards the afternoon the wind freshened to a gale, accompanied with snow and fog. Sudden and heavy squalls swept down, at intervals, from the mountains, so that we found it advisable to get our tenders, the kajaks, alongside, as our boat without their support might easily have been capsized. In this way we scudded, under a rag of a sail, through the Torsukatek channel ; but scarcely had we reached the end of it, when the gale rose to such a height, that our boat became quite unmanageable, and lay at length fairly in the trough of the sea; luckily for us, with her head towards the shore, which was not more than from sixteen to twenty fathoms distant. In this situation we drifted for some time, till we struck upon a

E

sunken rock, when we should inevitably have perished, had I not
instantly sprung out of the boat, and got her head brought round
to the wind.   By dint of great exertion we succeeded at last in
reaching the shore, where we fortunately found room enough,
though no more than barely room, to haul up our boat.   The
place where we encountered this danger received from the Greenlanders the name of Nah-ah (an exclamation of distress in their
language), in allusion to our sufferings there, during that and the
following day and night, from wet and cold.

On the 1st of November we left Nah-ah, and proceeded to
Ikigeit, where the heavy swell obliged us to make some stay.   I
discovered there some inconsiderable ruins, not noticed by Arctander : and Mr. de Fries has since found at this place a remarkable
grave-stone, supposed to date from the twelfth century, at present
in possession of the Royal Society of Northern Antiquaries, in
whose Transactions an account of it is inserted.

On my arrival at Nennortalik, the 2d of November, the Eastlander
Sidlit, and his three wives, who had arrived before me, paid me a
visit, and, on the plea of having come thither on my account,
demanded a gratuity.   I gave them to understand, however, that
their presence at Nennortalik was to me a matter of perfect indifference, unless they had come prepared to attend me to the East
coast in the Spring, and to render me whatever other services I
might require of them.   To this Sidlit, after some hesitation,
replied, that he would acquiesce in my wishes, provided he could
previously be baptized; on which I dismissed him, with the injunction to be diligent in his religious studies.   He came back, however,
as I had confidently expected, a few days after, and announced his
willingness to go, whether baptized or not; and with this understanding, I did not any longer scruple to deliver him, as I previously had
done to Ernenek, some goods in advance of the pay stipulated for
his services.

We now took up our quarters in the earth-hut prepared for our
accommodation, and were no sooner settled there, than we received
visits from all the native Greenlanders, men and women, of the
vicinity.   The women especially, and the unmarried ones above
all, (for the jealousy of their husbands acted often as a check
on the proceedings of the married,) were frequent in their calls.
A small magnet, shown them by Mr. Vahl, attracted, more than
anything else in our possession, the attention of our new acquaintances ; and no stranger arrived at Nennortalik without
coming to get a sight of this " Saviminersoak."   How it was
possible for it to sustain the weight of a piece of iron was to them,
of course, incomprehensible : the general belief among them was,
that it was besmeared with some glutinous substance, and, under
this impression, they invariably wiped it whenever an experiment
of its virtue was to be made.   These visits of the natives were at
first not unwelcome.   It did not last long, however, before they

grew to be so frequent, that we would gladly have dispensed with them. In saying this, 1 would not be understood as wishing to cast any imputation on the propriety of conduct of these poor people. It was, on the contrary, unobjectionable ; nay, their fear of seeming to intrude gave rise occasionally to the most ludicrous scenes. Whenever our servant, for example, prepared to lay our tea-table, so great a panic was sure to seize them, that they would spring up from their seats, and rush out of the house as precipitately as if the plates placed on it had been as many bears, or other savage monsters, threatening to tear them to pieces. This excessive delicacy of our guests we were ungenerous enough to turn against them, using it as a never-failing means, whenever it suited us, of getting rid of their involuntary importunity.

During our detention at Nennortalik, from the middle of October to the middle of March, nothing occurred worthy of mention. The Winter, on the whole, was mild, the thermometer being seldom lower than 13° or 14° below zero. While, indeed, throughout the greater part of Europe there was from 20° to 30° of cold, and the inhabitants of Naples were driving about its streets in sleighs, the snow was melting on the rocks of Greenland. It is evident from this circumstance, that the climate of Greenland is by no means so severe as it is usually held to be. In South Greenland, in fact, there is seldom more than from 16° to 18° of cold. Further north, about the Bay of Disco, and at the colonies of Omenak and Upernavik, the thermometer stands now and then, in Winter, at 30° below zero, (Réaum.,) or even lower ; and then, indeed, the cold is so intense that the very rocks are split asunder, and one often finds, on waking in the morning, his sheets literally incrusted with a coat of ice, and frozen to his cheeks and pillow. Still, even this degree of cold occasions, in my opinion, no more sensible inconvenience here than a temperature of 16° in Denmark, unless, indeed, it be accompanied with wind, particularly from the North, or N.W.; for, in that case, one is in constant danger of losing his nose or ears, unless he observe the precaution of thawing the frozen parts with snow before entering a warm room. It has been observed, and the fact is a curious one, that the severer a Winter is in Europe, the milder it is in Greenland, and vice versâ.

While Mr. Vahl was employed in ordering and arranging his plants, birds, and insects, and in making meteorological observations, my time was principally occupied with magnetical observations, and the phenomena of the aurora borealis, or northern lights. The former were—

1. Observations of variation, which gave the variation of the needle to be 51° 4′.

2. Observations of the intensity of the magnetic force, the results of which will be communicated in an Appendix.

E 2

3. Observations of the diurnal changes in the variation of the magnetic needle, which, in consequence of the faultiness of my instruments, yielded no result*.

The northern lights, (aurora borealis,) a remarkable and beautiful phenomenon of which the inhabitants of the greater part of Europe can form no adequate conception, are in Greenland and Iceland a thing of every-day occurrence, and serve materially to indemnify the polar regions for the want of solar light experienced by them, in consequence of the long absence of the sun below their horizon. It may be said to be of two kinds ; the one appearing uniformly between the magnetic E.S.E. and S.W., or W.S.W., in the form of a luminous arch, shining with a steady and more or less vivid light, its highest point being, in the magnetic South, from 10^0 to 20^0 above the horizon, and its legs seeming to rise out of the ocean. From this arch usually diverge rays towards the zenith, or a point in its vicinity. This description of northern light is colourless ; and I think I have observed, that it usually precedes, but still oftener follows after, some great change of temperature, especially from thaw to frost. The other sort of northern light, which, still more than the former, seems to stand in connexion with barometrical changes, flits from place to place in the semblance either of light luminous clouds agitated by the wind, and through which the light appears to diffuse itself with a sort of undulating motion, or of flaming rays, flashing, like rockets, across the firmament, most commonly upwards in the direction of the zenith, or, finally, like a serpentine, or zig-zag belt of vivid, undulating light, frequently coloured, which at one moment is extinguished, and the next relit. The most beautiful of this class of phenomena, meanwhile, is the *Corona*, a luminous ring near the zenith, of from 2^0 to 3^0 in diameter, with rays diverging in every direction, like prolonged radii, from its centre. This highly-interesting phenomenon seldom lasts longer than a few seconds, at the expiration of which an explosion, as it seems, takes place, scattering the luminous matter in every direction, and extinguishing it. The centre of the corona I found to be invariably situated to the east of

---

* Where the directive or horizontal power is as feeble as in Greenland, it is absolutely necessary, in making these observations, that the whole weight of the needle shall not rest upon its pivot, but that it be suspended by a silken fibre, so as to be altogether, or at least in part, sustained thereby. Though, with the aid of various instruments, I have failed to detect, either here or in North Greenland, any regular diurnal change in the direction of the needle, I conceive it right to mention, that Mr. Ginge, the missionary, who, about fifty years ago, made a series of observations at the colony of Good Hope, obtained the following results :—

1. That the variation is least at from nine to ten, A.M., and greatest at from nine to ten, P.M. †

2. That when the mercury in the barometer is most stationary, the variation of the needle is greatest.

† Captain Foster, R. N., on the contrary, found the greatest westerly variation to be about one, P. M., or when the sun was magnetic west.—J. C. R.

the meridian, at an elevation of from $81\frac{1}{2}°$ to $82\frac{1}{2}°$ above the horizon*. When the aurora displays itself in all its splendour, its light is brighter than that of the full moon. It has been asserted, that this phenomenon is sometimes accompanied by a low, hissing noise. I myself, in fact, have often heard the sound, but am satisfied that it has nothing to do with the aurora, but proceeds partly from the ice, partly from the wind sweeping over the snow and ling-clad hills. Whenever a more than usually vivid aurora displayed itself, I made a point of taking measures to observe its effect on a magnet suspended by a silken fibre, but never detected any agitation, or alteration in the direction of the latter, that could be attributed to this cause; though, I must add, that in making some like experiments, in the years 1823-24, at the colony of Good Hope, situated in lat. $69°$ 14′, I did think that some such effect was perceptible. That the substance-matter of the aurora borealis is liable to being acted on by the winds prevailing in different atmospheric strata seems evident, from the phenomenon itself, and as the changes of the weather depend again, in some degree, upon the winds, it is probable that a connexion exists between them and the phenomenon of the aurora. Many have hence inferred, that the appearance of the latter may safely be regarded as a prognostic of the former. This opinion, however, is, as far as I am aware, by no means well founded; and, in fact, all that may securely be relied on, with reference to this subject, is what follows :—

1. When the aurora borealis is vivid, and displays a variety of colours, boisterous or bad weather may be expectsd, and the wind may be looked for from that quarter where the aurora has disappeared, or been extinguished.

2. When, after a long absence, an aurora borealis appears between S.W. and S.E., in the form of an arch, from $10°$ to $20°$ high, and glowing with a steady light, it is a prognostic of approaching frost

The Greenlanders have a singular superstition connected with the phenomenon of the aurora borealis. They conceive it to be the spirits of the dead, playing at ball with the head of a walrus, and fancy that it draws nearer to them when they whistle,—a superstition at all events not more absurd than the idea long, and, indeed, still, prevalent in some parts of Europe, of its being ominous of war, pestilence, or famine.

The island of Nennortalik lies south of the large island of Ser-

* To determine the place of the corona in the heavens, I noted what stars lay round its centre at the moment of its formation, and then calculated, by means of the horary angle, the declination and latitude, the azimuth and altitude of the centre. The azimuth I found, in this way, to vary between 5° and 50° from S. to E.; the altitude, whose medium corresponded accurately with the dip of the needle, as above stated.

mesok, about a mile outside the firth of Tessermiut.   It is about four miles in circuit, and on the N.W. side perfectly precipitous. On its highest pinnacle, which is about 1600 feet above the level of the sea, are seen seven beacons*, said to have been erected by the Dutch.   The island produces black lead, and was anciently inhabited by the Icelanders, who, by the way, could not have subsisted here by raising cattle, but must have had recourse to seal and other fishery.   The harbour of Nennortalik is protected against the ice by the small islands and skerries lying off its mouth ; the north wind, however, blows here at times with so great violence, that ships seeking this harbour have need to be provided with good mooring tackle.   It is a curious fact, that when this wind blows most furiously at Nennortalik, the weather is usually calm and fair, or there blows an altogether different wind, off Sermesok, which is but four miles distant from it to the North.

EXPEDITION TO THE EAST COAST.

1829.

On the 25th of January, precisely the usual time of its return, the first stream of heavy drift-ice, of which we had seen nothing since the month of September previous, made its appearance.   The cause of its periodical departure from, and return to, the district of Juliana's-hope, it is not easy to determine.   It is well known that the heavy drift-ice usually every Summer besets the Southern and Western coasts of Greenland, from Cape Farewell to lat. 62° or 63°, frequently to 64°, and sometimes even as high up as 67°, the lat. of Holsteinsborg, as is said to have been the case in 1825. In September, or October, or perhaps still earlier, it disappears again, and the general opinion is, that it is swept away by the current westward towards America.   No such current, however, would seem, in fact, to exist, at least, to the best of my knowledge, there is none such to be met with in the district of Juliana's-hope† ; for which reason I am rather inclined to attribute this regular disappearance of the ice, towards the close of Summer, to another cause, its gradual dissolution by the heat of the Summer sun, and the sea's perpetually washing over it; the more so, because detached streams of it are often seen the whole year through, even at those seasons when the main-body of it has disappeared.   But how are

---

* *Varder*, pyramidal piles of stones, intended to serve as beacons.—*Trans.*
   † It is worthy of remark, however, that the current round Cape Farewell ceases from September to the end of January; not so the Davis' Strait current,—*that*

we to account for the *coming* of the ice to these coasts at a certain fixed period of the year? The following appears to me the most reasonable explanation of this phenomenon. The ice that, in January, reaches these coasts is, probably, part of a formation that has taken place on the East coast of Greenland in a high northern latitude, and from which it has, probably, detached itself as early as the Winter previous. It is, without doubt, identically the same ice among which the Spitzbergen whalers have navigated the Summer before. By the south-westerly current, known to prevail in these seas, it is carried down, between Iceland and Greenland, to past Cape Farewell, where it encounters another current that carries it up to Davis' Straits. But as the south-westerly current here spoken of is not accidental nor periodical, but constant, (it being the effect of the earth's revolution on its axis,) and as the Polar Sea contains such enormous masses of drift-ice, might we not, then, look to find Cape Farewell always beset with ice? Yet this, as well-informed persons testify, is by no means the case; the sea around this promontory being usually free of ice, or nearly so, from October to January. How are we to account for this? Either by supposing that the ice is broken up and dispersed by the hard southerly gales that prevail here in the Autumn and Winter, or that the whole mass of ice that in the Spring begins its progress from between Spitzbergen and Greenland, and which reaches the latitude of Cape Farewell towards the close of Summer, is then already near its period of dissolution. While, in the mean time, this process is going on with respect to that portion of the ice that drifts towards Cape Farewell, another and considerable body of it is carried by the current in towards the East coast, where, encountering the land, it accumulates into a compact mass, which only now and then yields to a strong, and long-continued wind from off the shore; and which, there being here neither swell nor current to act upon it, forms, with probably but little intermission, a constant and impenetrable barrier along the coast.

From the experience I had gained during my excursion in the Autumn to Prince Christian's Sound, relative to the navigation between Friederichsthal and Alluk, I judged the middle of March to be the most fitting time for the departure of the expedition, weather permitting, to the East coast. That time was now close at hand, for which reason, particularly as the Winter hitherto had been peculiarly mild, and promised to continue so, preparations with that view were commenced towards the close of February. Both our women's-boats were furnished with new skin-bottoms, the old ones being converted into tents for the accommodation of

---

continues throughout the year as the recent remarkable drift of our unfortunate whalers can testify.—J. C. R.

their crews; a stock of dried seals'-flesh and angmakset (*Salmo arcticus**) laid in; our provision-cases opened and examined; some women engaged as rowers, in place of others, who, though paid beforehand, now refused to go; and the crews of both boats appointed. The latter business, in so far as the women of the party were concerned, I left it to themselves to settle, in order that I might not needlessly separate those who might wish to be companions, and they arranged the matter, I must admit, in a manner no less satisfactory to me than agreeable to themselves, making a very fair and impartial distribution of their physical strength between the two boats. A third boat, intended to serve as a transport for the conveyance of provisions for our Greenlanders, was engaged to attend us for three or four weeks, or as far as the nearest inhabited spot on the East coast, where we hoped to be able to procure such provisions as the country yielded, in exchange for iron arrow-heads, knives, needles, beads, &c., of which we had an abundant supply. Lastly, the Eastlander Sidlit was ordered to have his boat in readiness for my use at any moment. The Greenland boat-women chose their own boatswain and boatswain's-mate, (if I may apply such terms to women,) whose duty it was to be ready at all times with their needle to repair whatever injury the bottoms of the boats might suffer. They selected, in like manner, their own cook, cook's-mate, and topman. The office of boatswain all of them seemed most averse from filling, and "black Dorothy," who was elected to it, made many remonstrances before submitting to assume it. They were, however, of no avail. A plurality of voices was in her favour, and she engaged to do its duties for the first week; for they had agreed among themselves to bear in turn the burden of all these charges. All being thus arranged, they seemed to look forward with pleasure to the time of our departure, a circumstance attributable no less to the care that had been taken to furnish them, in tents and clothing, with such protection as was possible against the inclement weather we might yet expect in April and May, than to the love of novelty so inherent in human nature, and their expectation of procuring, on the East coast, some of those variegated skins of the kasigiak (*Phoca vitulina*), with which they so much love to adorn their persons on Sundays and holidays, and which are said to be found there in greater plenty than in the rest of Greenland, and to be purchasable at a cheaper rate, being held there, in fact, in less esteem than other sorts of seal-skins. If the thought of being objects of envy to their poorer countrywomen of the East coast, in consequence of the display they had it in their power to make of beads and silk-handkerchiefs, or of the admiration their fair countenances were calculated, as they judged, to awaken in the

---

* *Mallotus arcticus*, Cuvier.

breasts of the gallants we should probably fall in with, had any part in producing this result, I shall not venture to decide.

On the 15th of March everything was in readiness for our departure. My instructions enjoined me to seize the first opportunity that might present itself in the Spring, of setting out ; and from all I had been able to ascertain, with regard to the state of the drift-ice at that season of the year, I had reason to believe that the early part of Spring was, in fact, the fittest time for navigating the sea along the south-eastern shore of Greenland. Meanwhile, we might still look to have a good deal of inclement weather, possibly even severe frost, and the delays we might experience in consequence, besides putting the patience of our boat-women to too severe a trial, might occasion an expenditure of our stores, but ill proportioned to the extent of ground got over by us. Before deciding, therefore, on the course to be adopted, I thought it best to take the opinions of Mr. Vahl and Mr. Matthiesen on the subject. I accordingly addressed letters to both those gentlemen, stating the arguments as well in favour of, as against, our departure so early in the season, and requested to be favoured with their sentiments. Both declared it to be their conviction, that the advantages that might reasonably be expected to result from our immediate departure, would fully counterbalance the evils that might, by possibility, accrue from it, and as this opinion not only harmonized with the tenour of my instructions, but coincided with my own, I determined to set out on the first occasion, and, to that end, took measures for obtaining, from time to time, intelligence of the state of the ice, which still surrounded the island in one solid mass*. One Greenlander, in particular, who dwelt upon the banks of the firth of Tessermiut, engaged to bring us a daily report of it from the bay south of Kangek, a promontory situated on the southern side of the said firth, and one or other of ourselves mounted every hour the lofty heights about us, which commanded a view of the whole ocean eastward as far as Cape Farewell.

To provide, as far as possible, against falling short of stores, I wrote to Mr. Wolff, superintendent of the colony of Juliana's-hope, requesting him to have a supply of bread sent us to Friede-richsthal, from whence it might be forwarded to, or fetched by us, if, after the expiration of three or four weeks from the day of our departure, we happened still to find ourselves in the vicinity of that place ; and Mr. Aröe of Nennortalik kindly undertook to procure a supply of such provisions as the country yields, with which the Eastlander Sidlit, as soon as a sufficiency should be got together, was ordered to set out after us. Finally, I made arrangements with the proper authorities, with the view of having

* It will be seen that we had done better, after all, in deferring our departure for four or five weeks more.

a boat with provisions sent to meet us on the East coast towards the close of the Summer of 1830. All these arrangements and precautions I looked upon as absolutely necessary, the two boats we were to take with us being scarcely capable of obtaining a year's provisions for the four Europeans destined to take part in the expedition, which, in all likelihood, could not be completed before September, or October, 1830, at earliest. For the Greenlanders that composed our crews, I laid in no more provisions in the transport-boat than would suffice for three or four weeks, as we calculated on being able to procure supplies on the East coast itself by means of barter, or by the dexterity, in fishing and the chase, of their fellows who were to attend us in kajaks. At the same time, I was aware that the East coast is but thinly populated, and that its inhabitants, few as they are, often experience such scarcity as to have little enough for their own use, and far too little to spare anything to others; as well as that, unless we made repeated stoppages for the express purpose of prosecuting the chase, not much was to be expected from the exertions of our kajakkers beyond a few birds occasionally, when and where we met with them in multitudes. As an encouragement, therefore, to activity on their part, I promised a reward in money, besides an extra portion of bread, spirits, coffee, or the like, to whichever of them should bring in a seal.

No favourable change in the state of the ice occurred until the afternoon of the 20th, when an easterly wind removed what remained about the above-named promontory of Kangek to a little distance from the shore. As my people, however, showed no inclination to quit their quarters, and as it would have been nearly dark before our boats could be loaded, I resolved, though unwillingly, to defer our departure till the next morning.

On the 21st of March, at ten o'clock A. M., we left Nennortalik our party consisting of four Danes, and fifteen Greenlanders (five men and ten women), besides the crew of our transport-boat, and a number of kajakkers, some of whom had been engaged for the purpose of taking our boats in tow when necessary, and others followed of their own accord, proposing to convoy us for a day or two. A northerly wind promised us, at starting, a quick run to Friederichsthal; but it soon veered to S. E., and came on to blow with so much violence, that we were obliged to run in for the land at the distance of about a mile east of Kangek. Between nine and eleven P. M. we had a brilliant display of the aurora, which, particularly towards the south and zenith, exhibited a succession of the most vivid colours.

On the morning of the 22nd we recommenced our voyage, but were speedily again arrested by the ice lying close up to a little island, east of Kangek. In the vain hope of some favourable change, we waited until the tide, towards noon, made it necessary for us to haul our boats ashore, at a spot scarcely more than one hundred paces in advance of that which we had left some hours previous. Scarcely had we got them in safety, when the ice was jammed in close upon the shore. We now despatched our Greenland sportsmen in quest of game, and got from them, on their return, some ptarmigans. All our attempts at fishing were, however, fruitless ; a thick snow fell during the night and following day. The ice had broken up somewhat off the island east of us, but a close stream of it lay between us and a group of islands in the bay between Kangek and Friederichsthal. Towards noon the weather cleared up, and our kajakkers set out with the view, partly of investigating the state of the ice, and partly of catching some eider ducks, fourteen of which they caught, and gave to our boat-women, who devoured them upon the spot. I myself ascended the highest eminence on the Kangek-shore, and had the satisfaction of perceiving from thence that the sea, from Friederichsthal to Cape Farewell, was clear of ice. East of that promontory, however, there still appeared to be some considerable masses, as there were also in the direction of the south, where, indeed, the ocean was covered with ice to the very verge of the horizon. We received to-day from Mr. Aröe of Nennortalik a present of some fire-wood, an article of which, from want of room for it in our boats, we had brought nothing with us, and which we were, consequently, obliged to look out for, at sea and on shore, as we proceeded.

In the afternoon of the 24th the ice began to move. By 3 p.m. we were in our boats, and, in all probability, would have reached Friederichsthal that evening, had not one of them sprung a leak, in consequence of which she made so much water, that it was found impossible to keep it under by means of baling. We ran in, therefore, for the nearest shore, got her hauled up, and set her boatswain at work to repair the damage, by sewing on a patch over the hole. By five o'clock we were once more in condition to proceed ; but the whole skin was found, on closer examination, to be in so ruinous a state, that I determined upon seizing the first favourable occasion of replacing it by a new one. After an hour's row we came to Nukalik, and there pitched our tents.

On the 25th a gale at S.E. that, several times in the course of the night, threatened to carry away our tents, compelled us to remain at Nukalik the whole of this, and the following days. We turned, meanwhile, our detention here to good account, by catching a quantity of game, particularly hares, which, being little sought after, are found here in great abundance. In a very short time the Greenlanders brought us ten of them, besides some ptarmigans ; they themselves never eat the flesh of these animals, as long as they have anything else to subsist on, reserving for themselves the entrails only of the ptarmigans, which they esteem a great delicacy. In a small fresh-water lake we found, and caught, some salmon. Near Nukalik are the ruins of some Icelandic buildings, of which Arctander seems to have had no knowledge. On the 27th, at 6¾ A. M., we left Nukalik, rowing through a tolerably wide channel within, or north of the above-mentioned group of islands,—a group consisting, probably, of upwards of a hundred small islets and skerries. We were now obliged, in order to obtain a supply of Greenland stores, to put into Friederichsthal, where I was shown by the missionary, Mr. de Fries, a copper coin found on the East coast, bearing the cipher of Charles the Twelfth, and the date 1718, the year in which that monarch died. Having concluded our traffic, we bade farewell to the civilized world, and continued our voyage as far as Koarak, opposite the lofty island of Nunarsoak. The wind had by this time freshened so considerably, that I thought it best to have our boats hauled up here at once, knowing there was no other place that we could reach before nightfall, where this could be accomplished. Several kajakkers had convoyed us hither from Friederichsthal, and on their leaving us in the evening, I requested some of them to return the next day, in case the weather should prove such as permitted of our proceeding, in order to attend us for a few days, and aid in taking us in tow. At eight o'clock this evening we saw an aurora borealis, in the form of a luminous arch stretching from N. E. to S. W., 30° high, and shortly after, three others stretching from E. S. E. to W. S. W., the loftiest of which reached nearly to the zenith. A stiff gale compelled us to remain at Koarak the two following days, and we availed ourselves of the opportunity to remove the damaged boat-skin, and substitute a new one. I ascended here the mountain Nah-ah, which rises to the height of about 1150 feet above the level of the sea. At its summit the wind blew in squalls from various points between S. E. and N. W. (passing through E.) while in the sound below it blew a steady topsail breeze at E. The latitude of Koarak I found to be 59° 59'. On the 30th, at seven A. M., we left Koarak. It had been my wish to pass, on this occasion, on the outside of Kangek-Kyerdlek, the southernmost promontory of Greenland, with the view of determining accurately the position of that important point; as my Greenlanders, however, were of opinion that we should be more likely to encounter ice by following this course, I abandoned the idea, and determined on taking the same route as I had done the Autumn previous. Kangek-Kyerdlek, or, as it is likewise called, Omenarsorsoak, is, unquestionably, the same headland which the Dutch have named Statenhook, and the English (or, as some think, our own navigators) Cape Farewell. In some of the latest English charts, Statenhook and Cape Farewell are laid down as two distinct promontories, the former name being assigned the southernmost extremity of the mainland, and the latter given to a group of islands (Kitsiksut) that stretch along the land between Nennortalik and Friederichsthal, at a distance from it of from eight to twelve miles. But there is, in fact, no remarkable promontory whatever about these islands, they being, on the contrary, so low as to be scarcely visible at a distance of more than twelve or fifteen miles, while Cape Farewell is spoken of by all navigators as very lofty. Captain Parry even believes that he saw it at the distance of forty leagues.

In the Spring of 1831 I ascertained the latitude of Omenarsorsoak to be 59° 48', and its longitude 43° 53' west of Greenwich. In different charts that have fallen into my hands, the latitude of Cape Farewell is variously given from 59° 25' to 59° 50', and its longitude (taking the mean of seven different tables) at 44° 20'. Omenarsorsoak, further, is very lofty, and is, besides, the only remarkable promontory lying below latitude 60°. It is highly probable, therefore, that Omenarsorsoak and Cape Farewell are one and the same. But from this point the land stretches away at once, on the one side in the direction of E.N.E., on the other in that of W.N.W., and thus no room is left for Statenhook, which, according to the charts above referred to, ought to lie in the same latitude with Cape Farewell, about 1° further east,— whence I conclude that not only Cape Farewell, but likewise Statenhook, is identical with the Omenarsorsoak of the Greenlanders. The European colonists in Greenland take the great island of Sermesok, north of Nennortalik, for Cape Farewell— an idea originating with Hans Egede, and which would be altogether undeserving of notice, were it not that we are probably to ascribe to it the error in the English charts, which, in so far as relates to the position of places in the district of Juliana's-hope, have been copied from Arctander's chart, appended by Eggers to his well-known work.

While engaged in towing our boats through the channel of Torsukatek, one of our kajakkers was so unlucky as to capsize, and the tow-line, which he was in the act of casting off, getting entangled about his boat, he was prevented from righting again with the ease and expedition usually displayed in similar circumstances by kajakkers. His comrades, however, hastened to his assistance, and my tender-hearted boat-women vied with one another in rendering him such services as his situation seemed to call for, one lending him a dry shirt, another a pair of breeches &c., for he was a good-looking fellow, and—which is of still more consequence in the estimation of a Greenland belle—a good seal-catcher. The channel of Torsukatek is bounded on either side by very lofty land; some of the highest points about it are said to contain pot-stone, which is not to be met with elsewhere in the district of Juliana's-hope. As we passed the Bay at Itiblirksoak, or, *the great place of transit* (to the firth of Friederichsthal)

—namely, which Eggers takes to be the Biargafiord of the ancients,
I tried to gather among the Greenlanders all the information I
could concerning the long reef and the Whale's hole, as it is called
(*Hvalshola*), which form two such remarkable features in its
chorography; but they, no less than their countrymen whom I
had previously questioned on the subject, when passing through
this sound in the Autumn, denied, to a man, the fact of their
existence. At Illoa we fell in, for the first time, with drift-ice;
it was not, however, so close as to cause us any detention. At
half-past five P.M. we hauled up our boats at Niakornak, the
north-west extremity of Christian the Fourth's Island.

On the 31st, as the weather during the night had been calm,
and the atmosphere clear, the sea, this morning, was found covered
with new ice. Nevertheless, at three-quarters past six, we left
Niakornak, and soon came to open water, but here and there
meeting with a stream of loose brash-ice proceeding from the many
ice-blinks occurring particularly along the main-land. Towards
noon we arrived at Ujararsoit, where we saw foot-prints of the
white bears in the snow. Having stopped here half an hour, and
gathered a little fuel, we proceeded again upon our voyage. As
we had a rapid current, however, to contend with, it was five
o'clock in the afternoon before we reached Kangerdlek, a little
firth about four miles east of Ujarasoit, running into the mainland in a northerly direction, where we erected our tents. One
of our kajakkers brought us in two small seals in the course of
the day, being the first we had caught since our departure from
Nennortalik.

On the morning of the 1st of April, the Friederichsthal people,
who had escorted us thus far, took their leave. We ourselves, at
day-dawn, launched our boats, and pursued our voyage through
Prince Christian's Sound. A little to the east of Kangerdlek
begins a sheet of ice that extends along the shore of the mainland
to past Puisortoarak, the most considerable ice-blink in the sound.
It is said to calve occasionally, and causes, when it does so,
inundations of the adjacent shores. The Greenlanders are of
opinion that at the spot now occupied by it there was formerly a
sound ; certain it is, that the land east of Puisortoarak assumes
at once a totally different character, being from that point more
low and level, and more uniformly covered with snow. The same
thing, however, may be said of Christian the Fourth's Island, on
the southern side of Prince Christian's Sound. From this
ice-blink a pack of brash-ice extended across the sound. It is a
sort of ice that, on account of its sharp edges, is peculiarly dangerous for skin-boats, as it easily cuts holes in their bottoms, and
at this place it was so compact, that the Greenlanders did not
believe it would be possible for us to pass it. Our ice-boards,
meanwhile, were rigged out at the boats' bows, and we succeeded
in forcing a passage through it ; we, however, soon encountered

at the eastern extremity of the sound the heavy drift-ice, that most formidable enemy, against which neither ice-boards, nor any other contrivance we could bring into play, were of the least avail, and which we had no hope or chance of overcoming but by patience. At three in the afternoon we landed at Kikkertak, a little island, situated at the distance of from one to two miles from the eastern extremity of Prince Christian's Sound. Here we discovered the ruins of some Greenland huts and graves, and other indications of its having been of old inhabited. Its present desolate condition is, no doubt, attributable to the same cause that has depopulated so many other places in the vicinity, the foundation of the missionary establishment at Friederichsthal, the native Greenlanders crowding thither to receive instruction from the Moravian brethren.

We were now obliged to remain at Kikkertak, in almost total inactivity, for twenty-five days*. We were, during the greater part of the time, completely shut in by the ice; sometimes, indeed, when it blew a storm from N.W., the ice would open somewhat within the sound; but not even all the violence of these storms produced the least effect upon the ice outside of it, which remained immoveable, jammed up compactly to the very shore. The only individuals of the party that, under such circumstances, might have employed their time profitably, were our kajakkers; unluckily, however, they proved to be either lazy, indolent fellows, or indifferent sportsmen, who, instead of procuring the means of living—as had been expected of them—for our boat-women, were not even able to provide for their own wants. The only exception to this remark was the Eastlander Ernenek, who proved to be an active, as he was a skilful hunter. When he set out on an expedition of this nature, he would frequently remain away two or three days together, but, when he did so, he was sure not to return empty-handed. Alone and unassisted he caught thus for us a greater number of seals than all the rest of my Greenlanders together, and on one occasion, having ventured to engage a bear in single combat, he brought with him, as trophies of his victory, its head and intestines, which are esteemed delicacies by the Greenlanders. He had, in the first instance, chased the monster on shore, but afterwards, on its taking the water, attacked it in his kajak. Great was the rejoicing among my boat-women when Ernenek delivered them his highly-prized booty; and "Ernenek-pitek," (or, *handsome Ernenek*,) passed from mouth to mouth till the last morsel of the delicious treat was devoured.

In the evening of the 12th some unusually brilliant coruscations of the aurora borealis were seen in the E. and N.E. They seemed to proceed from out of a thick bank of fog, about 6° or 8°

---

* The island of Kikkertak lies in latitude 60° 4', and longitude 43° 4' W.

above the horizon, and, after passing the zenith, appeared to be transformed into light clouds, for such were seen to flit past the moon in the south-westerly region of the heavens, while the northern was without a cloud. They had no sensible effect on the magnetic needle.

The Eastlander Sidlit came up with us on the 18th; as, however, he brought no provisions with him, I sent him back, accompanied by Ernenek, to fetch the stores laid up for us at Friederichsthal, of which we had every prospect of standing soon in need. At the same time I dismissed the owner of our transport-boat, taking into our own what remained of its cargo. In order, moreover, to save us as much provisions as possible for the use of our Greenlanders, I had made up my mind to send back with them the sailor who had come with us thus far in quality of cook, and whose services, considering the nature of the expedition we were engaged in, I did not look upon as absolutely necessary. He had, in fact, already got his things on board, and taken a pathetic leave of the Greenland boat-women, who shed abundance of tears on the occasion, when two of our kajakkers took it suddenly into their heads to quit us, a resolution which, notwithstanding all remonstrances and entreaties, and promises of liberal pay if they would remain, they lost no time in carrying into effect, and which now rendered the services of our cook— not as cook, indeed, but as sailor—indispensable.

At length, on the 26th of April, we saw "open water" outside the sound, and everything was got in readiness for our immediate departure, though the ice still blocked up the little island where we had been detained for nearly four weeks, so closely that we doubted very much if we should be able to get away from it. Keeping meanwhile a sharp look-out, we espied, at eleven A. M., an opening in the ice, just large enough to admit our boats, and determined on attempting it,

As we had not been able, at Kikkertak, to command an extensive view of the ocean, we now rowed straight across the sound, and landed on the opposite side, in a bay, capable, in case of need, of serving as a harbour for small vessels. Ascending the heights about this place, we ascertained the possibility of our getting past Igalalik, the extreme point on the side of the mainland, forming one of the chops of the sound; and set out, accordingly, with this intent, rowing along King Christian the Fourth's Island. We had not proceeded far, however, before we were stopped by some floes of ice, which the tide was drifting in-shore. Upon this I once more climbed the heights, and, perceiving from thence that it was still possible for our boats to pass between them, I hailed the Greenlanders and ordered them to pull away. They could not, however, be prevailed on to obey, until they satisfied themselves that their doing so would be attended with no danger, and, while they were thus employed, five or six minutes elapsed, which changed materially the face of affairs,   Another floe had, in the mean while, drifted in towards the shore a-head of us, threatening to bar effectually our further progress ; and the ice a-stern was settling fast to the land, thus cutting off our retreat ; while the shore itself, at the spot where we then were, was inaccessible.   We were, in a word, in a situation of great danger, and no choice was left us but to proceed, or to retreat at once, for a moment's delay seemed likely to be attended with the utter destruction of our boats.   In this emergency, I exerted all the strength I possessed, to fend off, by means of a boat-hook, the floe a-head, and, with the aid—first of Mr. Vahl, and, when they saw, from what he and I accomplished, that it was not absolutely impossible to force our way by dint of labour—of our boat-women, I happily succeeded so far as to make way for our boats, an opportunity of escape which, of course, we did not leave unimproved.

We found ourselves now in open water, able, for the first time, to hoist sail.   At 2 P.M. we were once more stopped by the ice a little to the north of Igalalik.   It was still possible for us to get on by passing outside of a chain of islands, stretching from this point along the coast ; but our Greenland women, who had no mind to proceed, having espied a snug spot ashore for pitching their tents on, and where there seemed to be abundance of fuel close at hand, pretended that it was blowing too hard for us to venture it.   The promise, however, of some coffee, in case we should reach Alluk, an island situated about four miles further north, before night-fall (for with coffee one can work wonders in Greenland), removed all difficulty.   It ceased at once to blow ; and we passed outside the islands above mentioned, which are, for the most part, of about the same height as the mainland adjacent, namely from 800 to 900 feet, and, with the help of sail and oars, arrived at Alluk at 5 o'clock P.M.   I here discovered, to my great concern, that the only chronometer I had brought with me was unfit for use.   On taking it out for the purpose of an observation, I found it was standing, and I could not manage to set it going again.   Some white whales, or belugas*, *(Delphinus albicans,)* said to be rarely met with on the west coast of South Greenland, were seen by us this afternoon not far from the shore.

Alluk rises to a considerable height above the adjacent mainland.   Its hills are steep, and present very much the same aspect as those about Friederichsthal.   The island, which is about six miles in circuit, consists, strictly speaking, of two mountains, divided by a huge ravine, the one to the east being the loftiest.   Vegetation here is tolerably luxuriant.   We found here, in particular, a great quantity of black crakeberries, as large, and nearly as well flavoured, as our own in harvest-time, when just arrived

* *Delphinapterus beluga,* Cuvier.

F

at maturity. On the western side of the island there is some
underland, affording convenient spots for pitching tents on. At
this island an annual fair is held by the Eastlanders, and the
Westlanders of Friederichsthal, who come here in the Summer for
the purpose of catching seals of the *cristata* species. In the
sound between Alluk and another island north of it, the winter-
ice was still lying a foot thick, a circumstance seeming to indicate
that the climate of the East coast is much more severe than that
of the West, where, the Winter previous, between the 60th and
61st degrees of lat., the sheet-ice did not, as I have been informed,
exceed from one to two inches in thickness.

As it blew too hard, on the morning of the 27th, for us to
think of proceeding, I ascended one of the highest eminences in
the island, and, for the first time since I had come to Greenland,
saw the sun rise out of the bosom of the ocean, or, rather, of the
ice, for the ocean, as far as I could see, was covered with it. Mr.
Vahl, who, later in the day, had set out on a botanical excursion
among the hills, came back in a great hurry, and announced that
he had fallen in with a huge white bear, which, as soon as it saw
him, had sprung up and stalked away. We were on the point of
setting out in a body in chase of him, but the wind just then
moderating, we made all haste to strike our tents, and left him at
peace, hoping to fall in again either with him, or some of his
kindred, at a more convenient time. Immediately after noon, we
left Alluk, whose latitude I found to be 60° 9′. I had entertained
the hope of reaching, in the course of the day, Kangerdlurksoeitsiak (laid down in the map as Lindenow's Fiord), the southernmost of the firths on the East coast, and but a short day's
journey from our last place of stoppage; but the ice was found to
be so firmly packed along the shore at Kaningesekasik (Cape
Hvidtfeldt) that we were obliged to abandon this purpose, and considered ourselves fortunate in finding, which we did not till after a
long search, a spot where we could haul our boats up, at Arfesearbik,
an island a little to the north of Alluk. In a tolerably deep bay,
south of this island, lay some sheet-ice, about a foot and a half
thick, and on it, near their ice-holes, some neitsersoaks *(Phoca
cristata)*. They were so shy, however, that we could not get a
shot at them.

It was not till the 29th, that the state of the ice permitted our
proceeding. Cape Hvidtfeldt is a lofty, precipitous headland, of
a blackish aspect, with slanting yellowish strata. From this point
begins Lindenow's Firth, the land about which was pretty generally
covered with snow. When this was not the case, however, were
observed signs of vegetation similar to those we had noticed further
south; indeed, the country hereabouts appeared to me upon the
whole less desert, or, in other words, better calculated to be a
place of habitation for man, than that in the vicinity of Prince

Christian's Sound. As the state of the ice, and the increasing gale, forbade our reaching Narksak, the only spot along the firth being as yet inhabited, we hauled our boats up at a place called Pinguarsok, about four miles from it, on the northern side of the firth.

On the morning of the 30th, the weather still continued to be too boisterous to permit of our rowing to Narksak, for which reason Mr. Matthiesen, accompanied by one of our kajakkers, proceeded thither, at my request, over land, and purchased some seal's flesh and blubber, which the sellers themselves brought us the next day. There were but four families then living at Narksak, consisting in all of twenty individuals, and all of them had made up their minds to quit it shortly, and emigrate to Friederichsthal. It is Lindenow's Firth, concerning which a report current on the West coast states, that a savage and cruel race of people, dwelling in the mountains, are accustomed to make, regularly every Spring, a descent upon the coast, when they drive away the Greenlanders there settled, and destroy their dwellings—a fable to which, as to many others equally veracious, Crantz attached implicit faith.

Having settled accounts with our Pinguarsok friends, we resumed our voyage, and, in the course of an hour, passed Nenneetsuk, a spot remarkable as having been the limit of Vallöe's progress northwards. Immediately afterwards, we were, however, stopped by the ice, which lay close up to the headland (Cape Vallöe) he had found it impossible to pass. We landed, therefore, and pitched our tents at Nenneetsuk, where we again lay icebound for upwards of three weeks. This long detention we endeavoured, however, to turn to some good account, by exploring every nook and corner in the peninsula—for such is Nenneetsuk, in fact, and not an island, as stated by Vallöe. The place bears evident indications of having been inhabited ; and we found, in one of the old houses still standing, a quantity of drift timber, consisting of red and white pine, still in good condition, a circumstance, by the way, which seems to show that the East coast is not so destitute of wood as some have thought. Among the hills we found several graves, and close by two of these, the kajak and hunting implements of the deceased, left in consequence of the belief prevalent among the pagan Greenlanders, that men are destined to pursue after death the same occupations that employed them during life, the only difference between the present and the future state being, that these employments are in the latter mere amusements, unattended with those perils and hardships which, in the former, are their constant concomitants : hence, their dead are made to take with them to the grave the implements that were most necessary and serviceable to them in this world— men, their boat and spear, and arrows; women, their lamp and kettle ; children, their toys, and, in general, the head of a dog, intended to show the helpless little ones the way to the land of spirits. In a natural cave beneath a huge mass of fallen rocks, we discovered several small boxes of European manufacture, some leaves of a Greenland psalm-book, and some female ornaments, such as beads, bits of red ribbon, &c., matters that have probably been here deposited as in a place of security, and which serve to show that the inhabitants of the country about Lindenow's Firth are no strangers to our settlements. In fact, we had already seen evidence of this fact, the Pinguarsok people having been tricked out in gay clothing of the latest fashion, chemises alone excepted, which the women here (for the men wear no linen) probably as yet considered too extravagant a luxury.

On the 9th of May I was witness of a remarkable phenomenon. Between two and three o'clock in the afternoon, one of the Greenlanders reported to me that open water was to be seen across the ice. As I had but half an hour before descended from our look-out station, whence I had seen nothing of the sort, the intelligence surprised me not a little. I lost no time, however, in remounting, and on getting to the top, actually beheld at the distance of about four miles, as it appeared, a large extent of open water, of that deep blue colour which the sea usually exhibits when it blows a fresh gale. But here and there were to be seen in it some inconsiderable streams of ice; and far off, with the aid of a telescope, three or four icebergs. Perceiving this, I really began to think there must be some truth in the opinion entertained by many persons, that the ice under certain circumstances sinks; for in no other way could I explain the so-sudden disappearance of such enormous masses of it as had occupied the sea a brief while previous. I was, however, soon undeceived, the whole proving to be a mere optical delusion. In the course of an hour the ice began to be once more visible in the direction of South, and by degrees the whole extent of water was again converted to a compact mass of ice, reaching as far as the eye could see. During the whole time, the atmosphere was perfectly clear, it blowing a gentle breeze from South-east, which, towards evening, veered to the South, and the mercury in the thermometer standing at + 4° (Réaumur).

In the morning of the 23rd, the ice having opened somewhat off Cape Vallöe, I despatched our kajakkers to examine more narrowly into its condition, while the rest of us struck our tents, and got our boats launched and loaded; and at a quarter past nine o'clock we took our departure from Nenneetsuk, whose latitude, taking the mean of several observations, I found to be 60° 28'. Shortly after, the kajakkers joined us, and reported the state of the ice to be such as would render it impossible for us to get past Cape Vallöe. Being, however, well aware that little dependence could be placed in the veracity of the Greenlanders, whose extreme

unwillingness to go far from home led them always to exaggerate
the difficulties and dangers in our way, I returned on shore, and
ascending one of the neighbouring heights myself, saw from its
summit, that the sea was actually open all along the coast. We
proceeded accordingly, and on reaching Cape Vallöe, found that
the sea was almost clear of ice to a distance of from one to two
miles from the shore, all the way to Kutek, which, as we were
informed, was the next inhabited spot upon this coast. The hills
on the northern side of Lindenow's Firth are higher than those
on the southern; but being, at the same time, steeper, they are
less covered with snow. North of Cape Vallöe occurs a deep
indenture in the land, out of which an ice-blink protrudes into
the sea. On arriving at Kutek, at 7 P.M., we found its houses
tenantless, their inmates having already taken their departure for
one or other of their Summer hunting-stations. Judging it still
possible for us to get on at least six or eight miles further, we
left Kutek, after having rested there an hour, notwithstanding the
angry looks of our boat-women, who had evidently calculated on
a longer stoppage. Their countenances cleared up again, however,
before long, on one of our kajakkers holding out to them the
prospect of reaching Ikarisieitsiak, a place not only known to be
inhabited, but to be the domicile of some old acquaintances of
theirs, who frequently had visited Nennortalik. We now passed
a deep bay, called Patursok, where two or three packs of ice threw
some obstruction in our way. The land about this bay is lofty,
but not rugged, and was covered with glaciers that reached quite
down to the sea. But here and there a solitary black pinnacle
was seen rising out of it, like a rock out of the ocean. North of
Patursok the land trends west by north, forming a firth, which on
the north is bounded by Illuidlek, a large and lofty island, of an
aspect precisely like that of the adjacent main-land. Shortly after
midnight, we arrived at Ikarisieitsiak, being a narrow sound
between two small, low islands, about a couple of gun-shots distant from Illuidlek, on one of which we landed, and pitched our
tents.

The 23rd of May.—Some dogs of the same white breed that
are to be met with in North Greenland (on the West coast) had
welcomed us on our arrival with their peculiar howl, giving proof
that we should find the island inhabited; and the next morning
showed that we were not mistaken in that inference. A family,
consisting of a man, his wife, and three children, proved to be in a
tent on the northern side of the island, at a place called Ivimiut.
This tent constitutes the Summer dwelling of the Greenlander,
from May to October he makes use of no other; and one must
admit that it is excellently well adapted to the purposes of people
who, during the whole Summer, are perpetually moving about,
at one moment far in the recesses of the firths looking for herrings,

roots, and berries, and at another among the islands along the coast in quest of seals, birds, and eggs. The ground on which the tent is to be pitched is usually marked out by a wall of about two feet in height, on which, as well as on the cross-beam of the door-frame, rest the rafters. Over these are then stretched two or three layers of hides, reaching down to the ground, where they are secured from being carried away by the wind by means of large, heavy stones. Instead of a door, a curtain is made use of, formed of the intestines of seals, in general handsomely ornamented, and so transparent as to admit a cheerful light into the tent. For the rest, the interior arrangements are precisely as in the ordinary Greenland houses, with the sole difference that a tent is seldom tenanted by more than two families together. While our boat-women were employed in preparing their meal of seals' flesh, we paid a visit to our neighbours at Ivimiut. On coming there, I found the children of the family at play outside the tent, and was surprised to see that, instead of taking instantly to flight, as not only children, but even many grown women do, on the West coast, whenever Europeans, strangers to them, make their appearance,— they appeared to look on us with perfect unconcern. When, indeed, we spoke to them, and they perceived from our pronun-ciation, that we were strangers, they evinced signs of fear, and crept trembling behind their mother. Another family, consisting of six individuals, was established on a point of land at Illuidlek, opposite Ivimiut. They paid us a visit, in company with the Ivimiut people, just as we were about re-embarking on our voyage. I observed, on this occasion, that the countenances of the two women had nothing in them of the ordinary Greenland physio-gnomy. Their whole appearance, indeed, presented none of the usual characteristics of their race, and, in particular, they had neither the prominent belly, nor the corpulence, of their country-women of the west coast. They were, both of them, above the middle size, and were remarkable for their clear complexion, their regularity of feature, and the oval form of their heads. They were more cleanly, also, than their countrywomen of the West coast, who, indeed, trick out their persons on Sabbath-days with beads, and ribbons, and variegated seal-skins, but are filthily dirty all the rest of the week.

We took our departure from Ikarisieitsiak at 10 A.M., with every prospect of making a good day's run, information having reached us that there was clear water beyond Kangek, the easternmost extremity of Illuidlek (probably the Cape Discord of the maps). But before we reached that cape, the east wind, which had set in to blow at the very moment of our embarkation, freshened so much, that we found it impossible to make head against it. We accordingly put back to Ivimiut, after having taken an observation of the latitude of Cape Discord, which was found to lie in 60° 52′.

The following day we made another attempt to get on, but with no better success. As my boat, by this time, had sustained considerable damage from being hauled ashore and launched so frequently, and as our boat-women began to be impatient at our frequent stoppages, I offered a reward to whichever of the natives of the place might bring us the earliest intelligence of its being possible for us to proceed.

The news, so much desired by us, arrived at length upon the 28th, but our Greenlanders had by this time settled themselves so comfortably in their new quarters, that it was not without many promises and entreaties that we prevailed on them to strike their tents. This, however, they did at length, and we set out once more upon our voyage. We had not proceeded, however, more than some eight or ten miles to the North, before we found the ice so closely packed, not an opening in it, however inconsiderable, being visible, as to leave us no alternative but to run in-shore, and land on the northern side of the bay of Kangerdluluarak, at a place called Serketnoua, which the kajakkers that had convoyed us from Ivimiut pointed out as the only one hereabouts where it would be possible for us to haul up our boats. A number of seals, of the species called by the Greenlanders uksuk (*Ph. barbata*), were seen on the ice-floes, and chased by the kajakkers. It was interesting to observe how courageously they defended themselves, (their eyes flashing as they turned to meet their enemies,) and seemed inclined to act even on the offensive. The land about Kangerdluluarak was found to be still more covered with snow than the country further South. In the interior of the bay, some four or five not inconsiderable ice-blinks protrude into the sea, one of them jutting out like a promontory, several cable-lengths in a south direction, immediately opposite Illuidlek. They were, all of them, branches of the glaciers that cover the high lands in every direction. Above those glaciers, however, rises a chain of mountains, forming a solitary exception to the uniform appearance of the country round, and no less remarkable for their beauty of contour, than for their height, which, I should think, must be upwards of 3000 feet, while the rest of the country, hereabouts, falls considerably short of half that elevation. On their steep sides, (which, in consequence of that very steepness, are free from snow, and contrast strikingly with the white low land round,) are seen some purple-coloured strata, probably of sand-stone, diverging, like radii, from the different summits to the icy base, and intersected by horizontal and arch-formed layers of a blueish colour, supposed by the Greenlanders to contain pot-stone. At Serketnoua we found some old houses, buried, like the whole face of the country, beneath the snow. The rocks, hereabouts, contained magnetic substances, possessed of such intense power, that the compass varied 14°, on its proximity to them being lessened or increased by from ten to twelve paces. The variation, as observed upon a floe of ice, was 51° 48'.

We now remained once more ice-bound for seventeen days. I found, by observation, the latitude of Serketnoua to be 60° 59', and its longitude 42° 35'. Snow and storms continued almost day after day, and contributed, not less than the want of their accustomed fare, to put our Greenlanders out of spirits ; for the peas and grits furnished them were but an indifferent substitute for the nutritive seals' flesh, with which they were now obliged, so frequently and for so long a time, to dispense. For the rest, nothing of any moment occurred during our detention at this place, except the killing of a bear, to which one of our kajakkers had nearly fallen a victim. The poor fellow had been sleeping on the ground in the open country, and was awakened by the hard breathing of the animal close by him. Springing up, he escaped to his boat, and felled him from thence with his arrows. The Greenlander who met with this adventure, and whose name was Ningeoak, was a lively, merry fellow, of some twenty years of age, very much addicted to antic tricks, in fact, the clown of the party. Like his fellows, each of whom had, on our setting out, selected a helpmate for himself from among the women of the party, he had made court to several, in succession, of his fair countrywomen, but had been refused by all of them on the plea of his being a "Nellursok," that is to say, a heathen, literally, an ignoramus. More than once he had begged me to make intercession with them in his favour, but all my efforts had proved of no avail. The dead bear proved, however, a more efficient advocate, his conquest of it, (for a successful bear-hunter is held, in Greenland, in high repute,) making so deep an impression on them, that I verily believe he might, if he had chosen it, have had them all. Ningeoak's pride had, however, been deeply wounded by their previous rejection of his suit, and, to revenge himself, he chose for his helpmate a superannuated beldame, the ugliest of the whole party.

In the afternoon of the 14th of June I observed, from the height, that the ice was less closely packed than, since our arrival at Serketnoua, it had seemed to be. We lost no time, accordingly, in making the necessary preparations for our departure, and, these completed, we left Serketnoua at nine, P.M. The land on the northern side of the bay of Kangerdluluarak is precipitous, and, of course, free from snow, but, at the same time, destitute of all kinds of vegetation. In the bay itself lie a number of small, low islands, or skerries, stretching along the coast from Omenarsuk, and, here and there, some sunken rocks, which, however, are not likely to prove an impediment to navigation, should any ships ever happen to visit the spot, as floes of ice, rising to the height of two or three fathoms above the water's edge, were seen to float freely over them. From Nouk the land becomes lower. It was, also, more than usually free from snow, the result, in all probability, of the sun's warmth, which, for some days past, had been sufficiently oppressive, notwithstanding that the mercury in the thermometer did not rise above 9·5°, Réaumur. The effect of the sun's heat had, indeed, been strikingly perceptible for eight days before we quitted Serketnoua, some ice-masses, several fathoms thick, having, during that interval, broken suddenly to pieces, and the small patches on the mountain-sides, where the snow had not lain, having been remarked to increase hourly in size. On the 15th, at two, A.M., we fell in with a pack, that barred our further progress. We looked about, therefore, for a fit tenting-ground on shore, and, after a great deal of trouble, found one on a small island, north of Nouk. In the afternoon, we were joined by the two Eastlanders, Sidlit and Ernenek, who brought us a small supply of stores. Next day, towards the evening, the ice along the shore began to open, though, further out, no water was to be seen.

On the 17th, at half past six, A.M., we resumed our voyage, and passed the two firths of Kangerdluluk and Ingiteit, both of which appeared to be blocked up with ice. Off the last-named lies a lofty island, called Omenarsuk, almost wholly clear of snow, its north-western side rising perpendicularly out of the sea. The promontories of Kaningesekasik, (Cape Olfert Fischer,) and Kangersukasik, (Cape Herlof Trolle,) between which it is situated, are, both of them, lofty and precipitous. Near the latter are two skerries, some hundred fathoms long, both divided, as it were, longitudinally into two parts. The ice about these skerries was again found to be close, which circumstance, together with its setting in, at the same time, to blow at N.E., a wind generally attended with severe squalls from off shore, would, probably, have prevented our further progress, had not Ernenek set us a good example, by forcing his way through the closest stream. At three, P.M., we passed Cape Trolle, and hauled into the firth of Auarket. This firth, as well as Ingiteit, is bounded on the south by lofty, precipitous mountains, bare as well of snow as of vegetation, while the land, on its northern side, is almost wholly buried under the snow. In the evening we pitched our tents at Taterat, a point of land from which the firth of Auarket properly begins, and the country about which, when compared with what we hitherto had seen of the East coast, might justly merit the epithet of fertile, as it not only was tolerably level and free from snow, but had even some spots well covered with grass and other plants. Taterat is the Summer resort of the inhabitants of the firth of Auarket, two families, comprising twenty individuals. They were a good-looking set of people, having little, in their outward appearance, in common with the Esquimaux race, a circumstance particularly remarkable in two young women of their number, whose slender forms, regular features, clear, ruddy complexion, and long, brown hair, fully entitled them to the epithet of beautiful. Brown hair seemed, indeed, to be not unusual among the members of this small community, especially among the younger ones : nay, it was even found, in several instances, to incline to reddish. A report had reached us, that, at a certain spot on the firth of Auarket, called Koremiut, lay a large mass of iron, which, from the description given of it, we concluded to be a cannon. Being desirous of obtaining some further information concerning it, we hired a boat, and, accompanied by some of the natives of the place, set out for the spot indicated, where we did actually find a small ship's cannon, whose calibre it was, however, impossible for me to ascertain, in consequence of the injury its bore had sustained from rust. A woman of the party, whom I took to be about forty years of age, stated that she could very well remember having heard it spoken of while she was yet a child. It has, in all likelihood, been driven on shore on a fragment of some whaler wrecked upon this coast. Having cleared the bore and touch-hole of the earth and sand, with which they were stuffed, I measured its dimensions, and then loaded and fired it off, to the great delight of the Greenlanders. The entire length of the gun, from muzzle to pommilion, was sixty-five inches and a half.

On our return from this excursion, we visited a natural vault, or grotto, beneath a rock, near Taterat, into which the sea enters. We found it to be about 150 feet deep, 100 wide, and from 100 to 120 high, exhibiting a regularity almost as perfect as if it had been artificially constructed. What contributed still more, however, to make this vault remarkable, was a singular, harmonic echo in it, which caught up and repeated innumerable times, every sound, even the lowest, uttered within it, and with a change of tone at every repetition. It had much the same effect to my ear as the solemn sounds of a funeral dirge heard from a distance; or rather, perhaps, as the wild music of the Æolian harp, it being impossible clearly to distinguish any articulate sounds. While we were there, sea-birds were flying about it, and within it, in flocks of thousands, taking pleasure, apparently, in listening to their own shrill cries, so melodiously re-echoed from the rocks. In the firth of Auartek are two considerable ice-blinks.

On the 18th, at seven, A.M., we left Taterat, and after a couple of hours' rowing through ice that, at some places, was tolerably close, we passed the promontory of Kunnuranak (Cape Tordenskiold). This is one of the best sea-marks along the coast. It consists of two mountains separated by a deep cleft ; the inner one, distinguishable by its round summit covered with perpetual ice, being considerably loftier than the outer, which is black, bare of snow, and flat on the top. I ascended this mountain to the height of some hundred paces, and saw, from thence, that the sea, in the direction of E. and S.E., was open, at about twelve or fifteen miles' distance from the shore. The ice in the firth of Aneretok formed again a barrier which we found impenetrable. Further in, however, we discovered a passage, profiting by which we arrived, at five, P.M., at Okkiosorbik, where we fell in with a company of about fifty Greenlanders, encamped, some on the mainland, and others on a small island near by. Here, for the first time, we were treated with the characteristic song of the Greenlanders, performed to the rude music of their drum, with its full accompaniment of gesticulation, and its chorus of " Eia-eia! Yah-yah! " exactly as described by Egede and Crantz. In its execution, on the present occasion, one old man especially distinguished himself, being incited to extraordinary exertion, either by the wish of yielding us amusement, or by the hope of some trifling reward. I know not how to give the reader a better idea of his performance, than by comparing it to the capers of a dancing bear. We learned, subsequently, that he was an angekkok, a character of much the same import among these savages, as the oracle among the Greeks of old. To him it is that the Greenlander, on every occasion of difficulty, or of moment, has recourse. If the seal, for instance, absent himself from the coast, the angekkok is called on to repair to that powerful female, who, according to a tradition current on the West coast, towed the large Island of Disco from Baal's River, hundreds of miles further North, in testimony of which fact a hole in a rock is still pointed out, where her tow-line was secured. This personage lives, says the legend, at the bottom of the sea, in a large mansion guarded by savage seals. Sea-birds swim about in her train-oil lamps, and the inhabitants of the deep flock round her, enchanted with her beauty, until the angekkok succeeds in seizing her by the hair, and, tearing off her head-gear, breaks the spell that bound them to her. If a Greenlander fall sick, it is the angekkok, again, who acts as his physician ; and so great is his skill in the healing art, that, far from confining his attention to the patient's bodily ailments, he ventures not unfrequently to prescribe for his spiritual wants. The song and dance being over, the aged angekkok advanced towards me, and asked permission to present his wives to me, for he had two. We sought in vain to purchase some provisions among the inhabitants of Aneretok. Like their neighbours at Auarket, they had none to spare. Indeed, in the course of the Winter previous, they themselves had fallen so short of the necessaries of life, as to be obliged to devour their tent-skins, and the soles of their old boots.

Next day the state of the ice did not admit of our proceeding, and I offered a reward to whoever might bring us the first notice of its being practicable. Finding that we purposed staying where we were, the natives now flocked to our tents, and we did our best to gratify their curiosity. My azimuth compass seemed especially to attract their attention; and Ernenek, who, from having frequently seen me employ it, had acquired some idea of its use, indicated to them very correctly, that the needle in it always pointed in the same direction. This, of course, surprised them greatly; but they were still more astonished on observing, that the card could be made to traverse in every direction, by means of a small magnet. How this could be brought about they were extremely curious to ascertain, and applied for information on the subject to their angekkok, who, however, so far from giving them the desired explanation, was obliged to acknowledge his own ignorance. With the use of fire-arms they were not unacquainted, most of them having frequently visited our settlements, where, indeed, every Greenlander, having the means, is sure to furnish himself with a rifle or fowling-piece.

The 20th of June, having committed to the charge of the Eastlander, Sidlit, whom I now sent back, a Report, addressed to the Board of Commissioners appointed to superintend my expedition, we left Okkiosorbik at eight, A.M. The land between this place and the head-land, or Kanjek, north of it (Cape Daniel Ranzau), is, like all the land about the firth of Aneretok, covered with snow, and has several large ice-blinks, one of which is said to occupy the site of what was formerly a sound. Under Cape Ranzau, which is a lofty and precipitous headland, we found the ice close packed; and here again I had Ernenek to thank that we were not obliged to put back; for he took the lead in his small, crazy boat, which seemed scarcely able to keep together, and our boat-women, who had implicit confidence in his skill, a confidence they could not have in me, or my European companions, who had but little experience in the management of the umiak among ice, followed readily in his wake. In the evening we pitched our tents on a point of land, in the bay between Cape Ranzau and Cape Cort Adelaer.

Next morning Ernenek set out for the purpose of investigating the state of the ice, and afterwards in quest of game. Towards evening he returned, bringing with him a large seal. Our other kajakkers, on the contrary, had remained, as usual, behind, leaving to us the care of furnishing them with provisions out of the stock we had in hand,—a proceeding which, as will presently be seen, was part of a preconcerted plan among them, entered into with the view of impeding our progress. Some of my boat-women had, already, some weeks previous, positively declared to me their resolution to go no further than Puisortok, a large ice-blink, from which we now were but a day's journey distant. I now, accordingly, inquired of Mr. Matthiesen if he, since then, had obtained any further information, concerning the intentions of the Greenlanders in that respect, and was told by him, in reply, that they would attend us as long as they saw we had a sufficiency of provisions for their consumption, but no longer. Now, if but two of the Europeans attached to the expedition were to be properly provisioned for the Winter to be passed on the East coast, we could not, at this rate, calculate on the company of the Greenlanders for more than two or three weeks longer, even allowing (which our experience of the navigation along this coast by no means justified us in allowing,) that their voyage home might be performed in a third part of the time we had taken to get to the point where we now were. Again, we could not depend on the chances of obtaining Greenland provisions, in anything like sufficient quantity, north of Puisortok, having failed to procure any at Auarket and Aneretok, which, we were told, were the two best seal-stations along the coast, especially as we were well aware that the inhabitants of that part of the country are frequently exposed in Winter to all the miseries of scarcity, in consequence of an unsuccessful fishery in the Summer. Neither could we place any reliance on the services of our own kajakkers in case of need; for but one among them knew anything of catching seals, and he could not be prevailed upon to go in chase of them, even when an opportunity offered, trusting, probably, by these means to force us the sooner to turn back, a consummation which now appeared to be the wish of all. It appeared, therefore, that we might still go on for two, or, perhaps, three weeks more; but, at the expiration of that time, that we should be under the necessity of parting company, and dismissing all the Greenlanders, and two of the Europeans, of the party. But, during this interval, we could not expect to get over much ground, probably, not more than fifty or sixty miles—thus achieving, in reality, little or nothing in the way of progress; and precisely within this limit lay Puisortok, an ice-blink which, in consequence of some local peculiarities, of which further mention will presently be made, we knew to be frequently impassable for years together. If, therefore, we kept together till we had passed Puisortok, and any difficulties should then arise to prevent its being repassed by the members of the expedition whom it was proposed eventually to dismiss, it seemed to Mr. Matthiesen and Mr. Vahl, as well as to myself, that we should place ourselves, and our boats'-crews, in risk of perishing of famine in the course of the next Winter. I proposed, accordingly, to Mr. Matthiesen, at once to send back one of the boats with Mr. Vahl, the sailor I had brought with me, and all the Greenlanders from Nennortalik, and to proceed in the other on our voyage; he, and myself, with Ernenek, and his family, on whose account I conceived I need not entertain any anxiety or apprehension, as I knew him to be a skilful seal-catcher, and was, besides, aware of his having many relatives on the East coast.

To this, however, Mr. Matthiesen objected, that if, notwithstanding the obvious danger of such a measure, we did determine on proceeding in the manner I proposed, it would be absolutely necessary to take, at least, two of the Nennortalik women with us, as it would be impossible for Ernenek's family to manage alone one of our large boats; that, if we did so, we must take stores enough for them, as well as for ourselves, if we would not expose them to the risk of famine ; and that a single boat would not, in that case, suffice, even supposing that we had a sufficiency of stores for the occasion. The objection seemed to me a just one ; and I determined, in consequence, on another plan, namely, on proceeding alone upon my voyage,— a resolution which I adopted the more readily as Mr. Matthiesen had, at the same time, stated, that he could be of no use to me, as interpreter, in my further progress North, he being unacquainted with the dialect spoken by the inhabitants of that region, as well as because it met the approbation both of him and Mr. Vahl, who agreed with me in thinking, that, with the stock of provisions now in hand, the great aim and object of the expedition,—the discovery of vestiges of ancient colonization on this coast,—could not possibly be attained, if more than one European were to partake of them.

Having thus made up my mind as to the course I should adopt, I sent for Ernenek and his two wives, acquainted them with my resolution, and asked them, if, upon condition of being liberally paid, and receiving part of the said pay in advance, they would engage to go with me as far as I might think fit to proceed, a proposal which they at once agreed to. Two old women of the Nennortalik party were, likewise, prevailed upon to go with us, tempted partly by the display of my beads and other trinkets, partly, perhaps, by the hope of finding on the East coast more faithful lovers than it had been their fate to gain at home : for report said, that the inhabitants of the East coast were accustomed, when visited by scarcity, to destroy their women, so that the sex was usually at a premium among them, every woman having three or four husbands. Finally, I yielded to the unanimous opinion of my companions, who represented to me the absolute necessity of my having a kajakker with me, and agreed to take Ningeoak, the clown, in that capacity, the more readily as one of the Nennortalik women who had engaged to follow me was his wife. As much provision as could be stowed away in our boat was now laid aside, all other necessary arrangements made, and official orders given to Mr. Vahl and Mr. Matthiesen to return, as well as a Report to the Board of Commissioners made out and intrusted to them, which done, I prepared to proceed as soon as an opportunity might offer.   The latitude of our halting-place was 61° 47'.

The 23d of June, Ernenek, who had made an excursion the day previous, for the purpose of ascertaining the state of the ice, returned with intelligence, that it now was possible, in his opinion, to pass Puisortok. I, accordingly, had my boat got in readiness this morning, hoping to get past this danger in the course of the day. From Cape Adelaer was seen, between N. and N.N.E., a tract of high land, bare of snow, its blue mountains giving it a pleasing aspect, very different from all we hitherto had seen on the East coast. I here took leave of Mr. Vahl, to whom I seize this opportunity of rendering my acknowledgments for his cheerful participation in the hardships and labours incident to our voyage, and his unwearied and conscientious zeal in the discharge of the duties especially assigned to him,—zeal, (of which the natural history of Greenland is already in possession of some of the good fruits,) which I trust will not be unappreciated by his country, —and hastened to reach that smiling land, where I hoped to find the end of the Ubygd, as it is termed, and the beginning of the so-much-lauded East Bygd. After rowing two or three hours, we were, however, obliged to land again at Sermenoua, a small peninsula, or naze, about five miles from Puisortok, the ice forming a compact mass, which we found it impossible to penetrate, and here we were under the necessity of remaining for three days. I observed that though the rocks about this place were, here and there, covered with a tolerably-thick stratum of soil, scarcely any traces of vegetation were perceptible. At the distance of some hundred paces from our encampment rose some huge ice-blinks, one of which I attempted to ascend. I was soon obliged, however, to desist from the experiment, having met with fissures and precipices which it was quite impossible for me to pass. The latitude of Sermenoua (i. e. the naze of land-ice) was found to be 61° 54′ 50″.

On the 27th, at sun-rise, Ernenek set out in his kajak, and shortly after returned with the news that we might proceed. At six, A.M., we accordingly left Sermenoua. As we neared Puisortok the ice became more and more close, and we were at length obliged to abandon our oars, which we found wholly useless, and to push ourselves along as we best could. We passed the ice-blink at the distance of from 100 to 400 fathoms ; it was, beyond comparison, the largest I yet had seen, being about a mile long. It rises perpendicularly about 100 fathoms, at which elevation it strikes off at an angle of from 30° to 40°, still rising to a considerable height, until it unites with the glaciers that cover the whole surface of the high land above. Being full of huge gaps and fissures, occasioned by its frequent calving, as also undermined to a considerable depth by the constant action of the waves and current, its condition is extremely infirm, and, in consequence, to approach it is an adventure of no little peril. Nor is this the only danger to be apprehended : the ice off this blink, even to a considerable distance from it, being said to shoot up from the bottom of the sea, in such a manner, and in such masses, as in many years to make it utterly impassable. How to account for the phenomenon to which I have just adverted I know not, unless by supposing that the bottom of the sea itself is hereabouts, like the dry land, covered with a thick crust of ice. But whether this crust is formed upon the spot, or is the remains of ice-bergs, and the heavy drift-ice frozen to the bottom during severe Winters, or a portion of the land-ice, which, loaded with stones and fragments of the crumbling hill, has protruded itself into the sea, is a problem impossible, perhaps, to solve. The Greenlanders state that there was formerly a sound on the inner, or land-side of this blink, which has been closed up by the encroaching ice. The colour of the sea off Puisortok was much diversified, being sometimes yellowish, and sometimes green or blue ; at some spots the water was muddy. The depth of water cannot be very considerable : I must, however, add that, on sounding, I got no bottom at twenty fathoms. During the three hours we took to pass this blink, it calved about twenty times. The masses of ice, however, which on this occasion were detached from it, were comparatively small, and we passed it without any accident, and without my having observed anything of that upheaving of the ice off it, to which allusion has been made, though the fact of its occurrence cannot be doubted, the very name of the place, Puisortok, being thence derived. This is, no doubt, the place spoken of by Vallöe, as the limit beyond which none dared venture by reason of a whirlpool, so vast as to swallow whole icebergs ; and it is worthy of remark, that he, too, makes mention of a sound said by the Greenlanders to have existed hereabouts, a sound once navigable, but which subsequently was blocked up by ice. On a point of land under the Kangek, or promontory, north of Puisortok, to which I gave the name of Cape Billé, in honour of Admiral Steen Billé, we found three Greenland families encamped. As soon as they saw us, they set up the usual cry of "Umiak ! umiak !" i. e. "A boat ! a boat !" and hurried to the shore to ascertain who we might be. On recognising Ernenek, the women flung themselves prostrate on the ground, setting up at the same time the usual Greenland funeral howl, a cry interrupted at regular intervals by some words uttered in a plaintive tone, conveying an eulogy of the deceased, and expressive of sorrow for his loss. Ernenek's wives had likewise lain themselves down howling at the bottom of the boat ; and, to complete the chorus, the dogs and children on shore added their cries to the rest. This lament, which lasted about a quarter of an hour, being finished, and my two Nennortalik ladies, who, unconcerned spectators of the scene, had all the while been attending to the duties of their toilet, having both put on their bead-trimmed jackets, anointed their hair with their disgusting substitute for hair-oil, and tied it into a knot with green silk ribbons (for red they had no right to wear *) and displayed on their persons all the handkerchiefs they were possessed of, we pulled in for the shore, to visit Ernenek's good friends, and learn from them the state of the ice, which we were told was open no further than to the island of Kikkertarsoak (Otto Rud's Island) about four miles further North. Of the Greenlanders we met with upon this occasion, one elderly woman wore her hair dishevelled, and another had hers cut off, and both were clad in male attire, —all signs of grief and mourning. For the rest, they were a dirty, miserable-looking set. It is, however, to be observed, that they were on a journey at the time, and this is an occasion on which the Greenlander puts on his shabbiest clothes. They were on their road to the fair held annually at Alluk, where they barter, with their countrymen of the West coast, bear, seal, and dog skins for articles of European manufacture, and especially for spear and arrow heads, knives, needles, handkerchiefs, and tobacco. These things they purchase at an exorbitant price; so much so that it would be at once a profitable speculation, and an important service rendered these poor people, to send, about the month of June every year, a boat laden with such articles from Nennortalik to this place of rendezvous. As soon as my boat-women had completed a bargain for some spotted seal-skins, for which they paid a few needles a-piece, we took leave of these poor people, and resumed our voyage. Off Rud's Island the ice was found to be impenetrable, and we hauled up our boat, accordingly, at a small naze, where there was just room enough for our tents, all the rest of the island being buried under the glaciers. Between Rud's Island and the mainland the Winter-ice still lay from two to three feet thick. The latitude of the southernmost point of this island was found to be 62° 7'.

On the 29th of June, there having blown a smart breeze from the West during the night, we concluded that the ice would be found to have opened sufficiently to allow of our passing. It was not, however, without much labour that we succeeded in reaching, towards evening, Malingiset, a small island about 1000 paces in circuit, and so much covered with snow, as to present the appearance of an iceberg. The whole extent of mainland between Rud's Island and Malingiset, a tract whose elevation, to the distance of three or four miles from the shore, scarcely exceeds 400 or 500 feet, is buried under snow and ice, yet here and there some short and naked naze protrudes from below the glaciers. On the N.E. point of Malingiset we found an old Greenland hut, and near it

---

* Among the Greenlanders of the West coast, as among the peasantry in some parts of Denmark, red is a colour used only by unmarried women. Wives, widows, and unmarried women having children, are prohibited its use, but may wear any other colour they choose.

G

two or three graves,—a thing of rare occurrence on the East
coast, the Eastlanders being accustomed to commit the bodies of
their dead to the sea, in consequence of the face of the country
they inhabit being covered, during the greater part of the year,
with ice and snow, and the scarcity of stones necessary for making
burial-places. Some old household furniture and fishing apparatus
lay scattered about the spot, and among the rest a sort of saw,
used, instead of a knife, for cutting blubber. It consisted of a
lance-formed piece of fir, along whose edges two rows of sharks'
teeth were let in, and secured by small nails made of bone. The
same sort of implement was formerly made use of on the West
coast. The latitude of Malingiset, by observation, was found to be
62° 20'.

On the 1st of July, at half-past five o'clock, A. M., we left Malingiset. At the bottom of the firth of Kangerdlurksoeitsiak (Mogens
Heinson's Fiord) which runs into the land to the distance of about
eight miles, rise some lofty and snow-free mountains, to a considerable elevation above the rest of the ice-clad country round.
Off the promontories Kasingertok and Nektoralik we again found
the ice close packed. This, indeed, we had observed to be the
case, under almost all nazes, or points of land, projecting to any
considerable distance into the sea. These promontories are precipitous, and therefore bare of snow; the first-mentioned is low
and narrow—the last, on the contrary, lofty and of a dark,
blackish aspect. Sea-birds, in flocks of thousands, were found to
have built their nests about it; nor could they have selected a
place affording them more perfect security, for these cliffs are so
precipitous, as to be quite inaccessible to man. The islands
of Nunarsoak, Omenak, and Omenarsoak, which we had got
sight of at Cape Adelaer, south of Puisortok, presented here a
singular appearance, owing to the effect of refraction. The many
conical and pyramidal peaks which characterize these lofty, snow-
free islands, seemed prolonged far beyond their actual height, and
over each of them, in the air, was seen an image of itself, but
inverted, which continually rose and sunk, at one moment dis-
appearing, as it seemed, behind the true peak, and in the next
re-appearing at an elevation above it of from 1° to 2°. The most
easterly and distant of these islands, Omenak, which I have called
in the chart Griffenfeldt's Island, appeared like a small globe,
separated from the rest, and suspended in the air at a great
height. Besides these objects, were likewise seen the inverted
images of a number of icebergs, which themselves were not—at
least from my boat—within the sphere of actual vision. Towards
noon we reached the large island of Udlosietit, said to contain pot-
stone. It was the first land in any considerable degree free from
snow, that I had fallen in with on the East coast; there was,
however, very little sign of vegetation about it, as far as I had an

opportunity of observing. The latitude of the S. E. extremity of this island is 62° 29' 50". As I was in the act of taking this observation, kneeling on the rock with my sextant in my hand, an Eastlander came rowing in his kajak towards the spot. He no sooner saw me, however, than he was seized with amazement and affright : and no wonder, for my European dress was a thing unknown in these regions, and a point of land concealed my Greenlanders and boat from view. He rubbed his eyes, looked at me again, and having satisfied himself that there was no optical delusion in the case, turned with all speed, with the intention of taking to flight. Upon this, however, I summoned Ernenek to the spot, who called out to him that he had nothing to fear, on hearing which he put back, and joined us, highly delighted, as it seemed, to find that I was neither a Tunnersok nor an Innuarolik, spirits believed by the Greenlanders to inhabit the mountains. At another place in the same island we saw an aged man sitting in a thoughtful attitude upon the rocks, his head resting on both hands. He seemed to look at us with perfect indifference, until we had got past him, but, this done, he took to his kajak and came out to us. He had a true robber-looking countenance, and his long black beard, his features overgrown with hair, his dark shaggy eye-brows, the black rings about his eyes, his wild and piercing look, and somewhat forward manner, formed a *tout ensemble* little calculated to inspire confidence. Nevertheless, I found him, on further acquaintance, to be a very friendly, serviceable person. We went with him to his Summer quarters, at Maneetsuk, a small rocky islet east of Udlosietit, where I found about twenty natives, his companions, domiciled in a couple of tents. They were, all of them, save a pair of breeches each, stark naked ; but on the old man's crying out to them, to come and see the Kablunak*, the women put on their jackets, and the whole party hurried to the shore to receive us. I would gladly have remained for some time at this place, as my boat-women were wearied with their day's-work ; but it was next to impossible for us to haul up our heavy boat at the spot. Contenting myself, therefore, with purchasing of them a few pieces of dried seals'-flesh, I continued my voyage as far as a place called Asiouit, where we found a covenient landing-place. A family of eight individuals, who were encamped there at the time, came down to the shore, as we drew near, to welcome us. They helped us in unloading our boat and hauling it on shore, and received for their pains a pinch of snuff a-piece, with which they seemed to be well satisfied.

---

* Such is the name usually given by them to all persons not native Greenlanders. On the West coast, the inhabitants of which have a knowledge of various European nations, it is the Danes especially that are distinguished by that appellation. The Greenlanders call themselves Innuit, *i. e.*, men. The word Karallit or Kaladlik is unknown among the Eastlanders.

On the 2nd of July, at six o'clock, A.M., we left Asiouit. We
now rowed through a quantity of heavy drift-ice along the land of
Nunarsoak, a tract of country very precipitous, and, of course,
free of snow, except in the ravines. Neither iceblinks nor glaciers
were to be seen about it, at least on its South side. Here and
there, its mountains were covered with dwarf-willow and birch;
though there were but very few spots where the vegetation could be
said to be luxuriant. On the whole, the face of the country was
bare and desert; but, nevertheless, its aspect was delightful to us,
who, for so long a time, had been accustomed to see nothing but ice
and snow. It was, moreover, highly beneficial to our eyes, which
had suffered greatly from the effects of snow-blindness, as it is
called, caused by the reflection of the sun's rays from the glittering
ice-coasts along which we navigated. I myself was, for a short
time, completely blind. The symptoms of this malady are inflam-
mation, attended by severe pain, and a suffusion of water whenever
the eye fell suddenly on the glaciers, when shone on by the sun.
The native Greenlanders, who, in their chase of seals, &c., are
sometimes exposed for a whole day at a time to the operation of
this intense light, are peculiarly subject to it: and to guard against
it in some measure, they wear shades of various sorts, some of
them very tastefully carved, and inlaid with bone.

From the western extremity of Nunarsoak project two low
isthmuses, one in the direction of East, the other of North, and
both named Kinarbik. Here two tents were pitched, inhabited by
fourteen individuals, who crowded about me inquisitively as I took
an observation for latitude, some of them even offering me their
aid on the occasion. As, however, the ground on which my
artificial horizon was placed, was not a fast and solid rock, I
thought it most advisable to do what I was about alone, and,
accordingly, gave them to understand, that it was dangerous to
approach my instruments; for to bid them go away, would have
been held by them an unpardonable rudeness. They conceived
from this that my sextant was a sort of fire-arm, and withdrew,
accordingly, to a respectful distance from it. The quicksilver in
my instruments they took for lead, and gave me to know, that they
were acquainted with the use of that metal in soldering. After
having satisfied their curiosity, as well as I was able, with respect
to the object of my voyage, the contents of my cases and boxes,
the material of which my clothes were made, &c., I prevailed on
some of them to go with me as far North as Griffenfeldt's Island in
their own boat, and to take in it a portion of our cargo, which was
too heavy for ours to carry without danger.

North of Nunarsoak lie some islands, which, like it, are free from
snow, lofty, precipitous, and with but little vegetation. On our
arrival at Griffenfeldt's Island, towards evening, we were received,
as previously at Puisortok, with a funereal howl, or lament, per-

formed, in this instance, by the members of a family there domiciliated, and consisting of nine individuals. Among them were two young women, relatives of Ernenek, to whom I gave some beads, receiving in return their "kujanak," or thanks, as well as a more substantial testimony of their acknowledgement, in the shape of a few pieces of fresh bears'-meat, and a dish of sorrel. I had soon, however, good reason to suspect that their conduct, in the latter instance, was not prompted merely by a sense of gratitude, as it was not unaccompanied by sundry questions, concerning the number of needles I had in store.

July 3. The ice, this morning, was found to have settled into the land, and to be so close, as to render it impossible for us force our way through it. I devoted the day, therefore, to an excursion among the mountains. The southern part of Griffen-feldt's Island consists of a single mountain of, I should suppose, 3000 feet in height, and terminating in three peaks, of which the central one is some hundred feet higher than the others. Its ascent is exceedingly difficult, its sides being everywhere steep ; and this is particularly the case with respect to its highest peak, which consists of a vast accumulation of loose stones, that roll down from under one's feet at every step. After a laborious ascent of five hours, I at length reached the top, which, in clear weather, commands an extensive view towards both South and North : the atmosphere, however, was on this occasion hazy, so that I had less benefit from my excursion than I had anticipated. My companion told me, that he had distinguished from the summit some lofty snow-covered peaks a little to the west of the Aneretok mountains, but much more distant. They were, probably, the tops of Niviarsiet, or the Maidens, in the district of Juliana's-hope. The mountain, to the height of 800 feet from its base, was abundantly covered with bushes, in many places, particularly with black crake-berry and with whortle-berry; but, above this limit, it was tolerably bare. Round the spot where we had pitched our tents, as well as at a few other places, there were some small meadows, if that name may be applied to patches of about four hundred square yards in dimensions ; and we found here, moreover, some scurvy-grass, for the first time since we had passed Puisortok. In the direction of E., and of S.E., the sea was open to a considerable extent, and the ice nearer the coast was not so compact, but that a ship, with anything of a favourable wind, might very well have sailed through it, except, indeed, close up to the land, where it was close packed. On my return from this excursion, I made a visit to the tent of our Greenland neighbours, the inhabitants of the place. Its owner was an elderly man, a widower, not much more than four feet tall, but nevertheless, I doubt not, a no less skilful seal-catcher than he was, to all appearance, a good housekeeper. Everything in his abode gave token of his being a person in easy circumstances. His boat and hunting-tackle were in excellent order, and his tent large and roomy, and provided with various household matters not often to be met with among the Eastlanders, such as an earthen vessel, a copper kettle, two looking-glasses, a couple of boxes with locks, &c., all of them purchased at the fair of Alluk. An unusual degree of cleanliness and order was, besides, observable both within and without his tent; but this may have been owing to the expectation of a visit from us, for cleanliness is not the most characteristic quality of the inhabitants of Greenland. A new bear-skin was spread over a box to serve me in lieu of a chair, and the best fare the house afforded was presented to me; bears'-meat, blubber of the narwhal, and a sort of conserve, made of blubber, roots, and berries, taken out of an old pair of breeches, that served the purpose of sweetmeat-jars. I made inquiries of these people concerning the state of the land to the North, and was informed by them, as I had previously been by Ernenek, that, at the distance of a couple of days' journey from Griffenfeldt's Island, it would again be found to be buried under snow. Of ruins of European dwellings they knew nothing, nor had ever heard of any legend or tradition concerning their country having formerly been inhabited by Europeans. Their country, they said, had no meadow-lands, the mainland being buried under snow and ice, and the islands that skirt the coast being, all of them, lofty and precipitous. They made mention, however, of one place, Ekallumiut, where, they said, some grass-grown fields were to be found. Ships, they thought, could not navigate the sea along their coasts, on account of the ice with which they are constantly beset. The latitude of the highest point on Griffenfeldt's Island is 62° 55'.

On the 6th of July we left Griffenfeldt's Island, and proceeded on our voyage, shaping a course through a sound, that runs the length of eight miles, due North, between the mainland and Tekkir-sok*. It is bounded on both sides by lofty, and, in some places, inaccessible mountains, but sparingly overgrown with black crake-berry and juniper-bushes. North of the sound, where the current flowed at the rate of from eight to twelve miles an hour, and was very irregular, the firth of Kangerdlurksoak, (Sehested's Firth,) runs into the land in the direction of W., or W. by N. It is filled up with ice of all sorts, and some considerable blinks were seen in the interior of it, where the land was buried under glaciers. From Akuliarisek, a naze, or point of land, forming the northern boundary of Sehested's Firth, the firth of Kasiartok runs due N.N.W., and from it branches off a sound running North of the Island of Asioukasik. We entered this firth, but found its navi-

---

* Whether Tekkirsok is an integral part of Griffenfeldt's Island, or not, is uncertain.

gation to be as difficult as it was dangerous, in consequence of the innumerable icebergs, and vast quantity of brash-ice, with which it was filled, and which proceed from a large ice-blink at the bottom of the firth. At three, P.M., we reached the mouth of the sound, Ikarisarsuk, and expected there to see an end to our labours for the day. Instead of this, however, we found the whole channel blocked up with Winter ice, from three to four inches thick, so that we were obliged to put back, and pass South about Asioukasik, which terminates to the East in three small promontories, each bearing the name of Kangerajek*, until we reached a small grassy islet off the eastern extremity of the firth, where, at eleven o'clock at night, we pitched our tents. The mainland hereabouts is high, and has many peaks, forming good land-marks. Being less precipitous than Griffenfeldt's Island, Omenarsoak, or Nunarsoak, it is, in some degree, covered with snow, though by no means so much so as further South. Patches of heath were everywhere seen on the hill-sides, down which flowed innumerable streams, forming here and there beautiful cascades, and falling into the sea with a noise that may be heard a long way off.

On the 7th of July we proceeded on our voyage. The promontory of Kotesermio, as also three skerries lying near it, are of a yellowish-brown colour. From this point we commanded an extensive view of the ocean, which was covered with ice as far as the eye could reach. It was only by hugging the coast, which trends from this promontory in the direction of N.W., that we could manage to get on. On a small island, called Anarnitsok, partially covered with a description of fine grass, we found three empty tents; their former tenants had, probably, taken their departure for some other fishing and hunting station in the vicinity. There is a bay here, running a couple of cable-lengths into the land, which, if it were but a little more secured against the ice, would form an excellent harbour. After half an hour's rest we again left Anarnitsok, but finding it impossible to make our way through the ice, under Kangek, (Cape Niels Juel,) a promontory on the eastern side of a large island, to which I gave the name of Skioldunge Island, and which stretches far up towards N.W., in the direction of the above-mentioned Ekallumiut, we landed, and pitched our tents on a naked rock, lying close under the island, a little to the West of the said promontory. A piece of drift-wood, of white pine, which we had seen on the ice as we came along, but had not taken the trouble to pick up, was now, as soon as our boat was unloaded, made a prize of, and chopped up into fuel, an article of which we were constantly in want. Being obliged to

* The word Kangek, which occurs so frequently in these pages, means *a promontory*. From it are derived the words, Kaningesekasik and Kangersukasik, *a large promontory:* Kaningoak, *a small promontory*, &c. Kangerajek signifies, I believe, *almost a promontory*.

remain at this place the following day, I had an opportunity of taking an observation for latitude, which I found to be 63° 12'.

On the 9th of July the ice had opened under Cape Juel. This promontory is of no very great height, scarcely more than from 700 to 800 feet. The quantity of garnets with which its face is speckled, give it a reddish-brown aspect. The ice, North of this point, consisted of much larger floes than any we yet had seen, a circumstance, however, which proved favourable to our progress, as they were prevented by the long tongues protruding from them, from coming into juxta-position, and formed thus small canals, broad enough, in general, for our boat to pass through. We were, nevertheless, often obliged to make a passage for ourselves, by hewing away the ice with our axes, and still more frequently to make long circuits in order to get on. North of the island of Omenarsuk, whose easternmost extremity is lofty, precipitous, and separated from the rest of the island by a cleft, that extends nearly to the water's edge, the ice became more open. On an island a little further North, we saw a few tents, abandoned, like those at Anarnitsok, by their inhabitants, whom, however, we shortly after met, in three umiaks and eleven kajaks. They, too, had to announce the death of friends, or relatives; for, on our approaching them, they flung themselves down, to a man, in the bottom of their boats, and commenced the usual dirge. Finding that it lasted, on this occasion, somewhat too long, I thought to put a stop to it, by letting my snuff-box go round among them, and actually succeeded, by this means, in obtaining a respite. It proved, however, to be but a respite after all, for, as soon as the box was emptied of its contents, they recommenced where they had left off, and howled their dirge out to the end. That their lamentation, however, was but an empty ceremony in which the heart had no part was evident, as well from their tearless eyes, as from their unconcerned good humour the moment after its completion. Curiosity induced them to put back, and acccompany us to the island of Kopetelik, where, towards evening, we pitched our tents. They were, like the generality of their countrymen of the East coast, a tall and well-made set of people. Most of the men had their eye-brows blackened, and some of them wore large mustachios. The women were tattooed on the chin, arms, and bosom. They, too, could give me no more information than the rest, whom I had previously questioned on the subject, concerning ruins, or other vestiges of ancient colonization in their country. Kopetelik, which ranks among the less lofty islands that skirt this coast, is partly buried under snow, partly a naked rock.

On the 10th of July, at six, A.M., we resumed our voyage, and found tolerably clear water as far North as a Kangek, rising boldly out of the sea a considerable height, to which I gave the name of Cape Moltke, in honour of his Excellency the Minister of State,

Count Moltke of Bregentved. North of this promontory the face of the country was again more covered with snow than it had been for some distance South, and glaciers were seen on the low and level upper-land, protruding at some places into the sea. At the island of Kikkertarsoak, which was surrounded by a multitude of icebergs, we fell in with an assemblage of some seventy or eighty Greenlanders, stripped, to a man, of everything but a pair of breeches each. We bought of them as much dried seal's-flesh and blubber as they could spare, and, forthwith, attended by thirty or forty kajakkers of their party, proceeded to Kemisak, a small, low island, where we found about 100 more Eastlanders in tent. On landing at this place, Ernenek and his wives fell down and kissed the earth ; a custom, it would seem, practised by the Eastlanders on coming to places they have never visited before. Kemisak was one of the prettiest spots I yet had seen upon this coast. Its valleys were, indeed, still, in a great degree, filled up with snow, especially those on its Northern side ; but, wherever this was not the case, the soil was covered with a vigorous growth of grass, and a number of sweet-smelling flowers adorned the rocks.

Very few of the Kemisak people had ever set their eyes upon a European ; and it was not surprising, therefore, that my arrival should cause much commotion among them. Old and young, in fact, crowded about me, and assisted in getting my things on shore, overwhelming me, as they did so, with a thousand questions, very few of which I understood. Some of the elder ones, in particular, were very inquisitive and importunate. Indeed, I have observed this to be very generally the case among the natives of this country. It was, however, an easy matter for me to get rid of them whenever I wished to do so. I had but to take my gun out of its case, and fire it off in the air, and the whole assemblage would immediately withdraw, or seek refuge in their tents. These people knew no more than the other Eastlanders I had previously fallen in with, of ruins, or of hot springs, such as, in Ivar Bardsen's Chorography, are said to have been found in some small islands in " Rafn's Fiord," in the East Bygd. Pot-stone, in like manner, which is said to have been so abundant in the East Bygd, that vessels of the capacity of ten or twelve barrels were fabricated out of it, was to be met with but at one small island in the vicinity of Omenarsuk. Nails, and bits of iron, or bell-metal, so frequently to be met with in the southern districts of the West coast, and which are evidently relics of the old Icelandic colonization, they had never either found themselves, or heard of being found by others, on the East coast. Grave-stones, and others, with Runic inscriptions, of which several have been found of late years on the West coast, and of which I myself brought home, in 1824, the first specimen, (found near the colony of Uppernavik, in about latitude 73°,) they had no knowledge of whatever. Ships they had never seen, and believed it would be impossible for them to approach their shores, by reason of the ice with which they were perpetually barricaded, as far as the eye can reach. Hares and rein-deer, which are said to have been a staple article of food among the inhabitants of the East Bygd, they only knew by name; and mice, of which a species has been met with some 400 miles further North—a discovery since frequently advanced in proof of the old Icelandic colonies having been situated on the East coast—were unknown to them *. The Amorroks, of which the people of the West coast frequently make mention, and which some hold to be wolves, or wild dogs, while others deny that they exist at all, they look upon to be fabulous monsters, as they likewise do the Erkil-liks. One of them, indeed, asserted very seriously that he had seen some of the last-mentioned among the mountains, about the large firth of Kangerdlurksoak, (Bernstorff's Firth,) which, in the latitude of Kemisak, runs into the land in the direction of W.N.W. They were shaped, he said, like human beings, but were somewhat taller, had a large snout, large bushy eyebrows, and a voice like the howling of dogs. On my asking him, if they rowed in kajaks, and caught seals like his own countrymen, or how else they managed to exist among these ice-clad mountains, he said, he knew not, but persisted in his statement, that he had seen many of them. I requested him on this, to show me the way to where they lived, but he excused himself on the plea of its being so far off †.

* Fortunately, it has since been ascertained, that these mice are of a new species, and, therefore, cannot be the descendants of the old Icelandic ; and the hypothesis built on their discovery falls, consequently, to the ground.

† Among those still inclined to combat Graah's opinion, that the East Bygd of the old Icelanders never was situated on the East coast, is Mr. Wormskiold, a gentleman of great erudition, who himself has visited Greenland. One argument, in support of his views, he deduces from the above passage of Graah's text, he being of opinion that the Erkilliks there mentioned are in reality no other than the descendants of the old Icelandic colonists. The tall stature, the large nose, and bushy eyebrows, are all characteristic features of men descendants of the old Northmen, as is no less the peculiar intonation of the voice in speaking, which the Greenlander, in his simplicity, compared to the howling of dogs. It is not a little remarkable, that as the Greenlanders of the East coast thus represent the country West of them to be inhabited by these Erkilliks, those of the West coast hold the country East of them to be the abode of a race of men differing from themselves in origin, as well as in various other particulars. In other words, both thus concur in representing the interior of the country as inhabited by a race of people different from the Esquimaux. There is a tradition of the West coast having once been visited by an individual of this race, named Grimmersoak ; and in this name Wormskiold finds another proof of the Northern origin of the race, to which he is said to have belonged, Grimmer (Grimmur) being an Icelandic proper name, and *soak* an Esquimaux word, signifying *great* or *big*. Wormskiold is decidedly of opinion that Graah would have discovered the real descendants of the old Ice-landic colonists, had he but penetrated into the interior of the country, in place of confining himself to a mere coasting voyage. The attempt, however, might have been attended with great peril, in consequence not only of the nature of the country itself, but of the superstitious fears of the native Greenlanders, who, very possibly, might have deserted him, and left him to perish in this desolate region.— *Trans.*

With respect to our chances of getting on, I was informed, that the ice further North was usually closely packed, and that no landing-place was to be met with for a long way along the coast. Five boats, they told me, had perished in the ice the year previous, on their way to Kemisak from Omevik, the nearest, and, in fact, only inhabited spot to the North. This last piece of information was not confined to my ears only, but reached, likewise, those of Ernenek's wives, one of whom began to make objections to our going further. This circumstance, however, did not disconcert me. In fact, I had been, for some time past, desirous of getting rid of them, having found their retinue of children a great encumbrance. For this reason, as well as because Ernenek himself expressed some apprehension of being unable, in the regions further North, to provide for his own and his family's sustenance the Winter through, in which case I should be obliged, sooner or later, to turn back, in order to take up my Winter quarters where we now were, I thought it best, provided other hands could be procured to supply their place, to leave them at once. With this view I lost no time in making application to several of the women of the place, displaying my beads, handkerchiefs, &c., and promising them a liberal supply of each in payment of their services. The catastrophe to which I have adverted had, however, made so deep an impression on them, that they, one and all, positively refused to accompany me. Failing with them, I turned, at length, half in jest, to a poor fatherless and motherless girl, of some twelve or thirteen years, named Kellitiuk, and asked if she would go with me, and, to my surprise, was answered—Yes. I took her at her word, and let her choose for herself some beads out of the stock I had as part payment in advance,—a procedure that did not fail to lead to the result I had anticipated; for scarcely had she finished sewing them upon her jacket, when two other girls of her age volunteered to follow her example. I was thus enabled to dispense with Ernenek's two wives, and, by these means, to spare not only a good deal of room in my boat, that hitherto had been occupied by their children and chattels, but, which was of still more moment, a good deal of provisions; for each of my new boat-women was ordered to take with her her own bundle of dried seals'-flesh. This arrangement concluded, a reward was now offered to the first that should bring me news of the ice being practicable.

From the 11th to the 13th of July we were obliged to remain ice-bound, at Kemisak, whose latitude I found to be 63° 36′ 50″, and employed the time in visiting the natives in their tents, and was everywhere received by them with kindness and civility, and treated to bears'-fat, dried seals'-flesh, and other dainties, with, sometimes, many apologies that they had nothing better to offer me. When I happened to remain at home, my tent was always

full of visiters, who frequently would sit whole hours looking at
the prints or books I showed them, and wondering, as it seemed,
how it was that they could not hear the latter speak, though they
held them close to their ears for the very purpose; for they
believed that every word I read aloud to them from a book, was
communicated to me by it in a whisper.

In the evening of the 13th of July I crossed over, in my boat,
to the mainland South of Bernstorff's Firth, with the view of
examining the state of the ice. I found it to have opened a little
under Kanjek, seven miles N.E. of Kemisak ; and, though the ice
between us and that point was still so close, that none believed it
would be possible for us to force our way through it, I determined
to make the attempt the next morning. The place where I landed,
Ikatamiut, displayed a tolerably luxuriant vegetation; and I made
a small collection of the various plants and flowers I met with on
my way. Some claps of thunder were heard, and some flashes of
lightning seen, in the direction of S.W., at about eleven o'clock
at night.

On the 14th of July, at five, P.M., we took leave of our friends
at Kemisak, and, by dint of great exertion, forced our way through
a sea, so much filled up with icebergs and brash-ice that, for the
greater part of the time, the water itself was wholly hidden from
our view, to the above-mentioned Kangek, a not very high, but
precipitous headland, from which the land stretches away in almost
a right line due-North. I gave it the name of Cape Mösting, in
honour of his Excellency, Mr. Mösting, Privy Councillor and
Minister of State. On reaching this point, we found the sea to
be again occupied with the ordinary drift-ice, which lay sufficiently
close, though not so much so but that, by changing frequently our
course, we were able to get along between the floes, without
running foul of them. The masses of which this drift-ice was
composed, were considerably larger than any we had met with
further South. Some of them were a mile in length and breadth,
and upwards of thirty feet in thickness. This extraordinary thickness is to be attributed, in all probability, to the snow that collects
upon them melting, when a thaw takes place, and settling into a
condensed and solid mass, which, by the next occurring frost, is
converted into ice. The coast, as far as Taterat, is bold, precipitous, and bare of snow; the upper-land, however, is here, as
everywhere else, covered with glaciers, protruding, wherever a cleft
or ravine occurs, into the sea. On the summit of one of these
cliffs stands a huge upright mass of stone, like a beacon, whence
the cliff itself has obtained its Greenland name of Innusuk, or
Innusursoak. About half way up the face of this cliff, a jet of
water gushes out of it. Taterat is a small, but lofty island, separated from the mainland by a narrow sound. It is about the
latitude of this island that Danel has placed the Herjolf's Naze of

the old chorographies, but most erroneously; for there is no point of land hereabouts answering to the description given of it, and Hvarf and Hvidsærk, two remarkable mountains, between which it is stated to have been situate, might as well be looked for anywhere else along this coast, as far as my observation goes, as here. A few miles North of Taterat a small firth, Otto Krumpen's Firth, runs into the land in the direction of West. The hills about it were completely buried under snow or ice. Still a little further North begins an enormous ice-blink, Cobberger Heide, which covers the face of the shore for many miles, reaching far up into the firth of Kangerdlurksoak (Gyldenlöve's Firth) which runs into the land in the direction of W., or W. by N. This ice-blink, like most large ones, rises perpendicularly out of the sea, but seems to be of a more firm and solid structure than is usually the case, though, at the same time, the vast quantity of broken ice that lay beneath it, covering the sea to a considerable distance from the shore, gave token of its calving frequently. This ice was so close, and its edges so sharp, that, notwithstanding the utmost caution, we could not avoid twice cutting a hole in the boat's bottom. Fortunately, however, this happened, in both instances, at places that could easily be got at, so that we found no difficulty in stopping the leaks with bits of blubber. As we could find no landing-place, we continued under way all night. At the distance of about two miles from the ice-blink above-mentioned, we saw a triple or quadruple line of icebergs, stretching up into Gyldenlöve's Firth. Some of them were of extraordinary magnitude, like those some-times met with in the northern part of Davis' Straits, particularly about the latitude of Omenak. Not a few rose to the height of 100 feet, and one, whose circuit at its base I took to be 4000 feet, rose to 120 feet above the level of the sea. Its full altitude must, therefore, have been about 900 feet*, and its cubic contents 900 millions, of feet. Yet, well as such a huge ice-mass may merit the epithet of Berg, (*mountain*,) it is inconsiderable when compared with some that other travellers assert that they have met with. Nothing is more curious than the great variety in form and appear-ance which these icebergs exhibit. Some of them resemble palaces, or churches, or old castles, with spires, and towers, and windows, and arched gateways; others, pyramids and obelisks; others again, ships, trees, animals, and human beings. A number of them together, seen at the distance of a few miles, present the appear-ance of a mountainous country, and have frequently deceived the eye of the mariner. Seen nearer, they look like huge hills of marble, and, when the sun shines on them, glitter like silver. We proceeded the distance of about six miles between the land and

---

* It has been ascertained, that not more than one-seventh or one-eighth part of an iceberg rises above water.

this chain of icebergs, hoping to find, somewhere or other, an opening in it through which to pass.   It was found, however, to be prolonged uninterruptedly until it came into contact with the land, and, as this was nowhere accessible, we were obliged to put back, and seek a passage outside of it.   In the course of the day we saw a good many atarsoaks *.   (*Pho. grœnl.*)   With their usual inquisitiveness, they raised themselves high out of the water, to look at us, but took care, at the same time, to keep at a respectful distance, safely intrenched behind the ice-floes, so that the shots which were sent after them were but thrown away.   After thirty-four hours' rowing we arrived at Aluik, an island inhabited by 130 persons, who, as we approached, came down to the shore, and received us in Greenland fashion, that is to say, helped us to get our things on shore, and to haul up our boat.   Scarcely had I got my tent up before it was crowded with the natives, who gazed with astonishment at everything they saw, raising, in chorus, a loud crescendo cry of "Ho! ho! ho! ho! ho!—Ho-i!" which was repeated a greater or less number of times, according to the degree of interest excited by the object.   The iron hoops and nails on my boxes and provision cases, particularly attracted the notice of the men, and one of them even tried to pick out a loose nail, while another took off the cover of a book-case, in order to examine it.   On my giving them to understand that they should refrain from such liberties, instead of being offended, they merely requested me to show them the contents of my many boxes and cases ; but as there were among them various matters which I supposed they stood in need of, and might have proved, on that account, a strong provocative of their cupidity, such as arrow-heads, knives, needles, and so forth, I thought it advisable, before complying with their wishes, to make them aware of the power of my rifles.   I, accordingly, sent a bullet through a piece of drift-timber lying on the ground at some distance from the spot, and was about to follow this up, with firing off a musquet loaded with shot, when a number of voices exclaimed, "Enough! no more! no more!" many of the by-standers making off, at the same time, with all speed to their tents.   Such is the terror felt by these people for fire-arms.   As soon, meanwhile, as I laid aside these so-much-dreaded weapons, they again collected round me, but I cannot say were as polite as their countrymen at other places I had touched at, in quitting my tent when I myself went out of it.   This circumstance, and the attempt made, as above-mentioned, by one of them to extract the nails out of my boxes, prevented me from being here quite at ease with respect to my security from theft, for which reason, as I was under the necessity of ascending the neighbouring heights, in order to observe the

* The Harp Seal.—J. C. R.

bearings of the coast, I had all my instruments removed to the tent of my boat's-crew, and took up my quarters there myself. But even this change in my arrangements did not altogether answer the purpose ; for, as there was not room enough in the tent for my provision-boxes, I was obliged to let them remain outside of it, and, consequently, to sit up all night, in order to ensure their safety—a precaution that, after all, proved to be super-fluous, as the natives, one and all, retired to rest at the usual time, and did not make their appearance again till the following morning. My boat-women, who had been as little pleased as myself with the familiarity and importunity of the Aluikkans, or, as they were generally designated, the Omerikkans, had, likewise, remained up during the night, in order to enjoy in peace and quiet the luxury of coffee, a drink which their inventive genius had taught them to prepare in an altogether novel way, the beans, after being roasted on a stone over the flame of a lamp, being ground by them between their teeth, and the very dregs (for the Greenlanders never throw away anything that can be eaten or drunk,) they, to wind up all, devoured with avidity.

The next morning I received invitations from the tenants of various tents; and, among others, from one individual who told me that he was a trader; for, be it mentioned by the way, they all took me for one, and had been wondering, therefore, why I refused to purchase the white fox-skins, which some of them had offered me for sale. The stock in trade of my new mercantile acquaintance was, however, expended, for which reason he was making preparations for a trip to Kemisak, where he purposed purchasing a fresh supply of old iron arrow-heads, knives, and other things of like description. In the tents I visited, I was treated with the usual dainties of blubber and seals'-meat. My entertainers, however, omitted the ceremony of licking the dirt off with their tongues, which, it is said, the Greenlanders of the West coast uniformly practised of old, when visited in their tents by Europeans*. To the good people of Omevik, European articles of luxury and fashion, such as ribbons, handkerchiefs, linen, and beads, were, for the most part, novelties ; and my two Nennortalik ladies, who did not let the opportunity escape them of displaying all their finery, made even a greater sensation here than they desired. The hide of a rein-deer, which one of them wore, was taken, like the material of my own clothing, to be the skin of a sort of dog, a circumstance which seems to justify the inference, that the rein-deer is altogether unknown at this place, as everywhere else further South along this coast. Very few of them seemed to have had any previous acquaintance with looking-glasses. Most of them, when they saw their own image reflected

* This practice is still prevalent amongst the Esquimaux of Melville Peninsula, and Boothia.—J. C. R.

in them, burst into a fit of laughter, and made a number of strange grimaces. One handsome young woman, however, became so enamoured of the glass I showed her, or rather, perhaps, of her own charms, that, after some demur, I made her a present of it. Brandy, to which the Greenlanders have given the name of *the maddening drink,* my new friends could not be brought to taste, notwithstanding that Ernenek showed them he entertained no fear of it. With my snuff, however, they used less ceremony; in fact, they took such quantities of it, that I was obliged to keep several people employed in drying and pulverising the tobacco leaves. Even young children take their pinch, whenever they can get it. I met, among these people, with but one instance of a man with two wives. For the rest they marry, it appeared, at a very early age ; two young girls, who could not have been more than thirteen years of age, were pointed out to me as already married. It is to be observed, however, that there was a great disproportion of the sexes among them, the males being at least one-third part more numerous than the females.

Here, too, as everywhere else, all my inquiries concerning ruins, and other indications of ancient European colonization, were fruitless. The natives told me the whole of their country was buried under ice, the small islands about Aluik excepted, and were astonished on being informed by me, that it had formerly been inhabited by Europeans. The glaciers, they believed, were continually on the increase, spreading every year further and further over the face of the country,—an opinion entertained no less on the West coast, and which seems, indeed, by no means improbable, for they evidently cannot have been produced all at once, but progressively ; and the causes to which they owe their present magnitude, must, in all likelihood, be still in operation, and the glaciers thus be perpetually undergoing increase. Several of them who were acquainted with the country to the North, to a long distance, positively denied the existence of any sound stretching across it; and I am very much inclined to believe, that nothing but the constant inquiries made by Europeans, concerning such a sound, has given rise to the report of its existence, the Greenlanders either thinking to gain favour by chiming in with their preconceived opinions, or, finding a malicious pleasure in sporting with their credulity, of their disposition to which several instances have fallen under my observation. That large indentation of the coast, in latitude 70°, known by the name of Scoresby's Sound, is, therefore, in all likelihood, no sound at all, but a deep bay, or firth. For the rest I may here take occasion to observe, that the said firth is, after all, no new acquisition to geographical science, it having been discovered, by a Danish navigator, named Volqvard Boon, as far back as the year 1761 [*].

[*] Wormskiold's Treatise, in the *Transactions of the Scandinavian Literary Society,* for 1814.

Aluik is a small islet very much covered with snow, and exhibiting but few signs of vegetation. The latitude, by observation, is 64° 18′ 50″. On the mainland, at the distance of five miles N.W. of it, is a lofty round-topped mountain, distinguished from the surrounding country by being bare of snow. Under a naze of a tolerably large island, completely buried under snow, N.E. of Aluik, a number of icebergs were seen aground. The channels between them were found to be filled up with drift and brash-ice. Towards the East the sea was somewhat open, but my boat-women refused to proceed in that direction, as it would lead them too far from shore. Having spent the whole night in vain endeavours to find a practicable passage to the North, we landed, on the 17th of July, at eight, A.M., at a very indifferent landing-place on a small island, (Gabel's Island,) six miles E.N.E. of Aluik. Its latitude was observed to be 64° 22′. It was high-water here to-day at three-quarters past four o'clock, and the day before, consequently, it being new moon, at about four. The difference between the high and low water-mark was from eleven to twelve feet. The greater part of this island was covered with snow. Scurvy-grass, (*cochlearia*,) very little of which I hitherto had met with on the East coast, sorrel, and black crakeberry-heath, were its only plants. In the evening I crossed over to another larger island, North of it, likewise very much covered with snow ; and from its highest summit, which rose from 400 to 500 feet above the sea, I saw open ice in the direction of E. and S.E., and, at about twelve miles' distance out to sea, a channel running to northwards.

On the 18th of July, at three o'clock in the morning, we resumed our voyage, and, after rowing five hours, reached the channel just mentioned. Towards noon we landed on a naked point of land, stretching out from beneath a precipitous headland, to which I gave the name of Cape Lövenörn. Close by this headland, to the South, are two large ice-blinks, both called Puisortut, and said to present the same features as the ice-blink of the same name further South ; North of it the whole country lies buried under the glaciers, which leave nothing of it visible, but, here and there, a peak, or point of land, as far as Peter Oxe's Firth, which was still filled up with Winter-ice, and did not seem to be of any considerable depth. From Cape Lövenörn, which consists of a light-coloured sort of stone, intersected by black strata, the land trends as near as possible N.N.W. It is, generally speaking, not very high: some few lofty mountains only being seen at the bottom of Oxe's Firth, the southernmost of them, which lies at the distance, probably, of from twelve to fifteen miles inland, being bare of snow, and looking like a decapitated nine-pin. Towards evening we pitched our tents on a small island, where, as well as at some others in the neighbourhood, we found a beautiful description of mica-slate. Its vegetable productions

H

were very inconsiderable, these being confined, in fact, to a sort
of small-leaved cochlearia and some black crakeberry-heath, the
latter growing everywhere along this coast, where the snow does
not lie.   I called these islands Nordbye's Islands.

The next day we crossed a bay, the land about which, like that
about Peter Oxe's Firth, was completely buried under snow, or ice,
with the exception of one naze, or, perhaps, small island, on its
northern side.   At noon, a light breeze at N.E. sprang up, accompanied with a cold fog, which speedily became so thick, that we
quite lost sight of the shore.   As the ice at the time was tolerably
open, we might have managed to get along by the aid of the
compass; but my Greenlanders, who placed no confidence in its
guidance, declared that we should go astray if we attempted it, and
I was, accordingly, obliged to humour them, and remain alongside
a floe of ice, till the weather cleared up, which it did towards
evening.   The phenomenon, so common during fogs, of objects
seeming to be further off than they really are, presented itself to
us here, under a peculiarly striking aspect.   The smallest hummocks of ice, looming like mountains, seemed to be a mile or two
distant, though, in reality, not further off than twice or thrice the
length of our boat.   Towards evening we arrived at some small
islands, to which I gave the name of Skram's Islands.   I ascended
the highest of them, and found the ice to be impenetrable, to the
distance of four miles to the North.   A deep indentation was
seen in the land bearing N.W., to which I gave the name of
Kiöge Bay.   It is surrounded by lofty mountains, unusually bare
of snow.   From this bay the land trends to the East.   This I had
been prepared for by Danel's, as well as Egede and Rothe's
voyage, together with the observations I myself had had it in my
power to make.   In fact, I had predicted it some days previous,
and my fellow-travellers were now not a little amazed to find, that
I had predicted rightly, particularly when I told them, that the
most easterly land in sight was a cluster of large islands; for I took
it to be no other than the five *Insulæ* of Danel.   The highest land
to the North here in sight was tolerably free of snow; and, though
I had by this time given up all expectation of finding the East
Bygd on this coast, the prospect of coming once more to a tract
of country, that had as yet been able to resist successfully the
encroachment of the glaciers, was most grateful to me.   The next
two days we were obliged to remain at Skram's Islands, whose
latitude is 64° 47'.

On the 22d of July the ice began to open.   At one o'clock, P.M.,
we took our departure from Skram's Islands ; and, after working
our way through a pack of ice of about four miles in breadth,
found ourselves suddenly, to our great satisfaction, in a small sea
perfectly free of ice.   We landed on an island, (Sneedorff's Island,)
where we found six old Greenland huts, and a number of graves,

in which lay, besides the ordinary Greenland implements of the chase, two images rudely carved in imitation of the human form, not unlike those presented to Behring, by the savages of the N.W. coast of America, and which he took to be idols, though it is very probable that, in fact, they were employed there, as they certainly are in Greenland, as mere children's toys.

Sneedorff's Island displayed a richer vegetation than any I yet had visited. Cochlearia, the round-leaved sorrel, and a number of wild flowers, exhibited a vigorous growth. The grass, however, that grew here, did not seem to thrive, except what covered the walls of the houses, the soil thereabouts being fattened with blubber, seals'-blood, bones, &c. At half past twelve at night we pitched our tents on a tolerably large island, about ten miles East of Sneedorff's Island. Here I was obliged by rain and fog to remain all the next day. Towards evening, the weather clearing up, I made an excursion among the hills. The island is almost wholly, particularly its southern and western sides, covered with glaciers, and its vegetation very inconsiderable. It is, in all likelihood, as Captain Zahrtmann has suggested to me, the same that Danel speaks of by the name Hvid Sadlen, and I have, accordingly, marked it down in my chart as such. North-west of this island, on the mainland, stands a remarkable round-topped snow-free mountain, called in the chart Cape King Frederick the Third, as neither Captain Zahrtmann nor myself, after a careful perusal of Danel's voyage, have been able to discover any point along this coast answering better than it does to the account given by that navigator of the said headland.

On the 24th of July, at five, A.M., we left Hvid Sadlen. N.E. of it is another tolerably large island, Œrsted's Island, the latitude of whose easternmost extremity is, by observation, 65° 5'. It is loftier than the last-mentioned island, its shores are for the most part inaccessible, and the whole of its western side is, like the greater number of the neighbouring islands, buried under a thick bed of snow that probably never thaws. Proceeding on our way, we passed between two islands, which I named Hornemann's and Vahl's Islands. The former, which is the loftiest of the whole group, I take to be 600 feet above the level of the sea. Both of them were almost wholly covered, like the rest, with ice and snow. A heavy rain fell in the afternoon; and my boat-women, wrapping themselves up in their water-proof jackets, exerted themselves to the uttermost to reach a landing-place, which they espied on an island north of Hornemann's Island, where we arrived at six in the evening.

This island, which I named Turn-back, was the farthest point North that we attained ; for when, after a detention of three days, we attempted to proceed beyond it, we found the ice to be impenetrable. A vast number of icebergs had grounded under the shore, and the spaces between them were blocked up by drift and solid field-ice. As I was unwilling, however, to turn back as long as any chance remained of our proceeding, though I had not the most distant hope of finding any vestiges of the old colony under a more northerly latitude than that we now were in, we returned to our tenting-place, at Turn-back, waiting patiently a favourable change.

On the 30th of July, towards evening, it blew a terrible storm at N.W., which, however, produced no other effect on the ice along the shore, than that of driving out to sea some large icebergs, bearing E. and E.N.E. of us, by which means I got a sight of two, or, perhaps, three large islands in that direction, distant from forty to fifty miles. These are, probably, the islands between which Danel states that he passed, in the year 1652, though they lie somewhat nearer the mainland than, acccording to his account, they ought. It is, likewise, in all likelihood, these same islands that the ancients called Gunbiörn's Skerries, and which, they state, lay mid-way between Iceland and Greenland, that is to say, (according to my interpretation of their words,) midway between Iceland and the Bygd in Greenland, which, in fact, they do exactly, if, by the Bygd, we are to understand the present district of Juliana's-hope, and keep in mind, that, in the early period of the Greenland colonization, those sailing for the colony did not shape a course direct S.W. from Iceland, but first steered West till they made the land, and then proceeded to the South along the shore*.

As there was still no prospect, on the 3rd of August, of our getting on, I determined, in order that my time might not be altogether wasted, to retrograde a step, for the purpose of exploring the country about Kiöge Bay. I judged it likely that this tract of country was inhabited, as I had been told at Omevik, that we

---

* In one of the Sailing Directions for navigating between Iceland and Greenland, attributed to Ivar Bardsen, the following passage, literally rendered into Danish, occurs :—" Fra Snefieldsnæs Vest n paa Island er kortest til Grönland og er det kaldet to Dages og to Nætters Seilads i Vester, ligge da Gunbiörnskiœerene ret midtveis imellem Grönland og Island, og var dette den gamle Seilads, men," &c.— Literally, " From Snefieldnæs, (situated on the) West (coast) of Iceland, the distance to Greenland is shortest, and it is said to be two days' and two nights' sail, in the direction of West, then lie Gunbiörn's Skerries exactly half-way between Greenland and Iceland, and this was the old course, but," &c.   Eggers has, in my opinion, satisfactorily proved, that the old writers have committed an error here in stating the distance to be a *two* days' sail to the West, and that, in place of *two*, we should read *four*. Wormskiold, on the other hand, who combats Eggers' statements, holds, that the error lies in the punctuation of the passage, I, for my part, believe that both are in the right ; and, while I read with Eggers *four* days, instead of two, I place, with Wormskiold, a semicolon after the words, " er kortest til Grönland," from which corrections it results, that the distance from Iceland to *Gunbiörn's Skerries* was four days' sail to the West, and Gunbiörn's Skerries being expressly stated to lie exactly half-way between Iceland and Greenland, that is, between Iceland and *the Bygd,* the distance between the latter, was eight days' sail. I think I have seen somewhere else in the old writings, the distance between Iceland and the Bygd given at seven days' sail, of which afterwards.

should find settlers at the distance of two or three days' journey from thence *. We pulled in under a precipitous headland, called in the map Cape Gudbrand, (Thorlaksen,) on either side of which the glacier expands, in order that we might, at least at one spot, set foot upon this portion of the coast, which is, in general, so effectually barricaded with ice, that it is impossible to get nearer to it than within from 300 to 400 fathoms. I collected here such specimens of botany and mineralogy as were to be found. At Sneedorff's Island I stayed two days, some seals having made their appearance, which I was desirous, if possible, of catching. All our efforts to that end were, however, fruitless. The latitude of this island is, by observation, 64° 57′ 56″, and its longitude 39° 20′. The variation of the compass was observed to be 56·4° north-westerly.

On the 7th of August we crossed over Kiöge Bay, and landed at two large islands, tolerably free of snow, on one of which, named by me Olè Römer's Island, we found three Greenland huts, the ground about which was covered with a more luxuriant growth of cochlearia than any I yet had seen. There was every appearance of this island having been inhabited the year previous, as we found some blubber, and various household articles, among which some lamps, that, by the way, were not made of pot-stone, put carefully aside. Some of these articles gave evident indication of their owners having been supplied with goods of European manufacture, such as knives and saws, things which they, in all probability, obtained by barter with their countrymen of the South. A large piece of drift-timber, which they had commenced cleaving asunder with stone wedges, lay near the shore. To the west of Römer's Island, a tolerably deep bay runs into the land; but the ice, with which it was filled, prevented us from going into it. Kiöge Bay, on the other hand, was as free of ice as it had been when I last crossed it,—a circumstance to be accounted for, perhaps, by a gentle, superficial current, which I observed in it, setting from the shore.

As neither Greenlanders nor seals were to be met with here-abouts, I turned back, on the 8th of August, towards the East. The ice had, during my absence, undergone no change, but remained immoveable, exactly as when I first examined it.

Danel's Islands were now plainly to be seen from Turn-back, as well as from two other islands, four miles N.E. of it. As I perceived that it would soon be necessary for me to return, in order to look out for winter-quarters, I went, on the 18th of August, to one of the last-mentioned islands; and, ascending its highest eminence, which rose to about 500 feet above the level of

---

* This was, I afterwards discovered, a mistake. North of Omevik the coast is said to be uninhabited.

the sea, erected a pile of stones about six feet high, and planted on
it the Danish flag, having previously deposited in the pile a silver
medal, presented to me by His Majesty, and bearing his image,
which I had brought with me for the purpose. I, at the same
time, took formal possession of the country in His Majesty's name,
and called it King Frederick the Sixth's Coast. The island where
I planted the flag, I called Dannebrog's Island, and its S.W. extremity, the latitude of which I found to be 65° 15′ 36″, Holm's
Naze, in honour of the late gallant commander of the Naiad.

On the 21st of August I made another trip to Dannebrog's
Island, but found the ice, as before, impenetrable. I now made
up my mind to turn back, for the country hereabouts was utterly
destitute of all means of subsistence, and the state of the ice, that
had now for three weeks prevented our further progress, such as to
preclude all hope of any speedy favourable change, innumerable
icebergs, fast aground, forming a barrier round the drift-ice that
lined the shore. Moreover, the stormy season was approaching
with rapid strides, and if even the ice should break up and disappear on its arrival, it still would be impossible for me to proceed
in so frail a bottom as a Greenland umiak through the heavy sea
I might then expect to encounter, along a coast unsheltered by
skerries. Finally, my people, if not absolutely in a state of mutiny,
were exceedingly averse from going further, and, indeed, would
not have held out even thus far, but for the bribes I daily offered
them of spirits, coffee, &c., my stock of which was now almost
exhausted. Add to this, that I was fully convinced it would be
vain to look for the East Bygd further north than latitude 65°,
a conviction forced on me by the following considerations. In the
first place, if the East Bygd lay at all on the East coast, the
district of Juliana's-hope must have formed part of the West Bygd.
Now, the distance between these Bygds the ancient writers have
stated differently, Ivar Bardsen declaring it to be twelve *vikur
siouar*, or forty-eight miles; Biörn Jonsen six days' journey in a
row-boat. If we take the latter statement to be correct, and, with
Wormskiold, estimate a day's journey in a row-boat of the ancients
at forty-eight miles, which I conceive, however, to be upwards
of twelve miles too much, we obtain 288 miles as the distance
between the two Bygds, from which it results, that the East Bygd
must have commenced somewhere between latitude 63° and 64°.
Now, calculating from the southernmost firth in the district of
Juliana's-hope where ruins are to be met with, I had gone over a
distance of about 440 miles, and must thus, long since, have passed
the point at which, according to this supposition, the East Bygd,
if it ever lay at all on the East coast, must have commenced. In
the next place, all the old Sailing Directions, as well for those
navigating from Norway to Greenland, as from Iceland to Greenland, seem clearly to indicate, that the Bygd lay further South,

namely, in about the same degree of latitude as that implied by Biörn Jonsen's statement of the distance between it and the West Bygd. Lastly, it is explicitly set forth in Gripla, an ancient M.S., that from Hvidsærk the land stretches away to the North, and the coast North of latitude 65°, as we know from the accounts of Egede and Rothe's voyage, as little answers to this description as that South of it.

At eight o'clock, A.M., we took our departure from Dannebrog's Island. The effect of this change of route upon my people was immediate and striking. They grew at once as active as they hitherto had been dull and indolent. Off White Saddle we found open water, and, for the first time since we had passed Puisortok on our way North, were enabled to hoist sail. Between ten and eleven o'clock, P.M., we pitched our tents on Sneedorff's Island.

August 22nd. We left Sneedorff's Island with a fresh breeze at N.E. The ice continued open as far as Skram's Islands, where we found some difficulty in getting on, it being found necessary to hew out a passage for ourselves through some floes. South of these islands we discovered a channel leading to Oxe's Firth. This we entered, and landed on a naze on the northern side of the firth.

August 23rd. We resumed our voyage at half-past six o'clock, A.M. From Cape Lövenörn we thought we saw the ice open in the direction of South, and shaped a straight course for it through a quantity of brash-ice, proceeding partly from the large ice-blinks along the shore, partly from the innumerable icebergs that still lay here, exactly as when we passed the spot on our way out. This ice grew more and more packed as we proceeded, until at length no water was to be seen. With our ice-board out at the bows, we tried to force our way through it, but found it impossible anywhere to reach the land. Night now coming on, and it begining to blow hard at S.E., with a heavy swell which set the ice in motion, our situation became very critical; for an inconsiderable leak, such as the sharp ice about us might very easily have occasioned, would, probably, have led to our inevitable destruction, as the darkness would have prevented us, in all likelihood, from finding and stopping it, and there were no floes near us large enough to have served us as a temporary place of refuge. My helmsman, indeed, was so impressed with a sense of our peril, that he thought it advisable to take to his kajak, in which, in the event of our boat's foundering, he, at any rate, might save himself. This evening, for the first time since April last, we saw the northern lights.

August 24. Day dawned after a most unpleasant night. Our dangers now became less; but the difficulties of our navigation, on the contrary, increased, the new-ice, that now began to form about midnight, having become so thick at about sun-rise, that we could scarcely break through it. At length, about nine, A.M., we found a channel not broader than our boat's length, between two

icebergs rising perpendicularly out of the water, to the height of
about 150 feet.   The fall of the avalanches, in Switzerland, is said
sometimes to be occasioned by the mere agitation of the air occasioned by a bird upon the wing; and the Greenlanders believe
that, in like manner, the dash of oars in water, or the rever-
beration caused by the utterance of a loud sound, is sufficient to
make an iceberg calve.   To attempt this passage under such circumstances was, therefore, hazardous in the extreme.   Having,
however, no alternative, we ran the risk, and in a few moments
a simultaneous shout of "Kujanak! kujanak*!" announced that
the danger was surmounted.   At one, P.M., we arrived at Aluik.
Here I was informed, that the snow-free tract of country, seen by
us to the North, consisted of some large islands, intelligence I was
the more disposed to credit, as it presented very much the same
aspect as the land about Nunarsoak and Omenak.   Grass and the
other vegetable productions were to be found there, it was said, as
in the mountains about Gyldenlöve's Firth, but no large fields,
(Narksak.)   One of my informers declared, that rein-deer, likewise, were to be found there ; but he was contradicted, and justly,
as I conceive, the skin of that animal being, as I have remarked,
a thing unknown at Omevik†.   Römer's Island, where we had
found the three houses, was said to produce pot-stone.   I presume,
however, either in very small quantity, or of a quality difficult to
break, as it was precisely here that I had seen some stones
hollowed out, evidently for the purpose of serving as lamps.   The
natives here had no knowledge of either Amaroks‡ or Erkilliks, the
latter of whom, they stated, dwelt on the West coast, while the
natives of the West coast, again, aver that they are to be met with
only on the eastern side of the country §.
   Having shared out some nails and needles among the natives of
the place, we left Aluik on the morning of the 25th of August.
The sea was filled with ice ; but the people at Omevik had told
us, that we should find more open water by holding further out to
sea; and, following their advice, we in effect avoided the dangerous
sharp-cornered ice, off the large ice-blink laid down in the map by
the name of Colberger Heide.   The drift-ice, however, was found
to be everywhere so thick, that it was eleven o'clock at night
before we got to land, at a small island off Krumpen's Firth.   It
was too dark to proceed further; and there was no place near us
where a boat could be hauled up.   I made up my mind, therefore,
to pass the night in the boat, while my Greenland companions

---

* An expression of thankfulness.
   † Wormskiold maintains, that this testimony of the Eastlander, in respect to
the existence of rein-deer in the tract of country spoken of, deserved more consi-
deration than it received at the hands of Graah.—*Trans.*   Reindeers' horns re-
cently cast, were found on Pendulum Islands in Lat. 74° N. on this coast, by
Captain (now Major) Sabine, R.A.—J. C. R.
   ‡ Wolves.
   § *Vide* Note, p. 90.—*Trans.*

laid down on the rocks, where they soon fell fast asleep, notwithstanding a drizzling rain that fell the whole night through.

August 26th.   As soon as day dawned, I walked round the
island, but found nothing worth recording.   At six o'clock I woke
my Greenlanders, who rose, wet, and stiff with cold ; and we
hastened to our boat, to warm ourselves at the oars.   Next morning we got to Kikkertarsoak, south of Kemisak.   Here I learned,
to my satisfaction, that all the natives of the place, with the exception of two families, had taken their departure to Ekallumiut ; for
I purposed visiting, as far as might be practicable, all the inhabited
points along the coast, with the view of laying in stores for the
ensuing Winter, and was glad to have an opportunity of touching at
this one especially, as I had been informed that large fields were to
be met with in the neighbourhood, and as the statements on
record of the distance between the East and West Bygds directed
suspicion towards it particularly, as the spot where the object of
my search, if it ever lay on the East coast at all, was to be looked
for.   For my part, I was thoroughly convinced that the East Bygd
would not be found there ; but I considered it, nevertheless, of
importance, to leave no spot unexamined, in order that—if no
more satisfactory result could be obtained—all doubt upon the
subject might be removed from the minds of others.

On the 28th of August, at six, A. M., we left Kikkertarsoak, in
company with the two families we there had formed acquaintance
with.   We kept close into the firth of Kangersinuk, the cliffs about
which I found were overgrown with heath, sorrel, angelica ; beach,
however, there was none, and little or no grass.   We spent the
night on an island situated a short distance within the sound, or
channel, leading to Ekallumiut, and continued our voyage next day
under convoy of eight women's-boats, and a multitude of kajaks
that had joined us during the night.   The Sound of Ekallumiut,
whose breadth is about a mile, trends, almost in a right line, due
N.W. and S.E.   The cliffs on both sides of it are high and precipitous ; but nevertheless, the ice, above which are seen projecting a
multitude of sharp pinnacles of rock, reaches often quite to the
water's edge, forming blinks that are said to calve large bergs.   Still
this was the handsomest tract of land I yet had seen along this
coast ;   at many places the vegetation was luxuriant, dwarf-
willows, juniper, black crakeberry, and whortle-bushes, and angelica
particularly, being abundant on the face of the cliffs,   Here, again,
however, there was no underland, with the exception of what was
furnished by, here and there, a projecting naze, and grass was as
scarce as it had been found to be everywhere else.   Just as we
doubled one of the nazes I have here adverted to, I saw, high up on
one of the hills, a number of small white objects, looking precisely
like a flock of sheep grazing.   They were in reality a party of Greenlanders, clad in white skins, collecting roots and berries ; but so

powerful was the illusion, that one not satisfied, as I was, that the
East Bygd never lay on the East coast at all, might very easily have
been tempted to believe that he had fallen in with traces of that
vanished colony.   I am the more careful to note this incident
because it serves to throw some light, perhaps, upon an ancient
legend, setting forth, that Amund, bishop of Skalholt (in Iceland),
being, on a voyage from Norway to his see in 1530, driven near the
East coast of Greenland, saw some of its natives on shore, driving
their cattle home.   The legend, indeed, goes on to state, that he
did not land in consequence of a favourable wind springing up,
which brought him *the night after* to his destination, a statement
quite sufficient of itself to determine the degree of credit due to the
story.   Having run through the Sound of Ekallumiut to the distance of about twenty miles, we found that its direction changed to
West.   The island which bounds it to the S.W., has here two
large ice-blinks, one of which was almost covered over with a thick
stratum of earth, stones, and rubbish, the débris of the rocks
between which it had forced its way.   A little to the West of these
ice-blinks a pretty little cove runs into the mainland in the direction of North, and on one of its banks we pitched our tent, in the
midst of a Greenland encampment consisting of thirty tents.

August 30.   The place we now were at, was the Ekallumiut so
often mentioned.   The cove, the length of which is between one
and two cable-lengths, has on both sides of it, but particularly on
the eastern, fields of considerable extent, covered with dwarf-willows, juniper-berry, black crakeberry, and whortle-berry heath, the
first-named growing to the height of two feet, and the whole inter-
spersed with a good many patches of a fine species of grass, which,
however, was very much burnt by the heat of the sun, except in the
immediate vicinity of the brooks and rivulets that, in great number,
ran down the sides of the hills, and intersected the level land in
every direction.   At the bottom of the cove, stretches an extensive valley, through which runs a stream, abounding in char, and
having its source in the glaciers, of which several gigantic arms
reach down into the valley from the height in the back-ground.   On
the banks of this brook the grass grew luxuriantly ; but it was far
from being, at many places, of a height fit for mowing, so that even
this spot, where grass was more abundant than anywhere else
perhaps along the whole coast, does not seem calculated to furnish
Winter fodder for any considerable number of cattle.   Various
flowers, among which the sweet-smelling lychnis, everywhere
adorned the fields.   The cliffs recede to a distance of from 200 to
300 paces from the sea, rising then, however, almost perpendicularly, far beyond the ordinary height, the clouds seeming to rest
upon their snow-clad summits.   Rock and ice-slides, are here
events of frequent occurrence.   Down a ravine on the S.W. side of
the cove, particularly, huge masses of ice were every moment pre-

cipitated, crumbling in their fall to dust, and accompanied with a noise like thunder. At this really beautiful spot, the natives of the country round assemble for a few days during their brief Summer, to feast upon the char that are to be got here in great plenty and of great size, the black crakeberry, and angelica, and to lay in a stock of them for Winter use, and give themselves up to mirth and merry-making. This evening they collected together in a body of some 200 or 250 persons, and began, by torch-light, their tambourine-dance, a festivity to which I was invited by frequent messages sent me during the night, but in which I was prevented by a slight attack of fever from taking part.

August 31.   On waking this morning, I heard the tambourine of my Greenland friends still going. I made haste therefore to join them, and though, when I reached the spot, they were on the point of breaking up, they continued their dance a little longer on my account. To form an adequate conception of the dance I witnessed on this occasion, it is absolutely necessary to have seen it. To describe it is no easy matter. The tambourine, as I have termed it, employed by them by way of musical accompaniment, is a simple ring, or hoop, of wood, with a piece of old boat-skin, well saturated with oil, stretched tightly over it, and furnished with a handle. This one of the party holds in his left-hand, and, taking his station in the centre, while the rest form a ring about him, and throwing off his jacket, strikes with a small wooden stick, extemporizing, after a brief prelude, a song, the subject of which is the chase of the seal, or some other, to them, important incident or event, the whole assembly joining, at the end of every strophe, in the chorus of " Eia-eia-a ! Eia-eia-a ! " During this performance, he makes unceasingly a sort of curtseying motion, and writhes and twists his head and eyes in the most laughable style imaginable. Nothing, however, can equal in absurdity the movements of his nether man, with which he describes entire circles, nay, figures of eight. This tambourine-dance is in high esteem among the Greenlanders. When about to take part in it, they put on their best holiday apparel, and the women take as much pride in performing it with what they consider grace, as our young belles in dancing a quadrille or a galoppe. It serves, however, not merely the purpose of amusement, but constitutes at the same time a sort of forum, before which all transgressors of their laws and customs are, in a manner, cited, and receive their merited reproof. When a Greenlander, to wit, thinks he has sustained a wrong or injury at another's hands, he composes a satirical song, which all his friends straightway learn by heart, and then makes known among the inhabitants of the place his intention of bringing the matter to arbitration. On the day appointed, the parties, with their partisans, assemble and form the ring, which done, the plaintiff, singing and dancing as above described, states his case, taking occasion to retaliate on

his adversary by as much ridicule and sarcasm as he can devise, to
which, when he has finished, the other, singing and dancing in his
turn, replies : and thus the cause is pleaded, till both have nothing
more to say, on which the spectators pronounce sentence at once,
without appeal, and the adversaries part as good friends as if
nothing had happened to disturb the harmony of their friendship.
In this way the debtor sometimes is reminded of his debt, and the
evil-doer receives a just rebuke for his misconduct.   In truth, a
better system for the prevention and punishment of offences, one
at least better adapted to the disposition of the people among whom
it obtains, could scarcely be devised, as there is nothing of which
the Greenlander is so much afraid as to be despised or laughed at
by his countrymen.   This apprehension, there can be no doubt,
deters many among them from the commission of offences, and it
is to be regretted that the missionaries, losing sight of this peculiarity in their temper, have abolished this national dance on the
West coast.

We remained three days at this delightful spot, which, in compliment to her Majesty*, I named Queen Maria's Valley.   During
my stay there, which afforded my companions the repose they
stood so much in need of after the hardships and fatigues we had
undergone, I did not leave a nook or corner of the country round
it unexplored, but found nowhere the least vestige of ancient European colonization, though the Icelanders, if they ever did settle on
the East coast at all, would scarcely have passed this spot by,
which, of all that I have seen on the East coast, is the best adapted
to the purposes of colonization, better, indeed, than any of those
sites in the district of Juliana's-hope, where ruins of their dwellings
are to be seen.   I collected here some specimens of mineralogy
and botany, of which our distinguished botanist, Professor Hornemann, one of the members of the Commission appointed to superintend the concerns of the expedition, has, since my return, assigned
the names and places.   A list of them will be found among the
Appendices.

On the 3rd of September we left Queen Maria's Valley, and
with us all the Greenlanders there assembled, who immediately departed various ways, with a view of repairing their Winter-dwellings,
the roofs of which either fall in of themselves during the Summer,
or are pulled down by the owners in order to purify the air within,
and dry the damp clay walls.   It was now high time for me, too, to
think of Winter-quarters.   The choice of the spot I left, however,
entirely to Ernenek, well knowing that the Greenlanders are seldom successful in seal-catching at places with the localities of which
they are not intimately acquainted; and he decided accordingly,
on a place called Nukarbik, on the South side of a tolerably large
island, between Cape Juel and Cape Moltke, where we found two

* The Queen of Denmark.

houses, one of them untenanted.   This arranged, and having
recommended Ernenek to collect the timber required for the roof,
and to his wives the reparation of the walls, I proceeded further
South in quest of provisions, for at Ekallumiut I had got nothing
but promises, on which I dared not venture altogether to rely.   As
the ice under Cape Juel lay close up to the shore, I went back the
way I came, through the Sound of Ekallumiut.   This sound turns
off at Queen Maria's Valley in the direction of S. E.   On both
sides of it were still seen numerous ice-blinks, one of them so much
covered over with stones and rubbish as to be scarce distinguishable
from the land, the more so, as some few blades of grass, or, rather,
some few sprouts of black crakeberry heath, were growing on it, here
and there, notwithstanding the coldness of the soil.   On a point of
land, called Kornouk, we found two dilapidated Greenland huts, in
which lay a great number of human skulls and skeletons, and near
them several graves, all, save two, open and untenanted. Doubtless
the wretched inhabitants of this spot had, to a man, perished here of
famine, during some severe Winter, and, foreseeing their inevitable
fate, previously dug their own graves.   The whole naze was flat, and
thickly covered with grass.   In a small fresh-water lake, the verdure
round which was of the brightest green, I found a couple of birds of
the duck family, with the names of which my boat-women were
unacquainted.   Due West of this naze, a firth runs into the land
the distance of three miles.   The cliffs about it are lofty and rugged,
rising abruptly out of the sea, so as to leave little or no underland,
and thickly studded with ice-blinks.   They showed fewer signs of
vegetation than the heights about Ikarisarsuk, or the Sound of
Ekallumiut.   About midway between Kornouk and this fiord lies
a small island, the only one of the sort I have ever seen.   It seems
a huge pile of stones heaped upon one another, no solid mass of
rock being anywhere observable, not even below the water's edge.
Still there is no indication of its being of volcanic origin.   Close
to it, on every side, the soundings are deep, as is the case indeed
everywhere in this sound, except in the vicinity of Queen Maria's
Valley, where the stream I have mentioned deposits sand in such
quantity that the whole cove is dry at low water.   At the southern
entrance of the sound we met three families, on their return from
the fair of Alluk, and learned from them Mr. Vahl's safe and
speedy arrival.   Shortly after it came on to blow hard from S. E.,
which prevented our further progress.   We therefore hauled up
our boat at Amitoarsuk, in lat. 63° 15', where I found a little bay,
forming an excellent harbour, with from three to five fathom
water, and good sandy bottom.   I gave it the name of Caroline
Amelia's Harbour.   It must, doubtless, be quite secure from drift-
ice, as the entrance into it is protected by a barrier of small islands
and skerries.   The almost constant impracticability of the sea, outside, makes it, however, highly improbable that ships will ever be

able to derive any benefit from it. Our next tenting-station was on
the northern side of the Island of Asiouikasik, in a cove into
which a char-stream, springing from a neighbouring mountain-
lake, empties itself. The sound North of this island was still, as
in the month of July, covered with a thick sheet of ice, a clear
proof that it had remained frozen the whole Summer through.
Here, too, there is good anchorage, with from five to six fathom
water. On the northern shore of Asiouikasik, in a small valley,
I saw some red snow, a phenomenon to be attributed, no doubt,
to the presence of some vegetable pollen.*

At Omenak, where I arrived on the 17th of September, I found
five families, all old acquaintances. Here I purchased about four
weeks' provisions, consisting of dried and rotten seal's-flesh, and
might, perhaps, have got a larger quantity, had I been able to
offer red ribbons, linen or cloth, in payment for it, articles which
are here in universal request, insomuch that I had been obliged,
some time before, to cut up a cloth petticoat into ribbons for the
purpose of adorning the heads and top-knots of the East-Greenland
ladies.

Winter being now close at hand, I dared not venture further
South. Stormy weather, however, prevented my setting out on
my way back till the 27th of September, on the morning of which
day I once more left Omenak. Four days after, on the 1st of
October, namely, we again arrived at our Winter-quarters to be, at
Nukarbik.

WINTERING AT NUKARBIK; TOGETHER WITH SOME REMARKS
ON THE CLIMATE, POPULATION, &c., OF THE EAST COAST.

1829-30.

I HAD expected to find, on my arrival at Nukarbik, our Winter-
dwelling ready to be roofed; but nothing whatever had been done
to it. Ernenek, with his own and three other families, had quietly
taken up his quarters in one of the houses, and left me, my kajakker, and two Nennortalik women, to manage as we might for ourselves. There was of course nothing left for us but to set to work
immediately, and this we did accordingly next morning; the earth,
however, was already frozen so hard, besides being covered with
snow, that we got on but slowly with our labour. The snow and
cold continued, till, at length, being absolutely unable to endure
living longer in a tent, we were necessitated to move in, notwithstanding that our house was very far from being ready. We took
possession of it, such as it was, upon the 28th of October. We

---

* *Algarum Species*, Brown. Ross's Voyage 8vo. ed., vol. ii., App. 195.—*Pro-
tococcus nivalis*, Hooker. See Appendix to Parry's Polar Voyage, p. 218.

had got a roof of sods only over one half of it, scarce even that;
heath to line the inner walls with we had none whatever; the entrance-passage had but one-third part of its proper length; the
floor was not begun, and the area of the house itself was full of
snow. Our first business on moving in, was, of course, to remove
the latter, which done, we stretched a tent-skin over us to serve
as a roof, and forthwith lit our lamps.. That our dwelling, unfinished as it was, was no less unhealthy than uncomfortable, it is
almost superfluous to state. The water poured down upon us
through innumerable holes in the roof, and streams of it ran down
the wall, and the floor soon became, of course, a paste of earth
and blubber, into which one sank several inches at every step in
walking over it. However, by means of spouts of skin placed beneath the roof for the purpose of carrying the water off, we succeeded, next day, in shielding at least our beds from the rain, so
that, on the whole, we were very well pleased with having ex-
changed our tent, which afforded no protection whatever against
the severity of the weather, for our present dark, cold, miserable
quarters. The house where we now were destined to spend five
tedious months, was about four yards long, by nearly as many
broad. We divided it into three compartments, one of which I
appropriated; one of my Nennortalik women with her gallant, the
clown Ningeoak, the second; and the other with Black Dorothy,
the third. My boat-women settled themselves, as far as circumstances permitted, quite in Greenland fashion; they ate, drank,
slept, and worked upon their brix, cooked their meals over their
lamps, devoured the vermin which they caught about their beds
and persons, sang psalms, laughed, cried, jested, scolded, arranged
their beads, put on and took off their finery, and ever and anon
anointed their hair with their urinary unguent. Ningeoak's whole
employment was to beat the tambourine and sing songs, save now
and then, when, with imperturbable gravity, he would deliver
speeches, fragments, probably, of sermons, picked up by him in his
travels. The most amusing part of his exhibition was that, whenever he lost the thread of his discourse, he would begin counting
in German, *ein, zwei, drey,* &c., as far as *sechs und dreyssig,*
where he would close with a solemnity of pathos which seemd to
make a deep impression on his hearers. For my part, I employed
the time of our detention here in learning the Greenland language,
and constructing a chart of that portion of the East coast I had
explored. For the rest, I was indisposed the greater part of the
Winter, so as to be unable to turn my attention to anything
beyond this.

In respect to stores, our prospects were at first far from cheer-
ing, and I found it necessary from the 1st of October to reduce
our hitherto abundant rations to half a pound of hard bread, and
three-quarters of a pint of barley and peas a day, besides once a

week half a pound of pork; and even with these very short commons, we had not more than enough for from thirteen to fourteen weeks' consumption. Thus circumstanced, and after having tried in vain to obtain board and lodging somewhere or other in the neighbourhood for one of my boat-women, I issued a sort of proclamation through the country, which thereabouts was thickly peopled, declaratory of my wish to purchase provisions of all sorts, bears and seals, as well as crows and ptarmigans, at whatever price. But my proclamation failed to produce the desired result; at least but very little of what I wanted was brought in, the people whom I had to deal with well knowing what it was to suffer want on this inhospitable shore, and, of consequence, when in possession of provisions, being unwilling to part with them, whatever might be the temptation. We should accordingly have been reduced to the utmost want, had not some of the natives of the place, led away by the glowing description of the settlements on the West coast made them by Ernenek and my boat-women formed the design, happily for us, of going with us to Nennortalik, with the view of fixing there their permanent abode ; for, entertaining this scheme, to their success in which they considered my good offices, and those of my party, indispensable, they, in order to conciliate us, never failed to bring us a portion of every seal they caught. But we did not long continue to derive benefit from this source, for as early as the beginning of January, the state of the weather and the ice put a stop to all seal-catching. In the month of February a scarcity of food began to be sensibly felt throughout the neighbourhood, and more especially at Nukarbik, and all the natives quartered there, as soon as their stock was finished, including their supply of mikiak, or rotten seal's-flesh, and even some skins, intended properly for boat and tent-coverings was exhausted, put their dogs to their sledges, and, with the exception of a solitary family, detained by sickness, set off in a body over the ice to join their friends and relatives further South, and see what they might have to spare. A late traveller observes that his sailors sickened to see the Esquimaux of Hudson's Bay eating their disgusting seals'-flesh and blubber ; the flesh of a young seal I can bear witness, from my own experience, is as nutritive as palatable ; and had we been provided with abundance of it, we should not have complained, but the fare we were obliged to put up with was coarse indeed, and nothing but dire necessity could have reconciled us to it. Nor, indeed, was scarcity of food the only evil we had to contend with. We were often short, moreover, of blubber, though we kept no more than two lamps burning, and as this is an article which the Greenlanders have no sale for, the circumstance serves to show how very small the supply of seals must be along this coast.

The climate on the East coast of Greenland is undoubtedly somewhat more severe than on the West. The Summer of 1829 began late, and passed away without a single day that could properly be called warm. As early as the close of August, the sea was every night covered with a crust of new ice, which by sunrise attained such a thickness that it was no easy matter, nay, sometimes impossible, to break through it with the oars; and by the middle of September all the bays and firths were covered with sheet-ice from an inch to two inches thick. The winter of 1828-1829 had been, it was said, unusually mild, and yet the Winter-ice lay still undissolved when the new ice began to form. Towards the end of October, sledging and hunting on the ice was in full train, and in November and December there were several days from eight to ten degrees of cold. Subsequently, indeed, and until the close of February, the weather was particularly mild, but at that date it again became severe, and the cold increased to as much as 16° or 17° of Réaum.; — 4° or — 6° of Fahr.

Everywhere on the West coast, the wind from S.E. is accompanied with an agreeable warmth, which suddenly causes the mercury in the thermometer to rise eight or even twelve degrees above the freezing-point, a circumstance which, together with the fact that some slight shocks of earthquake have been occasionally experienced in some of our colonies there, has led many persons to believe, that there are volcanoes in the interior of Greenland. If this, however, were the case, a similar degree of warmth should be experienced on the East coast when the wind blows from the N.W., instead of which the very reverse takes place; for here westerly winds are accompanied with a clear sky and sharp cold, and those from sea-ward with a milder degree of temperature, and almost always snow. This latter falls in an extraordinary quantity everywhere along the East coast, causing the glaciers with which the land is covered to increase perpetually, the loose snow upon their surface melting when it chances to thaw, and pressing down upon the strata below, or sinking through it, till the whole becomes one solid mass of ice, which never melts or undergoes change, until, in lapse of time, possibly not until some centuries pass by, it yields to the vast superincumbent pressure, and is precipitated into the sea in the form of icebergs. Vallöe speaks of a northerly wind being accompanied on this coast with a degree of warmth ; but he probably misunderstood the people from whom he derived his information, the natives of the East coast giving to North the same name which those of the West coast give to South, and vice versâ.

The flood-tide sets to the N.W., the ebb to the S.E. No permanent current is observable in the vicinity of the shore, the floes and icebergs often remaining stationary for many days together. But that a current exists, further out to sea, setting constantly

I

to the S.W., is evident from the great drift of ice between Iceland and Greenland, as well as from the fact that all the Dutch and English whalers, that, in the year 1777, were wrecked off Jan Mayen, drifted to the S.W. along the coast of Greenland. It is further evident that there is a considerable suction, so to say, of this current shorewards, the East coast being almost constantly beset with ice, reaching many miles out to sea, and seldom yielding to an off-shore wind. Towards the close of February, and in the beginning of March, this year, it was, indeed, removed, in the latitude of Nukarbik, as far as twelve or fifteen miles' distance from the shore ; but this was a most rare occurrence; indeed the natives of the place were much surprised by it, and declared that within their memory there never was so large a body of clear water seen along their coast *. This ice is, in general, so closely packed, that it would be totally impossible for a ship to make its way through it. When the wind blows from sea-ward it is often forced close up to the shore. Its aspect and quality are very various ; at one time it consists of huge fragments of broken icebergs, which it is quite impossible for one in any way to get over, at another of floes of various size, covered with a thick layer of snow, which, in Winter, furnishes excellent sleighing. Innumerable icebergs are at all times to be seen along the coast ; further out to sea they are of more rare occurrence, their settling so deep as they do into the water making them the less liable to be moved by the wind. They are frequently seen by hundreds, sometimes by thousands, forming a sort of barrier outside the drift-ice lying next the shore, and preventing its removal by an off-shore wind, thus throwing the greatest impediment in the way of navigating along this coast in women's-boats.

Along the line of coast between Cape Farewell and Dannebrog's-island, the following places were, in the Summer of 1829, inhabited :

Narksuk, in Lindenow's Firth	20 individuals.
Ivimiut	12 "
Taterat, in the Firth of Auartek . . .	20 "
Okkiosorbik, in the Firth of Aneretok . . .	50 "
Maneetsuk	8 "
Kinarbik	14 ",
Griffenfeldt's Island	9 "
Anarnitsok, in two tents, at most . .	20 "
An island between Omenarsuk and Kopetelik .	38 "
Kikkertarsoak	75 "
Kemisak	90 "
Aluik	130 "
At different places on the way to Alluk .	50 "

* Ernenek's wives, and some of the other natives of Kemisak, told me, on my return, that, during my absence, they had seen a ship (others said two) in the offing. I have reason, however, to believe that they were led by interested motives to give me false intelligence on this occasion, though the Greenlanders are, in general, not addicted to falsehood.

The whole population, thus, did not even amount to 600 souls, and at the present moment, does not amount to more than about 480, many of the inhabitants about Lindenow's Firth and Ivimiut, as well as a good many of those formerly living at Kemisak and Kikkertarsoak, having quitted the East coast, and taken up their abode at Friederichsthal and Nennortalik. According to all accounts, this coast was formerly much more thickly peopled. Those of its inhabitants who dwelt farthest South, long since emigrated to the new establishment of the Moravian missionaries, whence, very improperly as I conceive, pains are now taken to expel them, and of those living further North, a great many have been carried off of late years by famine, which, in some instances, has been so extreme among them, as to impel them to the terrible resource of butchering their fellows, a circumstance that has given rise to a number of reports and tales about the innate cruelty of the Eastlanders*. When reduced to these straits, it is the old and feeble that have, probably, been sacrificed; at least I know not how else to account for the fact that I met with no aged individuals on this coast to the North of Puisortok. To this dreadful alternative we ourselves might very possibly have been reduced at Nukarbik, had not the frost fortunately set in in February, and thrown its bridge across the sea, enabling those among us that had nothing left, to seek the aid of friends elsewhere. As early as the middle of that month, despair and horror were legible in every countenance.

The Greenlanders inhabiting the southern part of the West coast, have little in their exterior in common with the genuine Esquimaux, and the inhabitants of the country about the Bay of Disco in North-Greenland; and the natives of the East coast seem to me to have still less. They have neither the full, fleshy person, nor the prominent paunch of the Esquimaux, but are, on the contrary, slender, and even meagre. They are, moreover, distinguished from the Esquimaux by their form of head, and cast of countenance, which is handsomer, and more expressive. The women and children have, many of them, brown hair, and a complexion scarcely less fair than that of our peasantry, that is to say, when they scrape and wash off the filth that in general hides it from view. But as I should not venture to conclude, that the Esquimaux about Hudson's Bay have any claim to the honours of a Roman parentage from the circumstance of Sir Edward Parry's having seen "many a good Roman nose" among them, neither do I conceive that the natives of the East coast of Greenland are

---

* Ernenek's father-in-law, Sidlet, who, in 1828, gave me a meeting at Nennortalik, is said to have been twice present, by his own confession, on occasions of this nature. He is furthermore said on another occasion to have committed murder, and to have fled on that account, from his native place further South, to Kangerlurksoeitsiak.

descended from the old Icelandic colonies, because in some points they resemble Europeans. Their lank hair, their black, and somewhat Chinese eyes, their disproportionately large hands and feet, their temper and disposition, their manners, customs, and language, all indicate that they are of the same stock, originally, with the Esquimaux. They have, all of them, thick, arched, black eyebrows, and the men, in summer, paint a ring of black, with lampsoot under their eyes. Some few of them wear beards and moustachios, but by far the greater number eradicate the beard as it appears. They wear a ligature on their heads, for the purpose of keeping their long dishevelled locks behind; and many of them, a strap, worn cross-wise, over the breast and shoulders, to show if they increase or decrease in size. The women tie their hair in a large knot at the crown of the head, and cover it with a scrap of an old hide ; or, if possessed of one, a handsome ribbon. They are, moreover, curiously tattooed on the hands, arms, chin, and breast. I have even seen two men with their arms similarly tattooed. In their ears, the women wear a small triangular-shaped piece of lead, and, pendent from this, a string of beads half an ell long; while another, of the same kind, dangles from their forehead over the face.

Their clothing is composed of seals'-skins ; and the dress of both sexes is the same, with the exception of some slight difference in the cut of the jacket, that of the women having two skirts to it, in place of one. For the rest, the jacket, which is usually made of white skins, with the hairy side inwards, is sloped like a short petticoat, or shirt, closed, however, in front, and with a hood to draw over the head. Over this jacket the men wear, when at sea, or on the ice, another one, waterproof, made of seals'-gut. In Summer, when at home, or in Winter, when in their heated earth-huts, a scanty pair of breeches constitutes their entire dress. Their boots, the sole of which is shaped like a skate, are of waterproof skin. Those of the women look like cavalry-boots. For great occasions, they wear white ones, with a border of bear's-skin above the knee. All their articles of dress are edged with white-dog or seals'-skin, and their jackets have collars of the same, or of bear or foxes'-skin, or sometimes ravens' feathers. As the East-landers have not the same opportunities as their countrymen of the West coast to exchange their skins for coffee, &c., they are usually much better clad ; with the exception of the many father-less and motherless children among them—and of these, the girls especially, who frequently are bare of clothing—a circumstance serving to show, however, that there is no superabundance either of skins, or of charity, among these people.

The manners and customs, the huts, boats, implements, and hunting-tackle of the Eastlanders, are exactly as described by the Egedes, Dalager, and Crantz, to whose works I refer the curious reader, confining myself here to a brief notice of some of the peculiarities in their character and way of life, in which they differ most essentially from the West-Greenlanders.

The Eastlander marries at an early age. He selects his partner from among those of his own standing in respect of years, and is not influenced in his choice by any view to lucre, for a bride here owns seldom anything beyond the clothes upon her back ; with, perhaps, the addition of a lamp, a kettle, a few needles, and a round knife. Leaving such considerations to a more sophisticated state of society, what he chiefly looks to, in determining his choice, is fitness for enduring labour, personal beauty, and above all, chastity ; while on the other hand, the quality that recommends him most powerfully to the sex is, his skill in catching seals. It seldom happens that a man has more than one wife. When married, they lead, in general, a reputable life together; the women being more yielding and indulgent, and the men lending a hand in their domestic concerns more readily than is the case with the natives of the West coast. They by no means regard it, for example, as beneath their dignity, to drag the seals which they have caught, on shore ; on the contrary, they do this constantly, and if the weather be bad, carry it all the way to their huts, if it be not large*, and assist at the dressing of it. If, again, the state of the weather confines them within doors, they do not hesitate to attend to the necessary repairs of their dwelling, a duty which properly falls to the province of the women. In fact, jealousy is the only thing that now and then disturbs their harmony, and then a box on the ear generally sets things to rights at once; or, if the case be very serious, the parties separate ; all that is necessary for an offended husband to do, when things arrive at this pass, being, to set up a surly face, and without announcing where he is going, absent himself from home for a few days. The wife is sure to take the hint, and packing up her chattels, to repair with her children, to her friends and family. The affection the Eastlanders have for their children is excessive, and they that desire to conciliate the former, cannot do so as effectually in any other way, as by fondling the latter. Woe, on the other hand, to him that would rashly venture to chastise, or even to speak angrily to, one of these urchins ; and it is, therefore, a happy circumstance, that notwithstanding the little care bestowed on them, and their almost total abandonment to Nature and themselves, they conduct themselves so well as seldom to provoke reproof. It is a prominent feature in the character of the East-Greenlanders, that they look on begging, especially for food, as a disgrace. Rather than endure this degradation, I verily believe they would steal.

---

* The Uksuk and Neitsersoak (*Phoca barbata,* and *Phoca cristata,*) are sometimes so large, that it is no easy matter for five or six men to drag them the distance of a few paces only on shore.

Children, until they reach their fourth or fifth year, are carried
about by their mother, wherever she goes, upon her back. While
infants, they are cross and peevish to a degree, and scratch and
strike their parents ; offences for which they are never punished ;
particularly the boys, who, even at that early age, are looked upon
with a degree of respect, as the future masters and supporters of
the family. As soon as a boy can creep about alone, his father
gives him a little javelin, which he is taught to throw at a mark,
and he thus speedily acquires that dexterity in the management of
his weapon, on which, in after-years, he is principally to depend
for his own and family's sustenance. When he grows older, he is
provided with a kajak, and learns to battle with the waves,
to catch birds, and finally to strike the seal ; and the chase of the
latter is ever after his main business, and the chief resource for the
supply of all his wants, Without the seal, indeed, the Greenlander could not exist ; with it, he has all he stands in need of.
Its flesh and blood furnish him with food, its skin, with clothes,
boats, and tents, its blubber with light and fire, its sinews with
thread, its entrails with windows and curtains, and its very bones
serve to tip his darts, and shoe the runners of his sledge. It is,
therefore, not surprising that such importance should be attached
to this hunt, that when a youth for the first time comes home
with a seal in tow, the day is made a holiday, and the friends and
neighbours of the family invited to a feast, at which, while he
recounts, according to established custom, all the circumstances of
his chase, the maidens present lay their heads together to choose a
bride for him. As for the female part of the community, they
do nothing till their twelfth or thirteenth year, but play, fetch
water, and take care of the younger children. After this period,
however, it falls to their lot to sew, to butcher, to tan, to row
boats, build houses, and kill sharks, which last, in a moonlight
Winter-night, is their favourite employment.

In the interior of their dwellings they are filthy in the extreme ;
and not less so in their persons, their hands and faces being constantly begrimed with blubber. Their food is cooked in the most
disgusting manner ; their kettles, in place of being washed, are
licked by their dogs ; their meat is laid upon the dirty floor ; their
clothes and beds are full of vermin, and the rotten seals'-flesh, and
that abominable appurtenance of their ménage, the urine-tubs
kept for the purpose of soaking hides and anointing their hair,
diffuse an odour through their huts which I lack words to
describe.

Their intercourse with one another is marked with singular
urbanity. They know nothing, indeed, of empty compliments
and polite grimaces ; but in lieu of this, they are modest, friendly,
obliging, and forbearing. It is easy to see in their deportment
how desirous they are of pleasing, and how averse they are from

saying or doing anything improper or offensive ; things of which they, however, entertain notions widely different from ours. They consider it, for example, a great breach of decorum for a young man to offer a young woman a pinch of snuff; while, on the other hand, they make no scruple openly, and even at meals, to allow themselves free utterance in that sort of language which Holberg ascribes to a certain subterranean nation*. Towards evening, when the men, tired and hungry, are expected home from the chase, the principal meal is prepared. They give themselves, then, up to merriment, and beat their tambourine and sing, or recount the adventures of the day, cleaning and repairing their harpoons and spears the while, that all may be in readiness for the next. Their conversation, which turns for the most part, on the seal-hunt, and is replete with useful hints for a beginner in that art, is accompanied with so much gesticulation, that it is impossible to listen to it without interest, even though one does not understand a syllable of what they say. Whenever a seal has been taken, every individual dwelling under the same roof with him that caught it receives his or her share, which is greater or less in proportion to the size of the family, and of the seal.

During my stay at Nukarbik, we were visited almost daily by the people of the neighbourhood, and particularly by the young women, who, during winter, are accustomed to travel about in small parties from place to place, on foot, or in their sledges, drawn by dogs, sometimes to a distance of many miles, to hear and tell news. To us, however, they came less for this purpose, than with the view of getting a sight of my drawings, or myself, or of obtaining a pinch of snuff; taking the utmost care, whenever they did so not to approach me nearer than was absolutely necessary†. And I had frequent opportunities, on these occasions, to be convinced of the genuine civility and hospitality of these Eastlanders. When the barking and howling of the dogs proclaim the arrival of a party of strangers, the people of the place hurry to the shore to receive and welcome them, and invite them to their houses. The women are assigned a place in the brix, the men on the benches at the front and sides of the house, and if the number of new comers be so considerable that the house cannot hold them all, some of its own inmates retire immediately to another hut in the vicinity, in order to accommodate them. Their wet clothes are taken from them and hung up to dry, and dry ones lent them in their stead, and if a hole be discovered in their boots, the landlady sets to work straightway to patch it. The best the larder can

---

* An allusion to Holberg's *Niels-Klim*, which a regard to decency prevents me from making more intelligible.—*Trans.*

† The women, having never before set eyes upon a *Kablunak*, or European, were at first afraid of me.

afford is now produced, and laid upon the floor before them—but here begins a struggle between the entertainers and their guests, for regard to the rules of good breeding requires of the latter not to touch a morsel, however sharpset may be their appetites, until the former set them a good example. The meal discussed, and the strangers recovered from their fatigue, if there be a sufficient number present, the tambourine-dance is now got up, and terminates an entertainment that has at least the charm of genuine hospitality to recommend it. For the rest, this singing and beating of the tambourine is a pastime indulged in by the men during the whole day, when they have nothing else to do, but is never joined in by the women, except at their regular dancing assemblies (which occurred but twice during the winter I spent at Nukarbik), unless when paid to do it. Pay is, indeed, a word of magic power with them, at all times ; and they look to receive remuneration for every service, however trifling, that is asked of them. This in fact went so far, that if I but asked the name of the sun or moon in their own language, or requested leave to look at the tattooing on their arms, the reply was always " Won't you pay me ?" Nay, one of them had the face to demand a regular ground-rent of me, for permission to build upon his ground as he called it ; and, what is more, I agreed to pay it him in the form of a pinch of snuff, when he paid me a visit. In regard to their entertainments, I cannot say that they are distinguished by their number or variety of dishes. Dried, boiled, or rotten seals'-flesh, fucus, angelica, and berries preserved in blubber, constitute their bill of fare ; and in general even less than this contents them. The last party given at Nukarbik, while I was there, was, indeed, a regular pic-nic, every one bringing his, or her, own dish, for things were then at a low ebb in their larder. I should add, however, that, by way-of dainties, one is sometimes treated by them to the flesh of bears, belugas, sharks, dogs, gulls, and bull-heads, etc.

The Greenlander lives in a state of absolute freedom, and looks down with sovereign contempt on those of his own compatriots who take service with the Europeans, thus making slaves of themselves, as he conceives. He loves his freedom passionately, acknowledges no authority but that of his own will, and accounts to none for his actions, any more than he pretends to call others to account for theirs. None of them are invested with any power over the rest ; not even parents over their own children, who accordingly never fail to assert their independence whenever they conceive it to be infringed upon. This, however, is only observable among them during childhood ; those that were arrived at man's estate, I found invariably to be observant of their parents' wishes, displaying the most tender fondness for them, and never suffering them to want while they themselves had anything. Laws they have none, in lieu of which, they yield obedience to some prescriptive usages, of which I shall proceed to mention the most important.

Whoever finds a piece of drift-wood at sea, and lands it high-and-dry, is rightful owner of it; and where he leaves it on the shore, it will be suffered to remain, as safe from injury and molestation as if he had it under lock and key.

When a Greenlander has lodged his dart in a seal, and the creature, though wounded, escapes from him, and is subsequently caught by another, the property of it is his who struck it first. If the weapon he employed, however, was the larger javelin, or harpoon, to which a bladder is attached, and his line, in the struggle, has been broken, he that killed the seal (not he that struck it first) is its rightful owner. If two of them strike a seal at the same time, it is divided between them in equal shares, being cut in halves, for this purpose, longitudinally, hide, hair, and all.

If a seal be picked up dead, with a harpoon sticking in it, the harpoon is given back to its owner, but the finder keeps the seal.

If a whale be caught, every one present, whether he has lent a hand in catching it, or has been a mere spectator, nay, if he be nothing more than one whom chance has conducted to the spot, has the right to cleanse and take away what he pleases of the carcass. If an animal on shore is shot by two of them at once, it falls to him whose dart struck nearest the creature's heart, but the other also comes in for a share of the flesh.

If a Greenlander make a fox-trap, but afterwards neglect to set it, or to keep it in order, and another, seeing this, make use of it, the former can claim his trap, if a dispute arise; but the foxes that the latter meanwhile, has caught in it, are his.

If any one borrow the boat, spears, fishing-tackle, or other implements of another, and any damage happen to them, the loss is the lender's, if the injury be proved to be the effect of accident; if, however, it be attributable to carelessness and imprudence on the part of the borrower, he must make good the damage.

If any one make a purchase of another, and afterwards repent his bargain, he is at liberty, even after the lapse of a considerable time, to return the article, and even take back the price. For expensive articles, such as tents, boats, &c., credit is given. If the purchaser, however, happen to die before he has paid his debt, the creditor never makes any claim for payment of his family, though, in some cases, he takes back the article.

When a Greenlander dies possessed of a tent and a woman's boat, his eldest son inherits both, provided he be grown to man's estate, and be capable of keeping them in order. The rest of his chattels, whatever they may be, are shared between his wife and younger sons—for the daughters receive nothing. If he has no son, his brother is his heir, and if no brother, his most intimate friend; who, in that case, is bound to support the widow and family.

Whoever transgresses these, and some other established customs, incurs the penalty of being drummed out of the community. More serious crimes, as murder, are of rare occurrence; but when they do occur, are sure to be punished by a deadly vengeance wreaked on the offender, his children, or his children's children.

In regard to morals, the Eastlanders deserve much commendation. It is well known that the natives of the West coast, when Egede first came among them, were not only much addicted to theft, but that they even formed the project, more than once, of falling on, and murdering all the Europeans in the country; as also that, in former times, they have been known to entice sailors from their ships on shore, for the purpose of putting them to death, and making off with whatever they might have about them. There seemed no reason for expecting to find the Eastlanders any better than their neighbours. In fact, from time immemorial, they had been cried down as infinitely more savage and cruel. I have found them, however, to be the reverse of this, in testimony of which, indeed, it will be sufficient to observe, that, though they had constant opportunities of robbing me, night and day, during the nineteen months I spent upon King Frederick's Coast, I never lost so much as a needle—a circumstance the more surprising, because they all well knew what sort of articles I had with me, and because these were of all things precisely those which must have seemed most valuable in their eyes. Nor is theft the only crime of which I can attest their innocence. Rape and plunder are equally unknown among them. They are, in a word, a gentle, civil, well-intentioned, and well-behaved set of people, among whom one's life and property are perfectly secure, as long as one treats them with civility, and does them no wrong or injury. Their veracity and fidelity to their engagements are unimpeachable; and, as far as I have had an opportunity of observing, they are not obnoxious to the reproach of licentious habits; at least I never knew an instance of their exchanging wives, or saw or heard anything of those brothels of which Egede makes mention. In their intercourse with one another, they are hospitable, obliging, forbearing, and forgiving; except in cases of murder*. Swearing is a thing unknown among them, their language does not even boast a single term of abuse; and quarrelling and fighting they are no less strangers to. Their worst faults are—ingratitude, a total want of sympathy for the distressed and destitute (those excepted who are related to

---

* There have been instances, on the West coast, of vengeance being taken for a murder committed thirty years before: and even of its being wreaked on the children and grandchildren of the perpetrator, when he himself has escaped.

themselves), and cruelty to dumb animals, which, whether useful or useless to them, they torment and persecute without mercy. To this list of faults, I may add, insincerity and dissimulation.

They have no religion, or, at least, worship no Supreme Being, and know nothing of prayers, or sacrifices, or other sacred rites. Yet, they believe in the existence of certain supernatural beings, whom they figure to themselves, however, as not altogether incorporeal. The chief and mightiest of these is Torngarsuk, who is said to dwell under the earth, and is described sometimes as a bear, sometimes as a man with one arm, sometimes as a diminutive person not larger than one's finger. To him their angekkoks are obliged to make many a journey to obtain advice in cases of sickness, &c., &c. Besides this good spirit who is invisible to all but the angekkoks, they speak of many others, less powerful, spirits of fire, and of water, and of a spirit of the air, who, through the medium of the angekkoks, instructs them what they ought to do, or leave undone, in order to be happy. Each angekkok has, moreover, his own guardian spirit, or familiar, whom he conjures, and consults as his oracle. I have frequently been present on such occasions of conjuration, and will relate briefly what took place on one of them. The matter in hand was, to know if Ernenek was dead, or alive. He had been absent for several days, no one knew where; search had been made for him in every direction, but in vain, and his wives, alarmed for his safety, had recourse at length to an angekkok at Nukarbik, a smart young fellow, not one of the wisest of his generation, and, I suspect, a bungler at his trade, who promised them his aid. In the evening, accordingly, he came, and, the lamps being extinguished, and skins hung before the windows (for such arts, for evident reasons, are best practised in the dark), took his station on the floor, close by a well-dried seal-skin there suspended, and commenced rattling it, beating the tambourine and singing, in which last he was seconded by all present. From time to time his chant was interrupted by a cry of "Goie! Goie! Goie! Goie! Goie! Goie!" the meaning of which I did not comprehend, coming first from one corner of the hut, and then from another. Presently, all was quiet, nothing being heard but the angekkok puffing and blowing as if struggling with something superior to him in strength, and then again a sound resembling somewhat that of castanets, whereupon commenced once more the same song as before, and the same cry of "Goie! Goie! Goie!" In this way a whole hour elapsed before the wizard could make the torngak, or spirit, obey his summons. Come he did, however, at last, and his approach was announced by a strange rushing sound, very like the sound of a large bird flying beneath the roof. The angekkok still chanting, now proposed his questions, which were replied to in a voice quite strange to my ears, but which seemed to me to proceed from the entrance-passage, near which the angekkok had taken his station. These responses, however, were somewhat oracular, insomuch that Ernenek's wives were obliged to request some more explicit answer, whereupon they received the comfortable assurance, that he was alive and well, and would shortly make his appearance. The lamps were now re-lit, and an expression of terrror was very legible on the angekkok's face. He had, in all likelihood, received intelligence from one of his colleagues of Ernenek's safety; for, shortly after, Ernenek, as he had predicted, did arrive safe and sound, though much exhausted, having passed three days and two nights on the ice without food. Later in the day, a number of the younger persons assembled in my hut, and performed a scene, in which the mummery of the angekkok was travestied, and himself held up to ridicule : a circumstance from which it may be inferred, that these necromancers and their art are now-a-days held in no very high esteem among these people. Nor, indeed, did Torngarsuk himself appear to be much more devoutly revered by them, for they quietly endured to hear my Nennortalik women apply to him the epithet of evil one, meaning thereby the Devil. For the rest, these conjurations are frequently practised without any other design than that of pastime and amusement.

The sun, moon, and some of the stars, to which, by the way, they give the same name as the people of the West coast, they believe to have been Greenlanders, who have taken wing to heaven. When an eclipse of the moon takes place, they attribute it to the moon's going into their houses, and peeping into every nook and corner in search of skins and eatables, and on such occasions accordingly, they conceal all they can, and make as much noise as possible, in order to frighten away their unbidden guest. The northern lights (aurora borealis) they take to be the spirits of the dead playing ball with the head of a walrus. If a seal be caught at a time of scarcity, they always cast into the sea a small portion of its entrails, as well as all its bones. When any one dies, his surviving relatives abstain from certain sorts of food, and eat nothing at all in the open-air. The unmarried women, likewise, have many self-denials to endure, in order to avoid giving umbrage to the air, or moon, and thereby placing in jeopardy their reputation, or their life.

The prevalent diseases of the Eastlanders are ophthalmia, consumption, and pleurisy. Their method of curing ophthalmia occasioned by snow-blindness, as it is termed, is to make an incision in the forehead, or bore the eye-brows. They operate likewise for cataract, with no better instrument than a needle, or a round knife—not always, however, successfully, for I have seen several of them whose sight had been lost in consequence. Pleurisy, however, is the worst of the diseases with which they are visited; it prevails generally in the Spring and Autumn, and carries off many of them, both children and adults. It is a sort of an infectious cold, for which they, in a great measure, have themselves to thank, in neglecting to get their Winter-huts in readiness before the snow and cold set in, and in quitting these for their Summer-tents too early in the Spring. They are much troubled, besides, with boils ; but these, though sometimes large and painful, soon heal, and are seldom attended with any danger. Of the sort of white eruption, like what is called among the people on the coast of Norway, leprosy, which is tolerably prevalent among the Greenlanders on the West coast, the Eastlanders know nothing, the cause of which is, probably, that they eat neither herrings nor angmaksets. They are equally free from all descriptions of fever, a complaint which is very rare indeed, even among the Europeans domiciled in Greenland. I saw one individual afflicted with a sort of ring-worm about the waist, called by them "auinek;" he, however, speedily recovered, on applying to the part a gum-plaster. Fractures, wounds, and bruises, they cure by tight ligatures, and the application of blubber and urine. In serious cases, nature does often what their skill fails to effect. To a case of this description I myself was a witness, and I shall relate it circumstantially here, as it seems to throw light on more than one peculiarity in the character and manners of this people.

Early in the month of December one of the Greenlanders at Nukarbik had the misfortune to wound himself with a knife above the wrist. He made light of the accident, bound up the arm tightly, according to their custom, in order to stop the hæmorrhage, and went to his work as if nothing had happened. This mode of treatment, however, made bad worse : a tumor formed above the artery, as large as a tea-cup, the whole arm swelled, and the patient suffered acute pains. One evening, on his return home from a hunting-expedition, he consulted me. I knew not what to do with his case, and was very unwilling to incur any responsibility by giving him advice ; it was no secret, however, that I was in possession of a plaster which I had employed with success in many cases of boils, and, being urged to try its effect on him, I at last consented, the rather because serious fears began to be entertained for his life. I offered him one of my gum-plasters, accordingly, telling him, however, fairly, that I could by no means guarantee its producing any good effect—nay, even that it might possibly prove injurious ; a warning which, however, did not prevent his making use of it immediately. Next day, it had drawn somewhat, but the pain occasioned by it grew so acute, that the poor fellow fainted, and seemed to be at the point of death. As soon as I was informed of this, I hastened to him. On coming to the hut where he lay, I found him almost senseless, his friends sobbing and crying, and the children squalling, the only individual of them all that displayed any presence of mind, being his wife, who held him in her arms. With the aid of a spoonful of port-wine and lemon-juice, of which, in lieu of other medicine, I had brought some few bottles with me, he soon revived, but he had torn the plaster off, and would not put it on again.   For three weeks he lay in this condition, suffering the most excruciating torture.   A sage woman (not an Angekkok, though they are medical practitioners, as well as wizards), was then called in, who, tying a ligature about his head, raising it up, and finding it heavy, pronounced that he could not live.   The day after, I was told that he had refused all nourishment.   I thought this might proceed from loss of appetite, and had a mess of gruel prepared, which I took to him, together with a bit of bread, the best I had to offer.   Conceive, however, my astonishment, when the patient, in that mild way so characteristic of the Eastlanders, refused it, saying that his case was hopeless, and that he had therefore made up his mind to eat nothing, that he might not needlessly prolong his sufferings,   His wife, too, said the same thing, and pushed away the gruel with something like an air of anger, on my attempting to persuade him into tasting it.   From the moment of his announcing this purpose, both she and the children of the family seemed to have recovered their composure ; and though deep grief was legible in their countenances, not a murmur nor complaint escaped their lips*.   Whether he would have had the resolution to carry this design into effect, or not, I cannot say; for, three days afterwards, being Christmas-day, at nine o'clock in the evening, several of the inmates of his house rushed into my hut, with cries of " He is dying ! he is bleeding to death !" and took me back with them to witness a scene which it is difficult for me to describe, but impossible for me ever to forget.

On entering the house, I saw the sick man sitting upright upon the brix, holding out his arm, from which the blood gushed in torrents over a hide ; not a person supported him ; but while the women, sobbing and crying, were employed in throwing everything out of the house, clothes, beds, hides, provisions, &c. &c., as if to save them from a conflagration, the men, in turn, rushed up to him, face to face, and retired, uttering the most fearful shrieks.   The cries of the women, the squalling of the children, the terror and affright depicted in every countenance, the *tout-ensemble*, in a word, produced an effect upon my nerves, from which, for a long time after, I did not quite recover.   While this uproar and confusion was going on, the patient's wife would now

* It would appear that the terminating of their sufferings by a voluntary death, when no hope of ultimate recovery remains, is not uncommon among these people. Another instance of the kind, at least, has been mentioned to me by Mr. Aröe, of Nennortalik, a man on whose veracity reliance may be placed.   An Eastlander, he related, residing at Nennortalik, injured, I know not how, his foot : and after having tried various remedies in vain, being either unable, or unwilling, longer to endure the agony it caused him, begged his countrymen to throw him into the sea, a request which was complied with,

and then go up to him, and endeavour to prevail on him to consent to be buried alive under the snow, instead of being driven down in his sledge to the shore, by his son, as he had determined, and cast into the sea. At last the blood ceased to flow; he seemed scarcely able to breathe, and his whole frame was shaken with convulsions. I expected every moment to see him give up the ghost. He however did not die. After the lapse of a few hours, he came to his senses; the pain he had suffered, and the swelling in his arm had vanished, and on the following day he felt considerably better; nay, he began to entertain some hopes of recovery, and readily ate what I offered him. As I conceived the artery must have been injured, and was convinced that he could not bear the loss of much more blood, I prepared a sort of tourniquet, and applying it loosely to his arm above the elbow, directed his wife how to tighten it in the event of the hæmorrhage returning. This, as I apprehended, happened in the evening of the 27th, and my directions not being speedily enough attended to, the patient again lost a considerable quantity of blood, and seemed so ill in consequence, that none expected to see him alive next morning. The same scene 1 have described before, was now repeated, and his wife again endeavoured to prevail on him to consent to being buried under the snow, while he as obstinately insisted on being driven down to the shore, and committed to the deep. When a Greenlander is so far gone, as to seem incapable of noticing what is going forward about him, the preparations for his funeral are commenced. Our patient's wife, accordingly, was asking him every moment, " Do you hear? do you understand?" doubtless, in expectation of receiving no reply. As he continued, however, as often as she asked, to answer in a very audible voice, " Yes," she lost at last all patience; and, though he evidently was in full possession of his senses, and saw and noticed everything, as well as heard every syllable that was spoken, she began to make up his grave-clothes without more ado, and ordered two young girls, her adopted daughters, to take down from the walls the skin in which his body was to be wrapped*. The indifference with which this order was given and executed, was amazing: and the coolness with which the patient saw it done, was no less so. With perfect composure he looked on for a few moments, while these preparations for his transit to another world were being made, and then turned away his head, without uttering a word, or showing a sign

* The Greenlanders have such a terror of the dead, that they in general attire the dying in their grave-habiliments, to avoid the necessity of touching them when all is over. There have been instances, too, of their burying the old and feeble alive, when they have wrestled long with death, and are a burden to those about them. The latter was the motive here. I need not say that I had determined to prevent the barbarous act, and to take the sick man into my own hut till he should breathe his last, or be restored to health. But matters did not, as it happened, render my interference necessary.

that could be construed into fear of death, and fell, apparently, into a swoon. Shortly after, he was attired in his best clothes. The skin in which he was to be wrapped had already been stretched out in readiness, and the window opened through which, according to established custom, he was to be removed, as soon as the by-standers believed him to be actually dead, or as soon as their patience might be quite exhausted—everything, in a word, was completed in the way of preparation, when—the patient desired them to proceed no further, as he was better. He now called me to him, thanked me for what I had done for him, begged me to screw the tourniquet faster about his arm, (for he seemed to pin his hopes to it,) and regretting that I had lost my night's rest on his account, requested to have some lemon-juice. This I brought him, toge-ther with half a glass of port-wine and water, after drinking which he felt so much refreshed, that even before morning dawned, he seemed to us all out of danger—so that, in all like-lihood, it was nothing but the extreme weakness and other symp-toms consequent on the loss of so much blood, that we had taken to be signs of approaching dissolution. Nature now required no more assistance. The tumor on the wrist detached itself by degrees, until it hung by a slight sinewy fibre, and falling off at length, left a deep conical cavity, which filled up gradually of itself. The patient, however, recovered but slowly in other respects ; and seven months afterwards, when I saw him for the last time, he had not yet recovered so much strength in the hand as to be able to throw his dart, though he assured me he had followed strictly my injunction, to thrust the whole arm into a fresh-killed seal, as often as an opportunity might offer. Meanwhile, the tourniquet and plaster, which unquestionably would have borne the blame if he had died, now had the credit of his recovery. The angekkoks lost all their practice ; and, from that time forth, every one that had anything the matter with him applied to me, so that I soon saw I was held to be a great doctor, if not a very angekkok-poglik, that is to say, an angekkok of first rank, the master and superior of the common herd,

During this man's long and tedious illness, I had an opportunity of making some observations on the temperament and disposition of these people. Like persons of sanguine habit, they are easily moved to tears ; but they have, at the same time, a very sufficient share of phlegm, and as soon as they were out of the sick man's presence, they cared no more about him, but laughed and joked, and really seemed, as one of our profoundest observers of human nature has remarked, speaking of men of phlegmatic temper, to feel a sort of satisfaction—not in the sight, but in the thought of his sufferings, as giving a zest to the dull monotony of their exist-ence. Accustomed from early infancy, to torture and ill-treat the animals that are so unfortunate as to fall into their hands, they have, in fact, no feeling of genuine sympathy in their bosoms. Every one has enough to do with his own cares and troubles, and takes no further thought of those of others than a regard to self-interest demands*.

None of the other inmates of the house ever lent their sick comrade the least aid, but left this duty wholly to the two Nennortalik women, who, indeed, took the most watchful care of him whenever he was thought to be in danger ; though whether they did so out of christian charity, or from other motives, I cannot take it upon myself to determine, as they too, were unusually cheerful, and even merry, whenever they were out of his sight. During the first few days of his illness, all about him seemed to be much concerned on his account ; his wife never for a moment stirred from his side ; and the children never left the house, but sat sobbing and crying on the brix, denying themselves every gratification and amusement. More than once, I offered them some bread ; but the elder ones refused it of their own accord, and, for the younger ones, their mother forbade their accepting it ; the same, too, was the case with some tobacco ; and yet these are precisely the articles which they esteem the most. However, their patience yielded to the obstinacy of the sick man's malady; and not only did they cease to observe this abstinence, but, even when things were at the worst with him, seemed tolerably indifferent to the event. This, too, was not the only evidence they displayed of want of kindly fellow-feeling. The excessive heat that is felt in a Greenland hut in the evening, when all their lamps are lit, I thought could not but be prejudicial to the patient ; and I pointed this out to his wife, offering her the use of my own hut to prepare her meals in. Neither she, however, nor the other inmates of the house, would consent to any such arrangement, though it was evident to all that the sick man was actually always worse towards evening, than during the rest of the day.

Of the language of the East-Greenlanders I shall but observe, that it is the same that is spoken by the natives of the West coast, the Esquimaux of Labrador, and, in all probability, by the tribes inhabiting the north-east coasts of Asia, and the north-west of America, where many places are to be found, having genuine Greenland names ; as, for example, Umanak, Uppernavik, &c. There are, indeed, some differences of dialect between the languages of the East and West coast, as there are, no less, between those of the northern and southern districts of the West coast

---

* I have said above, that, in their intercourse with one another, they are hospitable and obliging : I have no doubt, however, that they are so out of sheer necessity, being perfectly aware that, without these virtues, it would be impossible for them to exist in the wandering state of life which the nature of their pursuits makes unavoidable. There are widows and paupers among them in abundance, who are left to provide for themselves as they best may, no one giving himself the smallest concern about them, or taking the least trouble to alleviate their wants, or mitigate their sufferings.

K

itself; these differences, however, were not so great but that my
Nennortalik women were able to converse with perfect ease with
all the Eastlanders we fell in with, a circumstance which enabled
me to make use of them, on all occasions, as interpreters, they
being likewise, masters of the Colony-Greenland, as it is called, a
jargon employed by the European colonists in their intercourse
with the natives, but which none of the latter but such as have
lived a considerable time at one or other of the settlements, are able
to comprehend*.

FRUITLESS ATTEMPT TO PENETRATE FURTHER NORTH— RETURN.

On returning from Dannebrog Island in August, 1829, I did not
resign all hope of being able to penetrate further North and East;
but, on the contrary, determined to renew the attempt the following Spring, if circumstances should permit. The stock of provisions I had brought with me being, however, by this time exhausted,
a small supply of bread excepted, it was necessary for me, in order
to carry my project into effect, to dismiss my kajakker, Ningeoak,
and my two Nennortalik women. I made arrangements, accordingly, for their return home with two families of the neighbourhood, whom I prevailed upon to set out as soon as possible, for
Nennortalik, charged with my despatches; and engaged in their
place, two other families, the heads of which, both excellent seal-
catchers, I promised to take with me to Nennortalik on my return,
and assist in the project they had formed of settling there, on condition of their first accompanying me on my intended expedition
to the North.

On the 5th of April we set out from Nukarbik, whose latitude,
taking the medium of ten observations, I found to be 63° 21′ 38″.
The whole island where it is situated, was, on my arrival there in
October, buried under snow, and so it continued to be when
I left it. Some patches of black crakeberry and juniper,
a little of the rhodiola rosea, and, in the immediate vicinity
of the houses, some sorrel†, were the sum-total of its vegetable
productions, a few species of moss excepted. By night-fall we

---

* There are, however, some few objects, the East and West Greenland names
of which are radically different. Blubber, for example, is called in the dialect of the
West Greenlanders, Orksok, in that of the East, Aberkak, &c. The word Konĕ,
(woman, wife,) which Fabricius has inserted in his Greenland Dictionary, and which
he conjectured to be a remnant of Icelandic, is, in fact, unknown by the natives of
the East coast.

† I have never met with any of the long-leaved sorrel on the East coast.

had reached, without difficulty, Cape Moltke ; but here we encountered a north-east gale, accompanied with snow, which continued almost without intermission fourteen days. The latitude
of Cape Moltke I found to be 63° 31'. At Ikatamiut, where we
arrived on the 14th, I found most of the Kikkertarsoak and
Kemisak people, who had fixed there their Winter quarters.
Among them was a man named Kamik, who frequently had paid
me visits at Nukarbik, and on all occasions been so troublesome
and forward, that he was very far from being a welcome guest.
To get rid of him, therefore, I had found it necessary to treat
him with somewhat less courtesy than the Greenlanders in general
deserve, and indeed appear to claim, as well of one another, as of
the Europeans whom chance may bring among them ; and my
stratagem had the effect desired, for he took his departure, looking
rather cast down, and returned no more. On meeting with him
here, accordingly, I had no reason to expect any very friendly
reception at his hands.   He appeared, however, to have forgotten
everything, and invited me to his house, the walls of which I found
hung with pictures, if I may so call them, figures cut out of black
skins, and representing seals, walruses, bears, and Greenlanders,
in which menagerie, after a short time, I recognised myself *.
Kamik was an angekkok, and seemed to enjoy a higher repute, as
such, than most of his colleagues. On my complaining to him
one day of the ice preventing me from proceeding on my voyage,
he boastingly said, it would be an easy matter for him, if he
pleased, to rid me of it ; nay, he promised to do so, if I would
show him the land of the Kablunaks, about which he had heard
so many wonderful things of my people. It puzzled me at first to
devise a means of gratifying this demand : I evaded the difficulty,
however, by placing my sextant in such a way that the heights
about Bernstorff's Firth, being reflected through the large reflecting glass, were seen through the eye-glass in the direction of due
East. He believed now firmly that he had seen an extensive
country in that quarter, nay, he afterwards declared, that he could
distinguish it with the naked eye, without the aid of the sextant ;
but, notwithstanding this fulfilment of the bargain on my side, he
begged for delay as to the execution of his part of it till the morrow—which morrow, of course, never came. For the rest, I was
informed by the natives of the place, that in very many years, the
state of the ice cut off all communication between Kemisak and
Omevik. I found the latitude of Ikatamiut to be 63° 37½'.

* They were all the handiwork of his children. On my inquiring of him how
many of these he was blessed with, he answered four. His wife, however, contradicted him, declaring there were five; nor could they agree about the matter
till they counted them on their fingers, the only arithmetical powers of which the
Eastlanders have any knowledge. Their names were, 1. Isueitsiak (Lamp-soot),
2. Ullo (Round-knife), 3. Amaut (child's-jacket), 4. Aberkak (blubber), and 5.
Utokak (old).

On the morning of the 20th of April, open water was seen about Cape Mösting. My Greenlanders, however, were unwilling to set out, nor did they make up their minds to do so, until they saw that I had actually begun to take down my tent. While our boat was being loaded, it began to blow from N.E., and the ice to set in to the shore. The people of Ikatamiut predicted accordingly, that they would shortly see us back again, and some of them assured me that all attempts at getting further North at present would prove fruitless, as the ice on the other side of Cape Mösting lay close to the shore. The Eastlanders, however, though in general not addicted to the vice of falsehood, were, I knew, not to be implicitly relied on, in regard to their reports concerning the condition of the ice. There was always something to be gained by our detention, and these poor people sought accordingly to prolong our stay by every imaginable pretext, which was, of course, the more excusable, because they could have no idea of how important it was to me to obtain correct intelligence. The Greenlanders of my own party I could even less rely on, for they were heartily tired of the expedition, and much preferred remaining where they were, wherever this might be, to going further. My only resource was, therefore, to see and judge for myself, and this I was very well able to do, now that I had learned how to manage a women's-boat among ice, a thing of which I knew nothing when I first set out. Indeed, had I been possessed of this accomplishment before, it would, doubtless, have been attended with much advantage; for I am satisfied that all we stood in need of, the Summer previous, to make much greater progress than we did, was some one skilled in their management of this sort of boat, and who, at the same time, had the interest of the expedition at heart. As it was, I had Ernenek to thank for getting on as far as I did. Without his aid, I am tolerably sure we should never have got beyond Puisortok.

We set out from Ikatamiut at nine o'clock, A.M., and kept in along Bernstorff's Firth the distance of eight miles. The northern side of this firth is, for the most part, covered with glaciers, that at many points protrude the length of several fathoms beyond the edges of the cliffs, and are generally, where this happens, of a semi-transparent and glittering blue colour. On its southern side the land is comparatively lower, but there likewise it is covered with ice and snow, except in the vicinity of Ikatamiut. One of the numerous large ice-blinks with which the shore on either side is studded, calved a very considerable berg shortly after we had passed it, which, throwing up the sea in huge foaming billows, caused a swell perceptible at the distance of upwards of four miles. At Cape Mösting the ice was found close to the shore. We were, however, lucky enough to find a small rock close to the shore, furnishing room enough for us to haul our boat up. Here we dug holes in the snow, and found them to be more comfortable quarters than our tents, which would have been perpetually upset in the violent gales, that, I knew by experience, were to be looked for here at this season of the year *. We had been in then but a few hours when the soft snow was congealed into a mass of ice, which by degrees grew to be so compact and solid, that even in the month of July it had not yet begun to thaw.

During our long detention at this spot, one of Ernenek's wives was delivered of twins, who died a few days after, and were buried in a cleft among the rocks †. The two little corpses, wrapped in skins, were removed through an aperture made for the purpose, in the back of the snow-cavern where they first saw the light. One of my boat-women was bearer, and the rest of the procession consisted of the mother, who followed sobbing and crying, and myself. The bodies were laid, side by side, on some old articles of clothing and thongs of dog-skin, and were covered over with a pile of stones to protect them from birds and beasts of prey. After the funeral, all the household chattels of the family were brought out into the open air, to be cleansed and purified, and the woman who had officiated as bearer hastened, as soon as she had performed that office, to wash her arms and hands in the sea, not for the purpose of removing the dirt and filth that lay on them, but merely to free them from the pollution contracted by the touch of a dead body. My kajakkers were particularly fortunate that day in their hunting expeditions. Ernenek alone brought home in the evening no less than four seals, and the other two three between them. As they had been badly off for eatables for some time past, having been obliged to put up with mikiak, or rotten seals'-flesh, this successful day's work could not fail to fill them with joy. The death of the two children, however, made it improper for them to display any outward sign of it; and their deportment was marked, accordingly, with a gravity and solemnity very much at variance with their true state of feeling, and little in unison with the tenour of their conversation, which, though carried on in an under-tone, without any approach to jest or laughter, turned on their usual topics. Such is the regard paid by the Greenlanders to conventional forms, to the observance of which they, indeed, attach even more importance than do civilized Europeans. This day, the 3rd of May, was moreover distinguished in the annals of our expedition, as being the first on which, since September last, we had seen any water thawed on the cliffs. Hitherto we had been obliged to melt snow over our lamps.

---

* These gales are so frequent on the East coast at this season, that, during the months of March, April, May, and the first half of June, seven days at least out of ten are stormy.

† From this incident, this rocky islet derived its name of "the Isle of Twins," (Tvillingöen).

I shall not abuse the reader's patience by giving an account of various small excursions to Bernstorff's Firth, and other attempts made by me during May and June, to get further North, but shall content myself with stating that they amounted to no fewer than eighteen in all, and that, on the 18th of June, the date of my last attempt, the ice continued to be frozen as firmly to the shore as on the day of my arrival at the Isle of Twins, two months previous. The state of the ice at this time was, indeed, such, that it was absolutely impossible to make one's way over it, or through it, a single mile's length North of Cape Mösting, on foot, or in a sledge, or in a boat. From the heights which I from time to time ascended, not the least open water was anywhere to be seen between N. and E.N.E., and the sky-blink seen frequently in that quarter plainly indicated that the ice extended in one unbroken field the distance of many miles from the shore. Towards the South, on the other hand, little or nothing of that phenomenon was this Spring observable, whence I inferred that my messengers must have had a quick run to Nennortalik *. The latitude of Cape Mösting was ascertained to be 63° 42'.

Two Greenlanders from Kemisak brought me, on the 21st of June, intelligence that a robbery had been committed at Nukarbik, in the truth or falsehood of which I felt much interested. I had left some cases at that place, containing a few clothes, books, &c., in order not to be encumbered with too much baggage. These I now learned, had been broken open, and robbed of their contents. In consequence of this information I set out the following day for Nukarbik, and, on reaching it, found that my cases had indeed been broken open, but that none of their contents were missing except about fifteen pounds of bread, which, I was told, had been carried off by the kajakker I had dismissed in the Spring, and who, I presume, had been impelled by want to take this step. All the other articles, among which were spear-heads, knives, beads, and needles, the very things most calculated to excite the cupidity of these people, were untouched, a striking proof of the respect felt by the Eastlanders for the right of property.

The country about Nukarbik now wore a much more pleasant aspect than when I left it in the Spring. The snow had disappeared from the steep cliffs, which now were overgrown with

---

* This sky-blink, or ice-blink, as it is usually termed by English navigators, is a whitish luminous appearance seen above ice in the lower region of the atmosphere bordering on the horizon. When seen under advantageous circumstances, says Scoresby, it not only furnishes a handsome, but a very available map of the ice stretching to the distance of some twenty to thirty miles beyond the limit of direct vision, and enables the experienced observer, not only to judge of the form and figure of the ice, but to know if it be field or drift-ice, open or packed, thin or thick. The reflection of field-ice is the brightest, but has a yellowish tinge ; that of drift-ice is of a purer white ; that of new-ice, of a grayish hue. The sky-blink over land (land-blink) is still yellower than that occasioned by field-ice.

angelica, dwarf-willow, juniper, and black crakeberry-heath, and sorrel. A luxuriant growth of grass covered the earth in the immediate vicinity of the houses, and on their walls was growing a quantity of large, juicy sorrel, with which we filled our bags, to serve as a refreshment on our further voyage.

After two days' rest we again set out, upon the 5th of July, from Nukarbik, with the view of making one more attempt at penetrating further North. The following day, as we crossed Bernstorff's Firth, Ernenek's other wife was taken with the pains of child-birth, and we made all haste to get ashore on a little naked rock on the North bank of the firth. The women of our party were immediately at work lending their assistance to the poor creature, while her lord and master, with the utmost *nonchalance*, lay himself down upon the rocks, and went to sleep. He was, however, soon awakened with the joyful news, that she had given birth to a son. The Greenlanders hold girls in no esteem, but boys, who they trust may grow up to be good hunters, and prove the means of support to their parents in old age, are always welcome. Accordingly, Ernenek no sooner heard the news, than he shook off his listlessness, and expressed his satisfaction at the event by saying to his wife, with an approving smile, " Ajungiladit," (*i. e.* You are not so bad).

With our new fellow-traveller in company, we pursued our voyage without any delay, and, the next day, reached the island of Taterat. Here we were joined by two families, that, the year previous, had travelled South in order to trade with the inhabitants of Kemisak and Kikkertarsoak, in the neighbourhood of which places, being prevented by the state of the ice from getting back, they had wintered, and were now on their way homewards, with the produce of their expedition, consisting of two or three broken spear-heads, a few old knives, and some score of beads. One of this party, the oldest, and indeed the only man advanced in years, that I met with on this coast, (I took him to be between fifty and sixty years of age) told me, that he had once been at a place called Sermelik, a large ice-blink, from six to eight day's-sail North of Omevik. Between it and Omevik, he said, the country was destitute of inhabitants, though, many years ago, two families had been settled there. Further North than Sermelik, neither he nor any of his countrymen had ever been[*], and the general belief was, that the country there was uninhabited. He further stated, that he had heard mention of a ship having been seen, many years ago, off the coast North of Omevik—probably that of Egede and Rothe, who, in their first expedition, penetrated, on the 20th of

---

[*] The Eastlanders have a very correct knowledge of the tract of country in which they live, but seldom undertake long journeys to strange places. Of all those I met with, between Friederichsthal and Cape Moltke, very few had ever been at Omevik, and but one or two North of it.

August, 1786, in lat. 65°, to within the distance of ten miles of the shore.

Umik had a large scar upon his back and shoulders, of which he gave the following account. A white bear having once come on shore at the place where he was domiciled, had laid hold of and carried off one of his children, a girl of six or eight years of age, as she was at play outside his hut. Alarmed by the child's cries, he hurried out, together with some other Greenlanders, and pursued the monster, which, however reached the shore, and springing into the sea with his prey, got upon the ice, whither the Greenlanders, without dogs, dared not pursue him. Armed with a couple of spears, he, however, set out in chase of it, and speedily came up with, and wounded the animal, who, turning round, struck down his enemy, and then quietly stalked off, leaving the child, as well as parent, on the ice. Umik, however, was too much infuriated to let him off so cheaply; instead of making the best of his way back, accordingly, he again seized one of his darts, pursued the monster, and as it turned upon him, struck it to the heart.

Though a thick fog completely hid the land from our sight, we set ut on the morning of the 5th of July, from Taterat, the latitude of which I had ascertained to be 63° 50′, and pushed on as well as we could towards the North. The ice, however, was close, and we had great difficulty in making any way through it at all. The Omevik people, who, like the Eastlanders generally, were in very small boats, got on infinitely better, in fact, without any difficulty. These small boats, indeed, are, in many respects, much to be preferred to those of larger size for this sort of navigation. For not only are they capable of being built much stronger, it being out of the power of the Eastlanders to get timber as large as it ought to be for boats of large dimensions,—but are likewise much lighter, (an important quality for a Greenland women's boat); and suffer less injury in their skin-bottoms, therefore, from the frequent necessity of hauling them on shore, or on the floes of ice: not to mention what is, in reality, however, their greatest recommendation, the facility with which one can thread in them the narrow and intricate passages through which it is necessary to wind one's way*. Arriving at the island of Ukasiksak at seven o'clock, P. M., we pitched our tents, and remained there, ice-bound, the whole of the next day. The name Ukasiksak signifies pot-stone; I found, however, none of it upon the island. Its latitude I ascertained to be 63° 57′.

On the 12th of July, at seven, A. M., we resumed our journey. On the western shore of one of the islands lying off Krumpen's

---

* My own boats were at least six feet too long, in my opinion ; and were not built of ash, which was another fault.

Firth there is a tolerably good place for hauling up a boat. Towards evening we reached Allikajek, a short naked isthmus of low land, under a lofty, precipitous shore, covered with snow, between two large ice-blinks. Here I ascended one of the neighbouring heights, and saw that it was still possible for us to make some little progress. My Greenlanders, on the contrary, maintained that it was impossible for us to get on, for which reason, I prevailed on one of the Omevik people to go a-head, and make the attempt, promising him a spear-head if he brought me back good news. Convinced, however, that no insurmountable obstacles were just now in our way, I succeeded in persuading my own boat-women to take to their oars, and, followed by the rest of the Omevik people, who had already set up their tents, we pushed off from shore. The unwillingness to proceed, which I had thus for the moment over-ruled, increased, however, apace. All hands declared it was impossible to force a way through masses of ice so closely packed, and finding that I could not convince them of the contrary, or, without their reluctant aid, accomplish anything, I at length submitted to return to Allikajek. Scarcely, however, had we unloaded our boat, when the kajakker I had sent a-head returned, and made so favourable a report, that my boat-women, after a brief consultation, sent a deputation to acquaint me with their having changed their minds, and being now desirous of proceeding immediately to Omevik. Of course I did not dream of interposing my *veto*, and, our tents being once more struck, we embarked anew at eight, P. M. In passing the ice-blink of Colberger Heide, it appeared to me to present a totally different aspect from what it wore the year previous, a circumstance to be probably accounted for by its having in the mean while calved some huge icebergs. It terminated now in a multitude of tall, blueish, semi-transparent peaks and pyramids, which appeared to be in a very frail and tottering condition, and at its base were seen a number of small, low skerries, which, the year before, had been buried under the ice. About midnight we came abreast of its most easterly extremity, and were rejoicing in the prospect of being among our friends at Aluik by sun-rise, when suddenly we encountered obstacles which we found it totally impossible to surmount. The drift-ice, namely, North of Colberger Heide, was found to be frozen into one vast solid mass, leaving not a drop of water visible.

We now again held council to decide on what was to be done; to return to Allikajek was a long and laborious journey. On the other hand, if we did not adopt this course, we had no alternative but to take up our quarters on one or other of the small skerries I have mentioned lying close under the ice-blink, for there was no place between Allikajek and Colberger Heide where we could haul up our boat. This measure we were aware could not but be attended with great and momentary peril. Indeed the Omevik people told

us, that some years previous, a party of men who had recourse to
it, had perished at this very spot, the sea, in consequence of the
ice-blinks calving, having inundated the rock on which they had
taken refuge, and swept away their tent and all that it contained,
Tired and exhausted as we were with our day's trial, we, nevertheless, resolved on braving every risk, purposing to set out the next
morning for Allikajek, and there await a favourable change. When
morning dawned, however, we found that our design could no
longer be carried into effect, the skerry where we had passed the
night being so beset with ice on every side, that it was just as impossible for us to return as to proceed. This day, the 13th of July, we
had a stiff gale from N. E., accompanied with a good deal of
snow.

For fifteen days we were now chained to this rock, threatened
every moment with destruction by the ice-blink, which calved some
hundred times a-day, resembling the discharge of musquetry and
cannon,   Huge masses, from time to time, were precipitated from
it, which, as they fell, were dashed into innumerable fragments,
causing the sea to sweep over the rock where we were perched, on
one occasion with such force as to carry away the boat and my
tent, which had been pitched nearest the water's edge, the distance
of several fathoms from the spot they stood on. However, we
suffered no material injury, as, fortunately for us, no solid bergs
were calved, during our long detention beneath the blink. It is
curious enough, by the way, that during the whole period of my
sojourn on this coast, I never saw an ice-berg detach itself from the
land-ice, though the many thousands of them that are to be seen
here at all times, some a-ground, some floating, prove clearly that
this must happen frequently.   One may almost be led to infer from
this circumstance, that their formation takes place in a higher
Northern latitude ; this, however, the Greenlanders aver is not the
case *.   The latitude of the skerry where we suffered this perilous
detention, is 64° 9′ 17″.

Towards the end of July, our situation, regarded in another point
of view, began to be alarming in the extreme, the small stock of
provisions we had laid in at Ikatamiut being at this time quite

* Egede states, that he never saw any icebergs North of the 65th degree of
latitude. He must, however, be understood as speaking here of the open sea ; for that,
near the shore, they are no less frequent North of this limit than South of it, I
can attest from my own experience in 1829.   Indeed Egede himself admits the fact
at another place, where he remarks, " The tract of country was extremely high,
abounding in rugged cliffs covered with ice and snow, indeed much more covered
with it everywhere than the land I saw further South. If any human beings
inhabit here, they must live in the interior, subsisting on the wild animals that may
there exist, and the fish frequenting the firths ; to find subsistence on the coast
must be totally impossible.   Even if I had been able to reach the shore, it would
have been impossible for me to land, on account of the barrier of ice that lined it."
That this land was a large ice-blink, perhaps the above-mentioned Sermelik, cannot
admit of doubt. Egede, it is to be observed, was at the time in lat. 65° 54′.

exhausted. Nor had any seals been seen since the 6th of July, these animals shunning places where the ice is very close*.   Add to this, that all our attempts at fishing with a line were unsuccessful (no bull-heads, though caught almost everywhere else along the coast, being to be found, any more than mussels, or fucus, all tolerable fare in time of need) ; that not a bird was to be seen, but now and then a solitary gull, that would make its appearance on the floes of ice, but always beyond reach of shot; that the rock we were on, so far from yielding any edible root, scarcely exhibited a sign of vegetation; and that the main-land opposite was covered with a stratum of ice, many fathoms thick.   In a word, after having killed and devoured a score of dogs, we were reduced to the necessity of living for several days on some old skins of seals caught the previous Spring, a sort of fare on which we could not have subsisted very long.   Satisfied of this, one of my Eastlanders, named Pauak, had given me notice as early as the 18th inst., that he would go no further, meaning to join the Omevik people, who, being like ourselves reduced to great straits, had made up their minds to put back to Kemisak.

Thus situated, I was obliged, of course, to relinquish all idea of penetrating further North, particularly as the season was, by this time, so far advanced, that, even if the ice did open so as to permit of my proceeding, I could not expect to get further than Dannebrog's Island, before it would be absolutely necessary to return, in order to be able to reach our settlements before the setting in of Winter†.

On the 25th of July, the day succeeding that on which I formed the resolution, the ice was seen to be open here and there, in the direction of North ; and the Omevik people seized the occasion to get away, as soon as the new ice, which, since the middle of July, formed regularly every morning, began about noon to disappear. In the hope of reaching a small piece of water, which we noticed under the ice-blink at about a mile distant North, and from which one of the Greenlanders had brought in some fucus and some bull-heads, we followed, shortly after, their example.   But that which, in their small boats, they managed to accomplish, proved quite impossible for us; and, after three or four hours' toil, we were obliged to return to the skerry.

Here, however, we could not think of remaining longer, for we

---

* The only living thing we caught, during our captivity at Colberger-Heide, was an aquatic bird of a species unknown to the Greenlanders.   It resembled an eider-duck (*Anas mollissima*), but was of smaller size, and had on each side of its bill a large, square black spot, surrounded by a red, tawny, and white border.

† If I had been ever so much inclined to remain another Winter on this coast, I should scarcely have been able to prevail on my Greenlanders to do so ; at any rate not further North than Ikatamiut, the inhabitants of which, many of them at least, had removed to Friederichsthal, and where, of course, there was less chance this year than the last, of our finding a sufficiency of provisions.

were now threatened with absolute starvation. On the 28th, accordingly, we left it, turning our faces South, in the hope of reaching some open water, seen some five or six miles off in that direction, and the attempt, fortunately, proved successful. We had still, however, a perilous and painful voyage before us; for five days and nights we were literally destitute of food of any sort, some bits of whales'-blubber disgorged by the sharks excepted, and were obliged to carry our boat, for the greater part of the way, over the ice, which, fortunately for us, consisted in a great measure, of large, and tolerably level floes. Had it consisted of the ordinary drift-ice, which is composed of rugged, unequal masses, confusedly piled together, it would have been altogether impossible for us to get along. During this most painful and laborious journey, I had frequent opportunites of admiring the patience, resignation, and perseverance of the Greenlanders. At last, upon the 2nd of August, we reached open water; and shortly after, to the great delight of all, a son of Ernenek's caught a little kasigiak (*Ph. vitulina*). It was devoured raw upon the spot, hide, hair and all. None cared to wait till it might be cooked, for we had tasted nothing, the two last days, but ice and snow. In the evening we arrived at Kikkertarsoarak, a small island in the vicinity of Ukusiksak. Shortly after, another and larger seal was caught, which added to the general joy. Indeed, I never saw them in such high spirits as they were this evening. Swimming, leap-frog, ball, and other games and exercises succeeded one another without intermission till they were summoned to their meal. In an old earth-hut at this place, I saw a number of skulls, one of which I took possession of, and brought away with me, secretly however, for the Greenlanders are very averse to any meddling with their burial-places.

Having rested after our fatigue at Kikkertarsoarak (*i. e.*, the large island's young one), we resumed our journey on the 4th of August. After passing Taterat, the ice again became close, so that we made but short days'-journeys. The tract of country between Cape Mösting and Cape Juel we found abandoned by the greater number of its late inhabitants, some of whom were gone to Friederichsthal and Nennortalik, and others to Udlosietit, North of Puisortok. In fact we met with none but three or four families, in the vicinity of Queen Maria's Valley, engaged in the char-fishery.

I have already mentioned, that I had taken into my employ, the year previous, at Kemisak, some boat-women, and, among the rest, a young fatherless and motherless girl, named Kellitiuk, whom Ernenek subsequently admitted into his family, intending to bring her up to be the wife of his eldest son, As we were in the act of loading our boat, on the 15th of August, with the intention of embarking and proceeding on our voyage, an Eastlander, of the name of Siorakitsok, came hurriedly to where we stood, walked into Ernenek's tent, and, seizing Kellitiuk by the arm, began without ceremony to drag her away, notwithstanding the most violent resistance on her part. I gazed with astonishment at this proceeding, which I took to be an ill-timed jest. I was soon convinced, however, of the contrary, by the howling and lamentation set up by the women in the tent, (this being performed not only on occasion of the loss of friends by death, but on many others, some of them trifling enough,) and I then recollected at once that this was no unusual way among the Greenlanders or providing themselves with wives, and that Kellitiuk's resistance was no proof of her aversion for her suitor, it being the established rule that young ladies in such circumstances should seem to be abducted forcibly. Ernenek's wives assured me, however, with tears in their eyes, that she had really been carried off against her will, that she desired nothing so much as to go with us to Nennortalik, and that she detested Siorakitsok; and I was the more disposed to credit their assurance, not only because he himself was a rude, brutal fellow, but because his mother (and as long as a Greenlander's mother survives, she is mistress of the house, and makes her daughters-in-law perform the offices of menials*) was scarcely better. It would have been an easy matter for Ernenek, who was a very giant in strength and stature, to prevent this impudent abduction. But the Greenlanders are a peace-loving generation, who eschew all interference in the affairs of others, and would, at any time, rather avenge than, by the interposition even of an angry word, prevent an injury. He accordingly looked on with perfect *nonchalance*, while his wives, and son, Kellitiuk's intended bridegroom, who was no match for Siorakitsok, rent the air with their lamentations. Meanwhile, Kellitiuk being one of my staunchest rowers, and having received, as such, a part of her stipulated wages in advance, I had a fair pretext for interfering in the business, and, Ernenek refusing to accompany me, I set off accordingly alone in chase of the ravisher, who, as soon as I approached, let go his prize and made off.

We now took our departure from Queen Maria's Valley, and arrived the following day at Anarnitsok, where we were hospitably received by seven or eight families of natives, all old acquaintances, there established. On learning that we were on our way home, they pretended to be much distressed at the idea of parting with us, and tried to prevail on us to spend the Winter there, as the season was, in their opinion, too far advanced for us to undertake so long a voyage as to Nennortalik.

On the 17th of August, at seven o'clock A.M., we were once more ready to get under way. As soon as the boat was afloat,

---

* For which reason a young woman, asked in marriage, has less regard to the qualities and character of her suitor, provided he but be a skilful hunter, than to those of his mother.

Kellitiuk jumped into it, laid herself down at the bottom under the thwarts, and covered herself over with all the skins and bags she could lay her hands on. This manœuvre augured some new danger, and, accordingly, I soon learned that Siorakitsok had just landed on the island, having his father with him to assist him. Nor did he long delay his operations, for, taking advantage of a momentary absence on my part, he leaped into the boat, and, without more ado, began pulling his intended out of it. Being informed of this by one of Ernenek's wives, who came running to me with the news, and begged me not to permit Kellitiuk to be carried off by him, and persuaded that the poor girl herself entertained a most decided aversion for the brutal fellow, I had already made up my mind to repel force by force, should he make any such attempt, besides that, the circumstance of her seeking refuge in my boat gave her, as I conceived, a claim on my protection. I hastened, therefore, to the spot, on reaching which, I found that he had almost succeeded in getting her out of the boat, while his father stood near by on shore, ready to assist in carrying her away, and all the Greenlanders of the place were looking on as unconcerned as if nothing unusual was going forward. I now dragged her from his grasp, and thrust him out of the boat, declaring that I had engaged Kellitiuk to go with me, as one of my rowers, as far as Nennortalik, and would not part with her till I reached that place. At the same time, by way of mitigating in some sort his disappointment, I recommended him to take Black Dorothy, whom I should not have been sorry to get rid of, as she had proved to be sullen and lazy during the whole period of our voyage, obliging me sometimes to have recourse to measures of severity in order to get her to do anything. The fellow listened to me calmly, and then, muttering some indistinct reply, went away with an angry air, and threatening looks. As I thought it not unlikely that he would take steps to avenge himself on me, I loaded my gun, and held myself in readiness to receive him. He, however, left the island, and I saw no more of him. His father, who had been a witness of the whole transaction, did not seem to be much concerned at his disappointment; but very good naturedly lent a hand in loading our boat, and bade us farewell with an air of perfect cordiality.

Our boat being at length loaded, and everything in readiness for our departure, behold ! Kellitiuk was nowhere to be seen. In vain did we wait for her two whole hours, and search the island in every direction, making her name resound from rock to rock—away she was, and away she remained. That it was quite impossible for her to have left the island, there was but one opinion ; and we therefore came to the conclusion, that she had made up her mind to go no further with us, and lay concealed in some hiding-place among the rocks, from whence she would come forth as soon as we were gone ; a surmise subsequently confirmed by information received from one of her companions, who said she had seen her make up her clothes into a bundle, and throw them on shore. Whether it was a lurking partiality for Siorakitsok that led her to take this step, or a sudden fancy to get married now that an opportunity offered, or, which I think more likely, it being a quality characteristic of all the Greenlanders I have met with, in a greater or less degree,—a feeling of pride, which made her think it a degradation to owe her escape to me, I cannot take it upon me to decide. One thing, however, was very certain—that she had been long deceiving us all; a circumstance which I regretted, because it caused me to part on bad terms with a set of people with whom, for upwards of a year, I had been living in uninterrupted harmony. For the rest, Ernenek's wife was one of our party who took her conduct most to heart ; and this for a very intelligible reason, that Kellitiuk had been accustomed to do all her work for her, it being beneath the dignity of the head-wife of so rich and great a man as Ernenek* to work, except by deputy. Seated on a bear's skin, in the middle of the boat, she was accustomed to issue her orders with an air of superiority, to encourage the others to row whenever they relaxed in their activity, and receive with a gracious smile, the roots and fucus which they gathered for her, whenever, for that purpose, she had the boat run in shorewards. If, as happened now and then, I desired her to lend a hand at repairing the boat's bottom, or the like, she invariably expressed her surprise at the demand, and asked me if I had forgotten what had happened in the Spring, adverting to the death of her twin-children, which event it seems, laid her under the obligation of abstaining for a time from every kind of labour, and on the strength of which she accordingly did absolutely nothing, till forced by circumstances. On parting with the Anarnitsok people, some of the men begged for a lock of my hair, on receiving which, they immediately plaited it with their own, or put it away in their boots, looking on it, I suppose, as a sort of amulet—for of keepsakes they have no knowledge. They all further expressed their hope that I would revisit them the following year.

For some days after, nothing happened worth recording. The ice continued to be close, and in particular, we found Sehested's Firth and the sounds between Griffenfeldt's Island, and the islands North and South of it, so blocked up with ice, that it was impossible for us to pass through them. Nowhere else, however, did I find the drift-ice presenting so formidable an aspect as between the mainland and Udlosietit†, where it was piled up to a height of from

* Ernenek, on my first interview with him at Nennortalik, was one of the poorest there ; but having, in payment of his services, received from me in advance a number of spear-heads, knives, and handkerchiefs, besides a rifle and a fowling-piece, and the promise of a boat and tent on our return, was now a man of substance.

† This name signifies, according to Mr. Motzfeldt's interpretation, *the Almanac.*

20 to 30 feet above the small islets and skerries lining the coast, barring completely all access to the bay North of Udlosietit.   At Asiouit, I met with about 80 persons, nearly all from the country about Nukarbik.   The greater number of them purposed to emigrate the year following to Friederichsthal, whither, in the course of the years 1829 and 30, about 120 natives of the East coast had already removed, comprising all the inhabitants of the country about Lindenow's Firth, as well as of Kutek, Ivimiut, and Auarket, so that now the only inhabited place, between Cape Farewell and Asiouit, was Aneretok, and even it was about to be abandoned by its inhabitants.   The whole population of the East coast, thus seems likely by degrees to settle in the neighbourhood of Friederichsthal.

As we were on the point of quitting Asiouit, on the 25th of August, we missed another of our party, a young girl of ten or eleven years of age, who had been in Ernenek's employ as a sort of servant.   She, like Kellitiuk, had run away and hid herself, while we were busied in loading our boat, though, as far as we knew, there was here no lover in the case.   Probably, one or other of the families settled there, being in want of a hand for their umiak, had persuaded her to desert ; though the reason of her quitting us, as stated by herself to one of her companions, was merely that she was tired*.   The latitude of Asiouit is 62°.

The western side of the island of Udlosietit was almost wholly buried under ice and snow.   From it, we struck across, in the direction of S.W., towards the mainland.   At Narksak, on a small plain, covered partially with a species of broad-leaved grass, found likewise elsewhere both on this and the West coast, and which, in Iceland, is commonly called wild corn, we saw ten Greenland huts.   Encountering, suddenly, a hard gale from S., accompanied with heavy rain, we landed on the 26th, at noon, on a naked isthmus of rock under the promontory of Kasingertok.

August 27.—I am now about to record an incident, the occurrence of which I very much regret, and which I mention chiefly as serving to show how necessary it is to be always on one's guard in one's intercourse with the Greenlanders, and what trifling causes sometimes suffice to rouse their fury.   On landing at Kasingertok, I found upon the rocks, a small piece of drift-wood, which I took possession of, and converted into a temporary bedstead, having so arranged my sleeping-bag upon it, as to prevent its falling into a pool of water among the rocks, above which, for want of a better situation, I had placed it,   Next morning, the weather being such as to prevent our proceeding, I climbed the neighbouring heights in order to examine the condition of the ice, and ascertain in what

* "Kasuonga," *i. e. I am tired*, is the usual apology of a Greenland servant when desirous of changing her situation ; and the announcement is generally followed up by her immediate departure.

direction we should steer when we resumed our voyage. This done, I descended, and, arriving at my tent, met Ernenek coming out of it, with the piece of wood in his hand, it belonging, as he said, to him. In removing it from its place, he had let my bedding, and some books that lay upon it, fall into the water, and there I found them. The interior of the tent was tolerably dark, and Ernenek, who in consequence was not aware what damage he had done, was, in reality, not much to blame. I was, however, a good deal annoyed by the accident, and told him, in rather an angry tone, that if the piece of wood did belong to him, he had, no doubt, a right to take it; but that, before doing so, he should have told me of his purpose, or, at any rate, been more careful how he proceeded*. To this, Ernenek said nothing in reply, but went away. Shortly after, the weather clearing up, I began to take down my tent, and cried out to Ernenek, as usual, " We will set off." As he made no answer, however, notwithstanding my repeating the same notice several times, I went to his tent, and asked him to come out and assist in launching the boat. To my astonishment, I I received for answer, that he meant to stay where he was. On this, I gave him to know, that if he did not obey my orders, he would forfeit his reward; and, without saying anything more, left him, with the intention of quietly returning to my tent, and submitting to circumstances, very well knowing that there is no making a Greenlander do what he has no mind to do.

I had not, however, gone many yards from the spot, when, hearing a noise behind me, I turned round, and saw Ernenek rushing towards me, like a madman, with a knife in his hand. I was without any means whatever of defence, having left my guns, which moreover, were not loaded, in my tent,—and in point of physical strength, he was infinitely my superior. Still, fly from him I would not; and, had I attempted it, he probably would have struck me down immediately. I thought it best, thus situated, to meet his fury with composure, and accordingly, when, trembling with rage, he seemed upon the point of thrusting his weapon into my breast, I asked him, with as much calmness as I could command, if, after conducting himself so well during the whole voyage, he really meant now, at its close, to take another course. These words, which it is probable he did not even rightly comprehend, had less effect in diverting him from his purpose, than the tone of voice in which they were uttered, and the air of calmness I assumed†.

---

* I made use, on this occasion, of the word " ajorpok," signifying merely it was wrong,—or improper. But Ernenek, probably, thought that I said " ajorpodit," one of the most offensive expressions to a Greenland ear, it being equivalent to telling him to whom it is addressed, that he is a dirty fellow. I certainly had no intention of paying him so poor a compliment, having, in reality, had reason to be pleased with him during the whole voyage.

† I have deemed it my duty not to suppress this incident, and have therefore told it precisely as it happened, though at the hazard of seeming to indulge in vaunt,—a

L

Whatever, at least, may have been the cause, the effect desired was produced. For some instants, we stood thus facing one another, he still with his drawn knife, and uplifted arm. Wishing, however, to put an end to this scene, I asked him, " What do you want ? will you go on with me ?" to which, in a decided tone, and grinding his teeth together as he spoke, he answered, " No, I will not ! nor will you, for you have no rowers." Having said which, he went back to his tent, and I resumed my way to mine, content to wait his pleasure, since I had no other choice. Shortly after, having taken my gun, and set off to shoot gulls, he followed and came up with me, followed by one of his wives, and begged that our difference might be forgotten, which I agreed to. I could not prevail on him, however, to resume our voyage, the ice being, as he said, too close, and the day too far advanced.

August 28.—Though the rain fell in torrents, Ernenek, contrary to custom, was the first to-day to strike his tent. At five o'clock we left Kasingertok, and forced our way through very close ice till dark, at which time we were still a couple of miles from the shore. We proceeded cautiously, pushing our boat on as we best could, until, close under the land, we came to what we thought was open water. Our oars accordingly were got out, and we rowed on smartly. In another moment, we struck on a blind rock, which, meanwhile, was so smooth and level, that the boat sustained no injury. On the 29th, between one and two o'clock, p. m., we reached the land North of Rud's Island, where my Greenlanders, spreading their skins upon the rocks, went to sleep, while I remained in the boat, to keep it clear of the ice, that threatened it on every side. Next morning, the drift-ice in the channel between the mainland and Rud's island was observed to be open ; further in, however, the Winter-ice lay still and unbroken. From the eastern extremity of Rud's Island, the sea was perceived to be open all the way to Cape Bille. I accordingly directed Ernenek to shape a course in that direction. His wife, however, gave contrary orders, directing the rowers to pull in for Rud's Island, that they might look out for a good tenting-place. From the moment I set out on my way back, I had made up my mind to conform as much as possible to the wishes of my boat-women in regard to the length of our days' journeys, the choice of tenting-stations, and so forth, as it was a matter of no great moment whether I arrived a day sooner or later at our settlements. However, after my fracas with Ernenek, which, no doubt was to be attributed, in part, to my too great indulgence, I deemed it advisable to assert my authority, and therefore repeated my orders, observing to the Greenlanders that it was their duty to obey, as they had engaged, on entering my service, to go where and when I pleased. On their still hesitating,

vice, for which none can entertain, in fact, a more sovereign contempt than myself.

therefore, I, without further ceremony, snatched the oar out of the steersman's hand, and, swaying the boat round, commanded them to give way—which accordingly they did. For the last fourteen days I had been seriously indisposed, and felt that I was daily growing worse. No doubt the main cause of it was the miserable fare I had been necessitated to put up with, being some year-old, sundried, and half-rotten seals' flesh, and, next to that, the extreme fatigue that I had lately undergone. Perhaps, too, my late squabbles with my Greenland followers may have, in some degree contributed to produce the same result. Be this as it may, I now became seriously ill, and on reaching the land in the vicinity of Cape Bille, was almost in a state of insensibility*.

On the 31st of August, we repassed Puisortok. The temperature of the sea, which I had frequently observed in the course of my expedition, and found to range between 28° and 34° was here 29·5°, precisely what it had been observed to be for some days previous, at several miles' distance from the blink.

At Okkiosorbik we met with about sixty natives, one of whom, an old angekkok, displayed a great degree of humanity, not often to be met with among the Greenlanders. Having learned from one of my people how ill I had lately been, and of the great scarcity of bread and tobacco among us, he commenced a search for a small quantity of the latter article, the last remains of his own stock, purchased at the fair of Alluk, and offered it to me, with many excuses for the insignificance of the gift. A little to the West of Okkiosorbik lies one of the largest plains I yet had seen on the East coast. It was overgrown with moss and a species or fine grass. The hills hereabouts were likewise covered with crakeberry-heath and dwarf-willows, and the whole country wore a much more smiling aspect than when I passed it in the month of June last year, at which time, it still had on its Winter dress. Black crakeberries and whortleberries were now to be seen here, in the greatest plenty ; plants which if they are not, in ordinary circumstances, of much value or utility to the natives of the country, are, nevertheless, calculated to be so under circumstances like those which we had lately been exposed to, their fruit having been, for nearly six weeks, our staple article of food. In fact, I attribute to these crakeberries chiefly, my not having perished on this inhospitable coast.

* As serving to illustrate the character and disposition of my fellow-travellers, it may not be improper to relate what follows : shortly after landing at this place, I asked one of my boat-women for a glass of water, but received for answer that there was none to be got, though there was a bucket full close by her at the moment. Ernenek, however, brought me some at last. It frequently happened, in like manner, that the kajakkers, whom I requested to collect some cochlearia for me on the rocks they might chance to land on (the Greenlanders themselves seldom making any use of that plant), paid no attention whatever to my wishes. This evening, on the contrary, they brought me some handfuls of it unsolicited.

The people at Aneretok did not think it possible for us to reach
Nennortalik, and endeavoured to persuade us to spend the Winter
where we were. None of us, however, had any mind to do so,
though some of us subsequently repented not having followed their
advice. On the 8th of September, we took our departure from Okkiosorbik, notwithstanding that the sea between the masses of drift-ice
was encrusted with new ice, which, since the close of August, formed
regularly every night, attaining by morning a thickness of two or
three lines. I had frequently occasion to observe, that when the
atmosphere was without clouds, the new ice began to form precisely at sunrise, and then increased with extraordinary rapidity
for an hour or two, though the mercury in the thermometer might
be standing at two or three degrees above the freezing point ; and
some degrees above what it stood at shortly before sun rise.   In
passing Cape Tordenskiold, I noticed that its northern face rises
out of the sea at an angle of from 70° to 80°. It is intersected by
a number of white veins, probably of quartz, and is easily distinguishable by its handsome chocolate colour, inclining to dark
gray.
    In the evening of the 9th of September, shortly after our arrival at
a small islet in the firth of Ingiteit, it came on to blow a severe
gale from N.E., accompanied with snow ; and the ice closing in,
in consequence, on the shore, we were obliged to stay there several
days, during which we made an excursion up the firth, in quest of
berries. This firth is scarcely more than eight miles deep.   On
its banks are to be seen a number of old, abandoned dwellings, at
one spot sixteen of them together ; being a greater number than
is usually to be met with in one hamlet anywhere else along this
coast, a circumstance which shows that the country hereabouts
was at one time somewhat thickly peopled.
    Off Cape Fischer, which we passed on the 15th of September,
we found the ice lying close up to some small skerries from ten to
twelve yards distant from the shore.   Inside of them the water,
indeed, was open, but, there being a heavy swell at the time, it
was dangerous for us to attempt the passage.   Rather than turn
back, however, we determined, after some demur, to venture : and
had well nigh paid dearly for our temerity, being cast with so great
violence against the wall of rock that formed the coast, that any
other boat, less elastic than the Greenland umiak, must unquestionably have been knocked to pieces.   As it was, we escaped with
the loss of some of our oars, which were snapped across, having,
however, narrowly escaped a much more serious evil, in consequence
of the stupidity of my Greenland crew, who, in the extremity of
their terror, rushed in a body to the larboard side, and were within
an ace of capsizing the boat.   This evening we saw a rainbow-like
parhelion, in the horizon to the East, just as the sun was sinking
behind the mountains : and shortly after it set in to blow hard

from North. We were lucky enough, however, to reach Serket-noua before the gale was at its height, Here we now remained eight days, exposed to all the miseries of cold, and famine, and sickness.

On the 30th of September, at about noon, it came on suddenly to blow a hard gale from W.N.W. Much as I had wished before that this would happen, I was very much annoyed at its happening just now; for at Kutek, where we chanced to be at the time, we had not been able to find a safe berth for our boat, it lying on a small skerry which the sea swept over at high water, and even there being but indifferently secured, in consequence of the want of stones to make it fast. And our apprehensions on its account soon proved to have been well founded, for, in the afternoon, a large hummock drifting down on it drove it from its moorings, and, before we could reach the spot, a sudden gust of wind carried it away. Destitute as we were of provisions, and of timber with which to build a hut, far distant from any inhabited spot, the greater number of us sick, and Winter at the door, we looked upon our boat as the sole means of rescue from our miserable plight, and on its loss, which now really seemed inevitable, as the sure fore-runner of our destruction. Speechless with horror, my Green-landers stood gazing at it, as it drifted away. Our alarm, however, was of but brief duration. The wind veering to N.E., drove it back on some floes lying close to where we stood, and we recovered it. A couple of its timbers were staved in, and its skin-bottom rent in divers places; but such damages we were accustomed to, and managed to repair without much difficulty. I myself, how-ever, in endeavouring to save it, sustained an injury in the right hand, which unfitted me for duty, or nearly so, for the rest of the voyage.

The storm ceased towards evening; but it still continued to blow sharply during the night and the whole of the day following. The ice, however, did not retire farther than three or four miles' distance from the shore, and began to set in again with great rapidity as soon as the gale ceased. We left Kutek on the 2nd of October; but had not yet reached Cape Vallöe when the ice closed in on the shore, so that it was with great difficulty we managed to get past that promontory. We arrived at Nektoralik after dark, and could find, of course, no place for hauling up the boat, which, accordingly, we moored in a small cove, and in which, according to my custom in such cases, I spent the night, while my companions took up their quarters on the shore. On previous occasions of this nature, I had made it an invariable rule to keep awake, in order to guard the boat from accidents, and had more than once been thus the means of saving it. On the present occasion, however, being exhausted with fatigue, for I had not closed my eyes for twice twenty-four hours, I fell into a sleep, which did not last long,

before I was awakened, and in a most unpleasant way. A hummock of ice having drifted into the cove, came in contact with the
boat and cut a hole in its bottom, so that, in a few moments, it
was in a sinking state. I got on shore in safety, with a gun in my
hand, which I fired off to rouse my Greenlanders, who, however,
either did not hear the report, or at least pretended not to hear it.
I set out, therefore, to the spot where they had taken up their
quarters, across a ravine at the bottom of the cove, a place difficult
enough to traverse even in broad day, and, notwithstanding the
darkness, fortunately reached it. On hearing what had happened,
some of them came forth; others, however, who either were sick,
or had nothing in the boat they cared about, did not stir, and could
not be prevailed upon to lend us the least assistance. All the rest
of the night, and the whole of the day following, we were now employed in saving what we could of the boat's cargo, a portion of
which being such articles as would not sink, was floating about
among the ice. I lost, however, on this occasion, some charts
that I had drawn up of different parts of the East coast, a box
containing specimens of mineralogy from the vicinity of the Isle of
Twins, and some other matters of minor moment.

I had hoped to find, either at Nenneetsuk, or Alluk, the boat
which, according to agreement, was to have been despatched with
provisions, to meet me on my return from the East coast. I was,
however, disappointed*. On the 8th of October, towards evening,
we reached Prince Christian's Sound, and, running into it, pitched
our tents upon its northern bank, three or four miles beyond Kikkertak. From hence I despatched Ernenek's son, and another
Eastlander who had accompanied us from Queen Maria's Valley,
they being the only individuals of the whole party that could be
said to be in tolerable condition, a-head of us to Friederichsthal, for
letters and provisions ; and not in vain, as the head-missionary,
Mr. Kleinschmidt, lost no time in sending me some bread and wine.
For some time past, indeed during the whole voyage homewards,
I had been in a state of utter exhaustion. These refreshments,
however, and the intelligence which shortly after reached me, that
my king and country were satisfied with the manner in which I had
executed my commission, acted as powerful restoratives, though
accompanied with information of the loss of some much-valued

* I afterwards found the cause of this to be, the return to Denmark of Mr.
Wolff, the superintendent of the colony of Juliana's-hope. Mr. Aröe had found
it impossible to do anything at Nennortalik, there being at that place a great lack
of hands, insomuch that he found it a matter of difficulty to have the most necessary business of the colony attended to, while at Juliana's-hope there are many
more than are required.
There seems, however, to have been some shameful neglect on this occasion, on
the part of the authorities in Greenland, and particularly those connected with the
colony of Juliana's-hope ; and the meritorious author, in not pointing out distinctly
where the odium should attach, has displayed more Christian charity than the parties merit.—*Trans.*

relatives, and I felt my strength of mind as well as body, improve from hour to hour.

The state of the ice, the illness of my crew, and bad weather, prevented our making long days'-journeys. On the 15th of October, however, we reached Nah-ah, whence I set off over-land for Friederichsthal, where I was received most hospitably by the members of the mission. Having offered here to furnish Ernenek with fresh hands for his boat, an offer, however, which he declined, I proceeded to Nennortalik on the 19th of October, where, much as I was pleased to meet with Mr. Aröe, its most meritorious superintendent, it grieved me to find him still occupying so subordinate a post. Some days now elapsing, and Ernenek not making his appearance, I sent a boat with provisions to meet him, and shortly after learned that he and his whole boat's company lay sick at Ikigeit, directly opposite Friederichsthal, where one of his children, and one of the Eastlanders that had come with us, had died. It was not till long after, indeed, that he was conveyed to Nennortalik; one of his wives, and his eldest son, a smart young lad, who had already begun to catch seals, being still sick when he set out, and dying shortly after. His boat had been sunk at Ikigeit, he and his whole party not having strength enough to land it. Mr. de Fries, however, had it afterwards taken up, and undertook, of his own accord, to have it properly repaired.

I now spent the Winter at Juliana's-hope, and, though I was not here in danger of actual starvation, still I may say with truth that I was indebted solely to the hospitality of the missionary, Mr. Esmann, and his wife, for not suffering various wants; the individual to whom it belonged to provide for the necessities of the expedition having forgotten, or rather neglected, to take any measures to that end, though he well knew that, on the spot, nothing was to be procured but ships' stores, and those sometimes of the most inferior quality*.

As soon as my health permitted, I resumed the survey I had left unfinished in 1829, of the districts of Juliana's-hope and Frederick's-hope. This task I should have been able to get on with much more rapidly than was actually the case, had I had a single individual to aid me, on whom I could place reliance. I had, however, none; the sailor who had come with me from Denmark having been sent back by the new superintendent of the colony (in conformity, as he said, with orders to that effect received by him,) some months before my return; and half the time, in consequence of my want of such a person, being lost, from the necessity I often lay under of raising with my own hands the requisite land-marks, as it was not always that I could prevail upon the native Greenlanders to do it for me.

* A portion of the bread, for instance, that was furnished me for the use of the expedition, was found to be scarcely eatable.

It was on the 11th of August, 1831, that I left Greenland in the brig Whale *. The ice that, some days before, had extended in one uninterrupted field from the very shore to such a distance that, from the tops of the highest hills, no water could be seen, had suddenly vanished, in what manner it is difficult to say, as no storm preceded its disappearance, and no current was perceptible †.

A few days after we encountered a severe gale from the E., which continued to the 20th of August, and carried us over to the coast of Labrador. On the 30th we saw Rona and Barra, and in the evening of the next day passed the Start Light at the Orkneys. The chronometer gave precisely the true longitude. In the Skagerak, the current was found to have set, between the 5th and 6th of September, to the East, at the rate of from one and a half to two knots an hour. Off the Skaw, however, it set, for several days together, to the N.W., at the rate of six knots an hour. In the evening of the 12th we saw the aurora borealis, in the form of an arch, stretching from N.E. to N.W.

On the 13th of September we passed the Castle of Cronborg. Here I left the brig, and went on board the guard-ship, commanded by Captain Thomsen, who accompanied me to Elsinore; thence I travelled over-land to Copenhagen, and reported my arrival to his Majesty, who was graciously pleased to express his satisfaction at the manner in which I had executed my commission.

---

* In this vessel came to Greenland the very sailor of whom mention has just been made, and who complained to me of the manner in which he had been sent home the year previous, though engaged to serve with the expedition for three years and a half. I pacified him by guaranteeing the payment of his full wages.

† I had before heard from the Greenlanders, that this sometimes happened ; but should still have doubted the fact, had I not thus witnessed it. The thing is possibly to be accounted for on the supposition of a violent easterly gale at some miles' distance from the shore.

APPENDIX.

APPENDIX.

No. I.

ON THE SITUATION OF THE EAST AND WEST BYGDS; WITH REMARKS ON EGGERS' AND WORMSKIOLD'S TREATISES ON THAT SUBJECT.

THOUGH the results of my expedition do not furnish any reason for believing that the East coast of Greenland was ever colonised by Europeans, there are still, however, some individuals who obstinately adhere to the opinion that the East Bygd, as it is called, was there situated. This voyage, say they, has, in fact, yielded no decisive results; for the traveller did not penetrate into the interior, or explore the bottom of those firths, or inlets, along the coast, where only vestiges of the lost colony were to be looked for. To this I answer:

1. That the Chorography of Ivar Bardsen, the only one we can at all depend on in this matter, by no means places all the inhabited sites of the East Bygd in the interior of the firths; but, on the contrary, states explicitly, that several, and these settlements having large buildings belonging to them, such as churches, were situated either on the islands off the mainland, or at the mouths of the firths, " on the right hand, and the left, as one sails in." Among the innumerable remains on the West coast, many are situated precisely as here described, at the mouths of the firths, and on the islands fringing the shore, as at the islands of Nennortalik, Sermesok, Ounartok, and Kakortok-Akia, or Mathias's land, and on the mainland at Friederichsthal, between Friederichsthal and Nennortalik, in the vicinity of Nukalik, at Kinalik, between Agluitsok and Igaliko, on the coast between Juliana's-hope and Tunnudliorbik, at the mouths of the firths of Tessermiut, Narksarmiut, Colony-firth, Tunnudliorbik, Arsut, and elsewhere. Now, if the East Bygd did lie on the East coast, I must have fallen in with many more ruins, so situated, than are to be met with on the West coast, since the East Bygd, judging from the number of its churches, must have been three times as populous as the West Bygd, which, according to the supposition I here combat, was the present district of Juliana's-hope.

2. The Greenlander is known to have an accurate knowledge of the localities of his native district, its shores and hills, its islands and its waters; an assertion no less true of the native of the East, than of the native of the West, coast. One day he is far into the firths catching char, the next in quest of roots and berries; at one time he takes up his abode at the mouth of the firth, at another among the islands. Nothing easily escapes his observation. In a word, he is as intimately acquainted with the geography of his country, as a pilot with the tract of sea he navigates. And this, I acknowledge, was one reason why, before starting for the East coast at all, I doubted greatly if I should there find any vestiges of colo-

nization ; the Eastlanders, who, now and then, had visited Nennortalik and Juliana's-hope, as well as those that latterly had taken up their residence at Friederichsthal, having never seen, or heard of, ruins, till they came to the West coast*.

In not exploring any of the firths on the coast to the bottom, I am, therefore, satisfied that I did rightly, well knowing, as has been observed, that where the Greenlanders themselves know of no ruins, there none are to be found. Even where ruins exist, one may search for them over and over again, if he have neither guide nor clue to aid him, without finding them, the greater number being so overgrown with heath and thickets as to be scarce distinguishable from the rocks. Had I engaged, therefore, in any such explorations, which, doubtless, both for myself and party, would have been a much more agreeable occupation than the perilous and painful coasting-voyage that we performed, we should, of necessity, have made much less progress, probably not have penetrated much beyond the 62d degree of latitude, and then the objection would have been, that the Bygd lay farther North. In such unprofitable searches, indeed, I did not waste my time; but, wherever I landed, I did not fail carefully to explore the country round, besides penetrating, to the distance of from ten to twelve miles, into five different firths—those, to wit, of Ingiteit, Auarket, Kasiortok, Kangersinuk, and Bernstorff: of which the three last-mentioned, as well as the Sound of Ekallumiut, are situated within those limits, (namely, between the 63° and 64° of latitude,) where the East Bygd, if it ever lay on the East coast at all, was, with most show of reason, to be looked for.

These observations will probably suffice for all who have no prejudices to relinquish relating to the matter here in question ; but the partisans of the old theory, which places the East Bygd on the East coast, will not yield the point, it is to be presumed, so easily ; and I shall therefore proceed to examine more narrowly the grounds on which they rest their conclusions, premising only a single observation on the meaning of the words East and West Bygd, or Böigd, for the information of those who may not have had an opportunity of making themselves acquainted with these minutiæ of the subject. It is a very general opinion—one, we might almost say, imbibed at the mother's breast—that East and West Bygd are the names, respectively, of two bays [*Bugt*], one of which lies on the East, and the other on the West, coast of Greenland. This, however, is a gross error ; these words denoting nothing more than two inhabited places (sites, or districts), one of which lay somewhat to the East of the other†. There is nothing in the terms themselves implying that they did not, both of them, lie on the same coast; and we find, accordingly, that several of the *savans* of former times, when the ruins on the West coast had not yet

* Wormskiold, indeed, says, in his Essay on the situation of Greenland, Viinland, &c. (in the *Transactions of the Scandinavian Literary Society*, for 1814), that he has heard of two places on the East coast where ruins are to be met with; but he neither mentions where they are, nor of whom he had his information : and as he himself does not seem to give implicit credit to the tale, it is likely that his authority was not the best. In the meanwhile, it is not impossible, that, by the two places here adverted to, may have been meant Friederichsthal and Ikigeit, both of which have been supposed by some to lie on the East coast, they taking Cape Egede, at Sermesok, to be Cape Farewell, the southernmost extremity of Greenland.

† From the Icelandic word, *byggia*, to build, (but also) to inhabit : whence the modern Danish, *bygge*, to build ; *bebygge*, to inhabit, &c.

been discovered, did actually assign both Bygds to the East coast, it; trending, as near as possible, N.N.E. and S.S.W.

The chief grounds, then, advanced in support of the theory which places the East Bygd on the East coast, are the following :

I.—The ancient sailing directions for those navigating from Bergen and Iceland to Greenland.

A.—Those of the Landnama-book, and Ivar Bardsen, run literally as follows:

" From the houses [Bergen] in Norway, you must sail steadily to the West to Hvarf in Greenland, passing North of [the] Shetland [islands], so that the horizon is seen in the midst of [between] the mountains, if the weather be clear, but South of the Ferro islands, so that the horizon is seen in the midst of [between] the mountains, and South of Iceland, so that you fall in with birds and whales.

" They who would sail direct from Bergen to Greenland, without coming to Iceland, should first steer West, until they meet (i. e. come opposite to) Reykianæs on the South of Iceland, from which they should then be distant twelve Icelandic sea-miles South, and then, keeping the same westerly course, steer for that part of the said Greenland which is called Hvarf. The day before the said Hvarf is seen, will be seen another white snow [covered] mountain, called Hvidsærk'; and between these two mountains, and Hvarf and Hvidsærk, lies a naze (Næs, point of land) called Herjolf's-næs, and near it a harbour called Sandhavn."

From the observation in the Landnama-book about birds and whales, it seems evident that the meaning was, to approach Iceland, probably, as Wormskiold surmises, to within eighty miles of it, as Ivar Bardsen says expressly twelve *vikur siouar*, which amount to about that number*. As a direct line, passing through a point lying eighty miles South of Reykianæs, must, if continued far enough, unquestionably strike the East coast of Greenland†, it has been inferred that the Bygd lay there ; and it does appear, indeed, at first view, that no other inference can be deduced from the expressions used. It should be kept in mind, however, that in those days, when the art of navigation was in its infancy, and neither chart nor compass were known, it must have been of moment for mariners, in voyages of any considerable length, to take new departures, wherever it was practicable ; for hence it was, as I conceive, that the direction to pass so near to Iceland was laid down, the rather that the additional distance thereby occasioned did not exceed from 90 to 100 miles, which, in a voyage like that from Bergen to Greenland, of 1400, was not worth taking into the account. This conjecture seems to me so natural, indeed, that I am only surprised that no one should have thought of it before. I am very confident that a seaman of the present day, if, without compass, chart, or

* Wormskiold is assuredly in error when he states that by the word "whale" is here meant the *Bal. mysticetus ;* for this is no more to be met with off the southern coast of Iceland, than the southern part of the East coast of Greenland. I take the *vikur siouar* to be equal to about one and a-half Danish (six geographical) miles ; for another of Ivar Bardsen's sailing directions states the distance between Snefieldsnæs and Reykianæs, which is eighteen Danish miles, at twelve *vikur siouar*.

† It would strike it at the ice-blink Colberger-Heide, a steep and rugged icy precipice, from eighty to 100 fathoms high, and many miles long, situated in a tract of country which is either buried under glaciers, or of which, at least, the coast is inaccessible.

quadrant, he was directed to sail from Bergen to Cape Farewell, would follow the exact course laid down in the Landnama-book.

The expression in the Landnama-book, " steadily to the West," seems besides to indicate that the general course from Bergen to Hvarf was West ; and this course leads precisely to Cape Farewell. If this, at least, be not the meaning, it is difficult to imagine why the sailing directions begin with those words. With regard, too, to the latter part of Ivar Bardsen's directions, " the day before Hvarf is seen, will be seen another white snow (covered) mountain, called Hvidsærk," sufficient attention has not, as I conceive, been paid to its import. If the Bygd lay on the East coast, I cannot conceive how Hvarf and Hvidsærk can have been so situated in respect to one another, that the mariner coming from the E.N.E. could see the one a whole day before the other, unless it be assumed that Hvarf lay some 80 or 100 miles in the interior of a firth, an assumption altogether gratuitous. If, on the other hand, we take it to be identical with the now district of Juliana's-hope, the difficulty vanishes ; for Hvidsærk then becomes identical with Cape Farewell, and Hvarf with Sermesok, which, of course, could not be seen, until the former was passed. Cape Farewell, in clear weather, can be seen from a distance of 80 miles, and, under very advantageous circumstances, even somewhat farther off; and this is precisely what a day's journey of the ancients may reasonably be estimated at. Whether, therefore, the ship bound for Greenland came from Iceland or from Bergen, taking a new departure from Iceland, Cape Farewell must, in general, have been seen the day before Sermesok. What still more tends to confirm me in the opinion that this island, or rather its southernmost promontory, is identical with Hvarf, is the circumstance that, along the whole of the East coast of Greenland, as high up as lat. 65° 20', there is not a single point which answers to the description in Erik Raude's voyage, of his sailing " West about Hvarf*,"—for such is the expression— and not *South about*, as they would seem to think who would make of Hvarf a headland at the entrance into one of the firths on the East coast.

B.—Ivar Bardsen's two sets of sailing directions for navigating between Iceland and Greenland, comprising the course followed by the ancients, and that adopted subsequently, run literally thus :

" From Snefieldsnæs [situated on the] West [coast] of Iceland, the distance to Greenland is shortest, and it is said to be two days' and two nights' sail in the direction of West, then lie Gunbiörn's Skerries exactly half-way between Greenland and Iceland, and this was the course formerly followed, but now the ice has drifted down from the North-bay†, and set itself fast so near to Gunbiörn's Skerries, that none without peril of life can follow it, as will afterwards be seen."

" In sailing from Iceland to Greenland you must take your departure from Snefieldsnæs, which lies at a distance of 12 ' vikur siouar' N.W. from Reykianæs, and shape a course to the West for 1 Day and 1 Night, and

* Eggers' Prize Essay on the True State of the East Bygd. Cop. 1793, p. 5.
† This can scarcely have been the real cause ; for the ice along the East coast of Greenland was, in all likelihood, much the same in the tenth century as it was in the fourteenth, and is now. The fact is, probably, that experience soon convinced them of the inconveniences and difficulties of the ancient course, which, if no ice indeed had been in the way, would have been a safer, though a longer, route for the seamen of those days.

then to the S.W. until you have got past all the ice above-mentioned lying at and about Gunbiörn's Skerries; you must then steer to the N.W. for 1 Day and 1 Night, which will bring you to Hvarf, where the above-named Herjolfsnæs and Sandhavn are situated."

Eggers, in my opinion, has long ago satisfactorily proved, that the "two days and two nights" mentioned in the former of these sailing directions is a corruption of the original text, and that we should read, in place of them, *four* days (four times four-and-twenty hours). Without this correction, Wormskiold's semicolon before the words "and it is said," etc., does not remove the difficulty: for the fact of Gunbiörn's Skerries being situated half-way between Iceland and Greenland, is not only only disproved by the experience of the Icelandic traders and fishermen, but by that also of the English and Dutch whalers. For the rest, I approve of Wormskiold's punctuation, and have already shown at page 100, that, by adopting it, together with Eggers's correction above-mentioned, the result arrived at is, that, following the ancient course, the Bygd lay at a distance of eight days' sail from Iceland. Thus interpreted, these directions show plainly enough, that the East Bygd was identical with the now district of Juliana's-hope; for the distance from Snefieldsjökel due West to Greenland is 400 miles, and thence to Cape Farewell, about 340, together 740 miles, or eight days' sail, at 92 miles.

Nor are the latter directions at variance with the theory which places the East Bygd in the district of Juliana's-hope. The "one day and night's sail" to the West is susceptible of a twofold interpretation. This course may, I conceive, have been laid down partly in order to enable the navigator the sooner to get sight of the coast of Greenland, and partly to prevent his getting too close to Cape Reykianæs, the sea about which is described as dangerous, on account of the frequent and severe gales that there prevail; and, on account of which it was thought advisable to give this cape a wide berth. The expression "until you have got past all the ice lying at and about Gunbiörn's Skerries," is to be understood, in my opinion, as meant of all the ice along the whole extent of the East coast; for it is difficult to imagine how some small rocks, lying in the middle of a channel 400 miles broad, should be able to place any impediment in the way of ice drifting from the North Bay (the Arctic Sea) in its course towards the S.W., in which direction we know that the current here actually sets. Besides, it is observed in the Royal Mirror (the *Kongs-Skugg-Sid, Speculum Regale*), in speaking of the ice in the Greenland sea,—" but this ice lies more in the direction of N. and N.E. from the land, than of S., S.W., or W.; for which reason, he that would reach the land, must sail round it, till he pass all the ice, and then sail in for the land*." Not a word is said here about sailing round the ice about Gun-

* The work goes on here to state as follows; "but it has frequently happened, that those sailing for this land, have held in for it too soon, and have thus got entangled in the ice, where some have perished, and from which others have with difficulty escaped; and the means of escape to which they have usually had recourse, have been to haul their boats up on the ice, and make the best of their way, with them, to the shore, abandoning their ships and all their goods on board them, to destruction. Some have managed to live, in this way, on the ice, for four or five days, others even a longer time." Precisely what is here described, happened, in 1777, off the East coast of Greenland, to some Dutch whalers, where it appears, that the ice, in the twelfth or thirteenth century, when *The Royal Mirror* is sup-

biörn's Skerries, the direction being explicit to sail round the land, an expression which is unintelligible, if by the East Bygd we do not understand the district of Juliana's-hope. The words, that the "ice lies more in the direction of N. and N.E. from the land, than of S., S.W., or W.," deserve likewise to be attended to; for if the East Bygd lay on the East coast, how comes there to be any mention of ice in the West? The one day and night's sail to the West, has been insisted on as a conclusive proof of the East Bygd's situation on the East coast. As this opinion has been asserted by a no less scientific navigator than Scoresby, I think it necessary for me to take some more especial notice of it, in doing which I hope to prove, that, by adhering strictly to the letter of the instructions where they occur, one cannot get to the East coast anywhere but in the neighbourhood of Cape Farewell, or at Cape Farewell itself. I do not even quote these sailing instructions of Ivar Bardsen's as proof of the fact, that the East Bygd and the district of Juliana's-hope are one and the same, for I look upon their accuracy, though perfect, as purely accidental: all I care for is, to prove how utterly groundless the position is, that these instructions lead naturally to the East coast, and cannot, by possibility, lead to the West.

To prove this clearly, and briefly, I have in the map laid down the course as prescribed in these directions; that is to say, I have marked off one day's and one night's sail (or, in other words, 96 miles distance) West; and from thence drawn a line in the direction of S.W. It will be perceived that, from no point in this line is it possible to reach the East coast after one day's and one night's sail in the direction of N.W., or, in other words, that there is no point in this line from which the East coast is 96 miles distant in the direction of N.W., until one comes quite down to Lindenow's Firth, in the vicinity of Cape Farewell, as also that a line drawn from Cape Farewell perpendicular to the said S.W. line, measures precisely 96 miles, or one day's and one night's sail. If it be said, that, as I took the liberty, at another place, of making two days and two nights into four times four-and-twenty hours, I ought here to understand the one day and one night mentioned as twice four-and-twenty hours, I am content to let the objection have its force, and only beg of any one who feels an interest in this question, to measure off 192 miles from Snefieldsjökel in the direction of West, and then to draw a line to the S.W. as before. He will find, that from no point in that line is the East coast 192 miles distant N.W.; while, on the contrary, this alteration may be admitted without at all affecting the correctness of my theory, if it but be admitted that, in the notation of the courses S.W. and N.W. an error of a single point has been made (the possibility, and even probability, of which, none will deny, who takes into consideration that the compass was not yet known), and if by Hvarf be understood Cape Egede at Sermesok. Upon this supposition, in fact, one might not only make Cape Farewell and Cape Egede on a N.W. course, but even Cape Thorvaldsen, at Nunarsoit, which lies 128 miles up along the West coast, for the course from Cape Farewell to

posed to have been written, was much the same as it is now. The translator of this curious book, the learned Halfdan Einarsen, was likewise of opinion that the East Bygd lay on the West coast; for he observes in continuation—"and therefore he that would reach the land, must sail round it in the direction of S.W. and West, till he has passed the ice."

this promontory is, as near as possible, W.N.W.; nay, if one were to steer N.W. by N., instead of due N.W., one might get still higher up.

II.—The distances between Iceland and Greenland, as laid down in the Landnama-book.

The passage in which this distance is given, runs as follows; " So say well informed men, that from Stad, in Norway, to Horn, on the East of Iceland, is seven days' sail to the West; but from Snefieldsnæs to Hvarf, in Greenland, which is nearest, four days' sail to the West. From Rey-kianæs, in the South of Iceland, to Aulduhlaup, in Ireland, it is three days' sail to the South; but from Langenæs, on the North of Iceland, to Svalbard, at the bottom of the sea*, is four days' sail to the North. From Kolbeins-ey† to Greenland, is one day's sail to the North."

It seems to me that the intention of the writer, here, could not be to determine the position of the East Bygd, but simply to indicate the distance of Iceland from the lands nearest and surrounding it, which, accordingly, is done in the most simple way imaginable, by noting the distance between four of its extreme points, on its North, South, East, and West coasts respectively, and the nearest land opposite to each. Now, if this be the case, we cannot look to these expressions of the Landnama-book, as fur-nishing any sort of proof of the East Bygd's being situated on the East coast. It is true that mention is made of the place called Hvarf, and we know that there was a place of that name in the Bygd; but, as Worms-kiold justly remarks, there may have been many other places in Green-land, as there are several in Iceland, called by that name. Indeed, there is reason to believe that a place so called did exist on the East, due West of Snefieldsjökel, that, namely, where Erik Raude, on making the East coast of Greenland, turned to the South‡, and the words " which is nearest" (that Hvarf which is nearest, not that which Erik doubled and sailed to the West of) seems to confirm this opinion. In another old copy of this work, it is said, that the shortest distance to Greenland, not to Hvarf, is four days' sail to the West; but by Greenland was understood not the Bygd merely, but the whole country, and, in all probability, Spitzbergen into the bargain. Finally, I must not neglect observing, that three of the five distances, here noted, are erroneously given; for there is no land at all to the North of Langanæs, nor any to the South of Reykianæs, within the limits specified, and from Kolbeins-ey to Greenland, the distance is 480 miles, or five days' sail, in place of one. With what security can inferences be deduced from a document so little to be depended on§?

* Here is not meant the bottom of the sea, in the usual sense of the word, but the *remotest parts* of the sea towards the North, the sea about the pole; as we say the *bottom* of a cove, of a firth, &c. &c.—*Trans.*

† Meve Rock.

‡ Hvarf means *a place of turning.*

§ The true distance between East-Horn and Stat, according to the best charts, is 676 miles; from Snefieldsnæs due West to Greenland, 396 miles. These two distances give, thus, the day's sail to be from 96 to 100 miles. The circuit of Iceland, again, from naze to naze, is, as near as possible, 752 miles; and as the time for sailing round it was said to be seven days, we obtain 107—8 miles as the amount of the day's sail. From Reykianæs to the nearest point of Ireland, (Urrishead), the distance is 688 miles, or seven days' sail, S.E. by S. If the Landnama-book did not expressly mention Ireland, one might possibly conclude, that by *Aulduhlaup* (*i. e.* the run of the waves) was meant some shoal where there

M

III.—The expression in Biörn Jonsen's Chorography; " Grænland horfer i útsudr, synst er Herjolfnes."

The word "horfer," according to Haldorsen's Lexicon, means " turns towards" (*fuces*), and several native Icelanders say that this is the only meaning it can have in the passage here cited, and by no means that of " stretches towards," which some persons, unskilled, as I suppose, in the Icelandic, have been desirous of attributing to it, solely because such an interpretation would better suit their views. " Reaches towards" has been rendered by the author of Gripla by the words " vikur til" (" ok vikur landinu til útsudr," *the land stretches towards the south-west*, namely, the East coast of Greenland all the way from Spitzbergen.) If, now, the word " horfer" here means " faces," the question of the East Bygd's situation on the S. W. coast of Greenland is so far set at rest, for there is no tract of land along the whole of the East coast, as far as lat 65¼°, that faces the S. W., unless, by Greenland, we understand the North bank of one or other of the firths on that coast *.

IV.—The expression in the same Chorography; " That er Stiarna er Afhvarf heiter à austanverdu landi."

Wormskiold's interpretation of these words, " The North-star is then towards that side where the land becomes easterly," must surely strike every reader as forced, besides being a very obscure and unnatural way of stating the simple fact, that the East Bygd lay on the East coast. But the translation is not only forced; it is, moreover, erroneous; for the word " that" does not signify " then," but " it," and the expression " à austanverdu landi," means " to the East of the country." The expression would then stand, " It is the star called the North-star, to the east of the country," words that are without meaning. I shall cite the whole passage, as it occurs in Eggers :—

" Grænland horfer i útsudr, synst er Herjolfsnes enn Hvarfsgnipa næst fyrir Vestan, Thángad kom Eirekr hin Raudi lengstoc letst tha † kominn fyrir botn Eireksfjardar. That er Stiarna er Afhvarf heiter à austanverdu landi, thá Spalsund, thá Dráugey, thá Saulvadalr," etc.

The word " Stiarna" is said, by those acquainted with Icelandic, to have no other meaning than " star." As this reading, however, makes nonsense of the whole passage, and as it seems odd that, in the middle of a chorographical description of the East Bygd, the writer should begin to talk about the North Star, in order to tell his readers on which side of the land the said Bygd lay, especially as he had already stated this in plain words a moment previous, I conceive the word must be an error, and that some other, perhaps, " Tharna" (this, *vulgò*, this here), or " Stadr" (place) should be substituted for it. If we adopt this correction, and place a comma, or semicolon, after " heiter," we make sense of the passage,

were breakers; for, in all old charts, not excepting even those in which the Faroe Islands are laid down rightly, a large island, called in some, Frisland, in others, Busse's-land, is laid down precisely in that direction, and at that distance from Iceland. The spot is indicated in modern charts, as *the Sunken Land van Buss*, and in most of the descriptions of the Atlantic, it is made mention of as dangerous on account of breakers.

* Some of the *savans* of yore imagined that the East and West Bygds lay, the former on the East bank, the latter on the West bank, of one and the same firth ; an opinion, which seems scarcely less extravagant than thatof La Roche Gallichon, who conceived the East Bygd to be in America.   † Sic in MS.—han?—ED.

which may be rendered thus: " Greenland faces the S.W., its most southerly point is Herjolfsnæs, and Hvarfsgnipa is next to it towards the W., the farthest point to which Erik the Red penetrated, he thinking himself then near the bottom of Erik's-firth. It is this place, that is named Afhvarf; and next it, at the eastern extremity of the Bygd, lies Spalsund, after which follows first Drangey, then Saulvadal," etc., etc. By adopting this reading, we, moreoever, supply another great desideratum, Biörn Jonsen's Chorography coming thus to point out in what way, in regard to relative position, the firths were numbered, it not seeming hitherto to state if they were numbered from the East or from the West.

What serves farther to confirm me in this opinion, is, as Eggers has remarked, that the author of this MS. would seem to have omitted something before the words, " oc létst han kominn fyrir botn Eireksfjardar," these very words occurring in the account of Erik's voyage, but in a very different combination. It is stated there, to wit ; " hit Thridea sumar fór hann alt Nordur til Snæfells oc létst hann kvaminn fyrir botn Eireksfjardar, *hvarf hann thá aptur*," etc., *i. e.*, " the third Summer he went all the way North as far as Snefield, and believed himself to be near the bottom of Erik's-firth, *thereupon he turned back*," etc. It was his thus *turning back*, perhaps, that gave the place the name of Afhvarf, and the spot so called lay, probably, in the vicinity of Snefield.

V.—That it is difficult, if not impossible, to find room on the West coast for the firths of the West Bygd, if the district of Juliana's-hope be the East Bygd.

To show the fallacy of this objection, I shall, in the first place, but cite the words of Biörn Jonsen, who, after enumerating the firths of the East Bygd, continues thus : " Thá er VI Daga ródr sex Mönnum til Vesturbygdar sex æringi, thá telr thar upp Firdi, thá er úr hinni vestri bygd til Lysufiardar sex Daga ródr, thadan sex Daga ródr til Karlbrída, thá thriggia Daga ródr til Biarneyar, XII Daga ródr umhverfis, Ey, Eysunes, Ædanes fyrir Nordan. Sva er talid, at CXC Bygda sie i eystri Bygd, XC i vestri ;" *i. e.* " It is a 6-days'-row for 6 men in a six-oared boat to the West Bygd, where begin the firths; and it is a 6-days'-row along this Bygd to Lysufiord, and from thence to Karlbrida other 6-days'-row, then a 3-days'-row to Biarney (Bear Island), then a 12-days'-row about, Ey, Eysunæs, [and] Ædanes to the North. It is said, that there are 190 Bygds in the East Bygd, 90 in the West."

No one that knows anything of the subject here under discussion, whatever be his opinion in regard to the site of the East Bygd, will deny, that, by Biörn Jonsen's Biarney we are to understand the large island of Disco, possibly together with the islands, and groups of islands, round it[*]. The words " XII Daga ródr umhverfis " have been, if I mistake not, generally understood as meant to apply to Disco, and that it was intended thereby to be said, that to row round Disco, and the islands about it, required twelve days. Instead of gratuitously assuming, that the day's-row of the ancients was forty-eight miles, Wormskiold ought rather to have taken this passage

* It has hitherto been a question, whether we ought to understand this word as signifying *one* island, or *more*. It occurs here in the plural, but it would be strange, indeed, if groups of islands lying many miles distant from Disco, were to be included with it under one denomination.

for his guide, and he then would have obtained a very different result, it
making the day's-row to be but twenty-four, instead of forty-eight miles*.

I, however, entertain a very different opinion concerning the meaning
of this remarkable passage, and believe that the expression, "XII Daga
ródr umhverfis" (a 12-days'-row about) does not refer to the antecedent
Biarney, but, omitting the comma after it, to the places mentioned subsequently, Ey, Eysunæs, and Ædanæs. " Ey," I take to be no other than the
" Ey," or *island* of Disco itself, which, rather than any other, may be
κατ᾽ ἐξοχὴν so designated, especially as its proper appellation occurs immediately before; " Eysunæs," to be Noursoak (the Great Naze), situated
between the Waigat and the Firth of Omenak, a point satisfactorily made
out, as I conceive, by Professor Finn Magnussen on etymological grounds†;
and " Ædanæs," to be Svartehuk, in which opinion I am supported by the
authority both of Finn Magnussen and Wormskiold.

By following the direction of the land from Fortune Bay at Disco, along
the Western shore of that island, and then striking across to Hare Island,
opposite to Noursoak, thence to Unknown Island, thence to Svarthuk, and
then back through the Waigat, round Disco, to Fortune Bay, a distance is
obtained of from 420 to 440 miles, which, divided by twelve, gives the day's-
row to be thirty-five or thirty-six miles‡, which ascertained, we shall now
see, how far the twenty-one days' journey, in a row-boat, from the East
Bygd to Biarney, will bring us, taking the East Bygd to be the district of
Juliana's-hope, and Biarney to be Disco.

The ancients, in making their voyages in row-boats, kept, in all probability within the rocks and skerries that fringe the coast of Greenland, and
were thus obliged to pass over a greater distance than they might have
done by shaping a straight course from place to place. My experience
enables me to estimate the increase of distance thereby occasioned at about
four miles to every fifteen or twenty, or about eight miles in a day's journey

* The circuit of Disco, Hare Island, Prince's Island, Green Islands, Dog Islands,
Crown Prince's Islands, and Rothgun's Island, scarcely amounts to 280 miles in all.
Wormskiold is in error, therefore, when he states that it very nearly amounts to a
twelve-days' journey of forty-eight miles a day, in other words 576 miles. Another
important error committed by him I may take this opportunity to touch on, as it
lies at the root of his whole calculation. He takes the distance between Juliana's-
hope and Good-hope to be 304 miles, and that between Good-hope and Disco,
452; arriving thus at the conclusion that these distances are to one another as six
to nine, or as the distance above given in days' journeys between the Vesterbygd
and Lysufiord to that between Lysufiord and Biarney. But this is evidently incor-
rect; for the distance between Juliana's-hope and Good-hope (whether you go
outside of Nunarsoit, or through the channel of Torsukatek) is precisely equal to
that between Good-hope and Disco, both being as near as possible 304 miles. The
firth of Good-hope, therefore, cannot possibly be the Lysufiord of the ancients,
which is to be looked for farther North. The location of Karlbrida at Holsteinsborg
is a still greater error; for Holsteinsborg lies exactly midway between Good-hope
and Disco, while the distance between Lysufiord and Karlbrida is to that between
Karlbrida and Biarney (according to Biörn Jonsen) as six to three.
† Antiquarian Annals, 1827.
‡ Even this was a very good day's work. Every one, acquainted with this mode
of travelling, must at once admit that forty-eight miles is a great deal too much.
With five hands at the oars, besides the occasional help of kajakkers, etc., and in
a light boat, I have never got over more than thirty-four miles in one day. In
general, a mile in Greenland falls somewhat short of full measure, and one is sometimes deceived, thus, into the belief that he has got over more ground than has
actually been the case.

of thirty-six*. All that is necessary, then, is, to mark off, from Biarney (Disco) 588 miles (according to the letter of the above passage, and without allowing for sinuosities, 756), and—the distance from Juliana's-hope being, in effect, greater by from fifteen to twenty miles,—it results that there is abundance of room on the West coast for the whole of the West Bygd, even if Juliana's-hope be taken to be the East Bygd.

On the other hand, if we apply these data to the hypothesis of Worm-skiold, Biarney comes to be off Fish-firth, between Good-hope and the Sugar-loaf (Sukkertop), in lat. 64° 45′, 268 miles South of Disco, unless, indeed, as he has done, we arbitrarily assume a point in the West Bygd from which to count the six-days'-row to Lysufiord. But what right have we to do this? Lysufiord is everywhere made mention of as one of the firths of the West Bygd, and Biörn Jonsen's words, " Thá er ur·hinni Vestribygd til Lýsufiardar sex Daga ródr" are not to be rendered, " it is a six-days'-row beyond the West Bygd to Lysufiord," but, " it is a six-days'-row *along* the West Bygd to Lysufiord." Thus understood, the passage throws light, not only on the distance between the two Bygds, but also on the size or extent of the West Bygd.

In consequence, then, of what has been set forth, I am of opinion, that the West Bygd began in lat. 62° 30′, this being exactly six days' journey, or 168 miles, from the firth of Immartinek, the most northerly and westerly firth in the district of Juliana's-hope, where ruins are to be found. In other words, it began close to, and North of, the iceblink of Frederick's-hope. Lysufiord must then have been situated at the distance of six days' journey farther North, that is to say, in the neighbourhood of the Sugar-loaf (Sukkertop); and, Karlbrida, other six days' journey North, or in about the 68th degree of latitude; from whence to Biarney, or Disco, finally, is about three days' journey.

Nor is this hypothesis, resting, as it does, on reasonable data, to be over-turned by the objection, that, at the spot, where it places Lysufiord, neither many, nor large, ruins have been found: for, in the first place, I have not pretended to fix precisely the position of this firth, but only conjecturally, by calculation of days' journeys from the East Bygd, so that it very possibly may lie a few miles more to the North, or, which I look upon as more likely, some fifteen or twenty South of the Sugar-loaf (Sukkertop); and, in the next, who as yet has given himself much trouble to obtain information about the ruins to be found in Greenland, or, if he be possessed of any, through the medium of the natives, has thought it worth his while to make it known? Many a person, as Wormskiold rightly observes, has lived a length of time in Greenland without seeing any of the antiquities that surround him. At Good-hope, the Europeans have now been settled for upwards of a century, and yet but one man, the Rev. Mr. Thorhallesen, has, in all that time, furnished any information of the kind, and even he has confined his notice to but some few of the many ruins to be met with in the firth of Good-hope, and the adjoining district of Amaraglik. What

---

* I have shown above, that Wormskiold gives more than 452 miles as the distance between Good-hope and Disco, though, measured in a right line, it does not exceed 304 : giving thus four miles to every seven as the increase of distance occasioned by following the sinuosities of a voyage within the skerries ; for the last thirty or forty miles cannot be admitted here into the account at all, as there is no sailing within skerries from West Eiland to Good-haven (in Disco).

should we have known about the ruins in the district of Juliana's-hope, had not Bruhn and Arctander been sent there for the purpose of exploring and describing them ?   And, after all, though they spent two years upon the spot, how incomplete is the account of them which they have furnished, and how many a ruin does there exist, well known to the native Greenlanders, but which no European to this day has seen. It is but of late, indeed, that a proper search for them has been commenced. The results of it we have yet in prospect.

There is, farther, one circumstance which I must not neglect to mention, as serving to account for what may prove to be the fact, that not very many ruins may be discovered in the West Bygd. This comparatively inconsiderable settlement was destroyed, or at least ceased to exist, 150 or 200 years before the much more important East Bygd, which last, moreover, as being the seat of the bishop, the lagmand, or justiciary, and probably no less so of the wealthiest and most influential of the colonists, possessed, doubtless, larger, more splendid, and more lasting edifices. The ravages of time on the relics of the West Bygd we may thus reasonably conclude to have been much more destructive, and, if, in addition to that cause, it actually was laid waste with fire and sword, as stated in the letter of the Pope to the Icelandic bishops, what probability remains, that, after the lapse of 500 years, many vestiges of it should still be left ?

Nevertheless, vestiges of ancient colonization *have* been met with in the tract of country between the 62d and 67th degrees of latitude, and, what is singular enough, the ruins so discovered have been found grouped, as it were, at precisely as many different spots, as, according to the accounts transmitted to us, there were firths in the West Bygd, namely; 1, at Krabbë-firth ; 2, Fish-firth, both in the district of Fishernæs, and mentioned by Vallöe, who, however, had not himself seen them, but had his information from the Greenlanders ; 3, 4, 5, the firth of the Amaraglik, with its two arms ; 6, 7, 8, the firth of Good-hope, with its two arms. Of these six firths, Thorhallesen observes, that they abound in ruins. Some of them he had himself seen, and two he describes as seeming to be the remains of churches*. 9. At Kin-of-Sal, in the Sugar-loaf district, mentioned by Crantz, occupying the site where I take Lysufiord to have lain ; 10, the firth of Ikertok at Holsteinborg, mentioned by Thorhallesen, who, again and again, declares that it is very uncertain if there are not still more ruins to be found between Holsteinsborg and Good-hope, there being in that tract of country a number of firths, the banks of which are covered with grass and thicket.

I have already stated in the Introduction, that Ivar Bardsen has given the distance between the two Bygds to be twelve *vikur siouar*, or (eighteen Danish) seventy-two miles, instead of a six-days' journey in a row-boat. If this be correct, we might expect to find ruins a long way South of the point where I, following the authority of Biörn Jonsen, have taken the East Bygd to have begun ; and, in fact, ruins do exist at the firth of Arsut, situated at about the distance of seventy-two miles from Immartinek, in

* One of these, near Ujararsoak, Dr. Pingel, as well as Wormskiold, takes to be the ruins of a church : and the other on an arm of Amaraglik was no less so, probably, as Thorhallesen relates, that he saw "human bones sticking out of the green-sward, which the Greenlanders stated to be the bones of the old Europeans (*Kablunaks*), and which, in that belief, they were careful not to touch."

the district of Juliana's-hope. In Ivar Bardsen's time, (who probably
lived a couple of centuries before the author of the Chorography Biörn
Jonsen has transmitted to us) it is likely that a larger extent of the country
was inhabited; and hence their discordance. Had Ivar Bardsen not
expressly mentioned this distance of twelve *vikur siouar*, use might have
been made of these ruins at the firth of Arsut to overturn the theory of
Eggers; but as it is, the observation cannot otherwise than confirm it;
for, if the *West* Bygd was the district of Juliana's-hope, the *East* Bygd
must necessarily have begun at the southernmost extremity of the East
coast; but this tract has now been twice explored (by Vallöe in 1752, and
by myself in 1829), and no vestiges of ruins found, and its natives have too
frequently visited our southernmost commercial and missionary stations
without giving information of any such, to admit a doubt of the existence
of any below the 61st degree of latitude. Indeed, Wormskiold himself
does not pretend that it is the case.

Wormskiold's reasons for taking Baal's River to be Lysu, or Lysufiord,
and Amaraglik to be Svar, or Svartfiord, are so weak that they have
scarcely any claim whatever to serious consideration, not even if it was a
settled point that Lysufiord derives its name from its clear sky, and Svartfiord from its dark, or cloudy*. That Arngrim Jonsen, who has contributed
more than any one else to cause confusion in this matter, has mentioned
Svartfiord immediately after Lysufiord, is another very good reason for
taking the former to be Amaraglik; for another order in the enumeration
of the firths is observed by Thord Thorlaksen, and still another by Bussæus,
in his Danish version of Arngrim's work. The supposition of Tunnudliorbik being Hornëfiord, I look upon as equally groundless. There are
two firths, or inlets, so called, in Iceland, both taking their name from
isolated mountains at their entrance, with summits shaped somewhat like
a short horn. But the mountains of Niviarsiæt are far up in the interior
of the country, have no resemblance whatever to horns, indeed differ in no
respect from the other lofty mountains of the interior, and are not to be
seen from the firth of Tunnudliorbik, or its vicinity, unless one ascends the
heights. On the southern side of Tessermiut (Fuel-firth, East of Nennortalik) is a mountain, which, seen from certain points, particularly from the
East, may be said to have some likeness to a horn; but I dare not venture,
on that account, to maintain that Tessermiut is Hornëfiord (though the
East Bygd likewise had a firth of that name), for this would be building
on a quicksand†.

* Thorhallesen believes the name of Lysufiord to have been derived from the
light-coloured ground at its bottom, and from a sort of fish, *whitings*, supposed by
him to be found only in Baal's River, a supposition which he afterwards discovered
to be erroneous.
† I state this, and what follows, not from the idle wish of showing the false
grounds upon which this or the other individual has built his conclusions, but
solely because such erroneous statements and opinions, if suffered to remain uncon-
tradicted, pass very easily into fixed articles of faith. Such, probably, was the
origin of the fable, which sets forth that Snefieldsjökel in Iceland, and Hvidsærk
in Greenland, could be seen at once from a point between them. Now, no one
that has given a thought to the subject, can reasonably take Hvidsærk to have been
situated farther North than lat. 65°, in which parallel there are no particularly lofty
mountains on the East coast of Greenland, none that, even in clear weather, can
be seen at a distance of 65 to 70 miles, much less 200. From Straumsnæs, near
the North Cape, the distance to Greenland, N.W., is perhaps scarcely 200 miles,

Wormskiold's conjectures touching the situation of Hvidsærk on the East coast, in lat. 65° 2′, of Herjolf's-næs in lat. 65° (he probably means 64°), and of Hvarf between the other two*, we may here pass by without farther notice, as no arguments whatever are advanced in support of them; for, that Danel saw some islands in lat. 65°, and named a mountain in lat. 64° Herjolfsnæs, can scarcely be considered such. On the other hand, I should think myself to blame, if I omitted saying a few words with respect to his location of Korsey (Cross Island), and Œllumleingri.

Of the former it is said in Ivar Bardsen—" Farther to the East, towards the ice-mountains, is a large island, called Korsey, where there is abundant hunting of white bears, though not without permission of the bishop, as the island is the property of the see. Beyond it, to the East, nothing is to be seen, at sea, or on the shore, but ice and snow." This Korsey, Wormskiold makes out to be Jan Mayen; it is, however, to be remembered that Jan Mayen lies sixty-five geographical miles from the nearest point of Greenland, and 800 miles from what he maintains to have been the site of the East Bygd. Can it possibly be imagined that the colonists of Greenland were in the habit of hunting bears at so remote a spot, it being kept in mind that, in the time of Ivar Bardsen, their only means of conveyance were row-boats? Besides, the concluding words of Ivar Bardsen's statement is quite at variance with such an hypothesis; for, in the first place, there is no land either to the East, or to the West, of Jan Mayen; and, in the next, it is well known that the northernmost tract of the East coast of Greenland,—that between the parallels of 70° and 74°,—is less covered with ice and snow than the country further South†. As to the cross observed by Wormskiold in Zorgdrager's map, this, I magine, was not intended to intimate its being Korsey (or Cross Island), but to mark the grave of the seven Dutchmen who, in 1643, attempted to winter at Jan Mayen, but were all found dead when the Dutch whalers came, the year after, to the island ‡.

But still less can the large bay, or inlet, in lat. 70°, which our countryman Volqvard Boon first discovered in the year 1769, but which now bears the name of Scoresby's Sound, be taken to be the Œllum-leingri of the ancients; for Ivar Bardsen says of it (Œllum-leingri),—" It is narrow at the entrance, but broader within; it has no current; it is full of small islets, with abundance of birds and eggs on them; it has poor land on both sides, overgrown with grass as far as it has been explored," &c.; whereas Scoresby's Sound has strong currents, no islets, birds, or eggs, and, instead of being narrow at its entrance, is four or five times wider than any known firth, or inlet, whether on the Eastern or Western coast of Greenland.

and here, from an intermediate point, both lands might be seen, but no more Snefieldsjökel than Hvidsærk. However, this may very possibly have given rise to the tale.

* Properly speaking, it was Herjolfsnæs that lay between Hvarf and Hvidsærk, not Hvarf between Hvidsærk and Herjolfsnæs.

† Scoresby speaks of some tracts of meadow in Jamieson's-land, lat. 70½°, as beautiful as any in England. We cannot but suspect, however, that, had he seen them himself, he would have found them not quite so beautiful, notwithstanding that his descriptions are in general somewhat highly coloured.

‡ They died of scurvy. Their journal was found, brought down to the 31st of April, 1644.

The southernmost tract of Greenland is very imperfectly known*. But enough we do know of it to be well aware that there are places in it which correspond in a great measure with the description given of Œllum-leingri. At Illoa, or Illoamiut, Arctander states that he saw green fields; and, in two of the entrances into this firth (the sound between Kangersoak and Cape Farewell, and that between Nunarsoak and Kangersoak), there are numerous small skerries, holms, and islets, making them narrower at their mouths than farther in†. Here are rapid currents, and no want of birds or eggs. In all respects, in fact, but that of depth, Illoa corresponds with the description given of Œllum-leingri; in that one point, indeed, they differ, Ivar Bardsen stating that Œllum-leingri runs so far into the land, or, in his words, " is so long, that none knoweth where is the end of it." The reader will, however, call to mind what I have before remarked in regard to a firth in the vicinity of the ice-blink at Frederick's-hope, to which all access is now cut off but over land. Besides, we are not to forget, that Ivar Bardsen is not to be implicitly relied on as to all his details—witness his statement about Himinraki. One might much more fairly, I conceive, deny the location of the West Bygd on the West coast, because no such Himinraki is to be found there, than refuse to place the East Bygd in the district of Juliana's-hope, because we are somewhat at a loss what to do with Œllum-leingri. A Greenland firth may, in the lapse of 400 years, very materially change its aspect; but what we are to think of Himinraki and the perils that environ it, we are quite unable to conjecture.

Having thus shown what may be reasonably urged against the weightiest of the arguments adduced to prove the location of the East Bygd on the East coast, it may be permitted me to advert to a passage in an ancient work, which seems clearly to establish that Hvidsærk was situated at the southernmost extremity of Greenland. I allude to a passage in the Gripla, a document, as far as I am aware, of unquestioned authenticity, and which is free from the interpolations so frequent in many of the other ancient MSS. transmitted to us. It runs thus in the original, and as rendered by Eggers ‡:—

" Baierland er vid Saxland, hiá Saxlandi er Holsetuland, Tha Denmark. I gegnum fellur Siór austurvegn. Svithiod liggur fyrio austan Danmörk, Noregr fyrir nordan, Finnmörk nordur	" Baiernland er ved Sachsenland, næst Sachsenland er Holstenland, saa Danmark. Igiennem falder Söen östre Veien. Sverige ligger Œsten for Denmark, Norge Norden for, Finmark

---

* When I came to Friederichsthal, in the Spring of 1831, with the intent of exploring this part of the country, my rowers refused to go further, fearing that I meant to revisit the East coast. Mr. Kleinschmidt, however, got me others, who took me as far as Cape Christian. Somewhat to the East of this headland, we were shut up by the ice for fourteen days, and this was of itself a greater length of time than I then could well devote to that purpose. Cape Farewell itself I did not reach, but determined its situation trigonometrically.

† Of the tract of sea between Cape Farewell and the bottom of Illoa, only the inner portion, properly speaking, can be called a firth. But the whole of it may, nevertheless, have been so denominated, as the epithet is somewhat loosely applied in Greenland, it being given, for example, to several sounds, or channels between islands, as to Ikersoak (called Bredefiord—Broad-firth), to Nardlunek (Woodfirth), and perhaps still others.

‡ The following is a literal translation of Eggers' Danish version: "Bavaria is by Saxony, next to Saxony is Holstein, then Denmark. Between flows the sea

af Noregi. Thá víkur til Landnordurs of Austurs, ádur enn kemur til Biarmalands, That er skattgillt under Gardariki. Frá Biarmalandi liggia óbygdir nordur allt til Thess, er Grænland kallast. Enn Botnar gánga Thar fyrir, og víkur Landinu til útsudurs, eru Jöklar og Firder, Eyar liggia Thar uti fyrer Jüklunum. *Fyrir einn Jökulin gieta Thar ey rannsakad, fyrir annan ei hálfs Mánadar ferd, fyrir Thridia vikuferd, er sa næstur Bygdinne, er heiter Hvítserkur. Thá víkur Landinu til Nordurs, enn sá ey vill missa Bygdina, stefni hann i Utsudr.* Gardar heita Biskupsstóll i Bottnenum a Eyriksfirdi. Thar er Kyrkia vígd hinum helga Nicolas*. XII Kirkiur eru á Grænlandi í hinne eystri Bygd, IIII í vestri Bygd."

Norden for Norge. Saa viger (Landet) til N. O. og Ost, da kommer man til Biarmaland, hvilket er skatpligtigt til Gardarige. Norden for Biarmaland ligge ubygte Stræninger indtil det (Land), der Grönland kaldes. Og Bugter gaae der ind ad, og viger Landet til S.V., (der) ere Jökler og Fiorde, Oer ligge der úden for Jöklerne. *Fra den ene Jökel er Veien (Nord paa) urandsagelig, fra den anden (til den förste) er ½ Maaneds Fart, fra den tredie (til den anden) en Uges Fart, denne (tredie) er nærmest Bygden, og hedder Hvidserk.* Saa viger Landet til Norden, og hvo ikke vil forfeile Bygden den styren i S.V. Gardar hedder Bispestolen i Bunden af Eriksfiorden. Der er en Kirke viet til den hellige Nicolaus*. 12 Kirker ere paa Grönland i Œsterbygden, 4 i Vesterbygden."

Eggers, as appears above, has rendered the word "fyrer" by "fra" (from); but it will likewise have been observed, that, in order to make the sentence in which that word occurs intelligible, he has been obliged to interpolate several words not found in the original. To ascertain how far his interpretation is correct, we must first endeavour to determine what it is we are to understand by the *Jökels* here spoken of.

Down to the close of the last century the general opinion was, that Spitzbergen was an integral part of Greenland. Now, as we know that the whalers of our own time have not been able to penetrate to any considerable distance beyond this island, we may safely infer that the ancients, with their very inferior means, could not do so either; and I am, therefore, disposed to think, that, by one of the Jökels above-mentioned, we are to understand some iceberg or iceblink or other, at Spitzbergen†. If we assume the first-mentioned Jökel to have been so situated, we are then, according to Eggers' version, to look for Hvidsærk at the distance of twenty-one days' journey from thence. Now, if we estimate the day's

towards the East. Sweden lies to the East of Denmark, Norway to the North, Finmark to the North of Norway. Then runs (the land) to the N.E. and E.; then one comes to Biarmaland, which is tributary to Gardarige [Russia]. To the North of Biarmaland lie uninhabited tracts as far as that (land) which is called Greenland. And inlets go therein, and the land runs to the S.W., (there) are Jökels and Firths, islands lie there outside of the Jökels. From the one Jökel the way (northwards) is inexplorable, from the second (to the first) is ½ month's run, from the third (to the second) a week's run, this (third) is nearest the Bygd, and is named Hvidserk. Then the land runs to the North, and he that would not miss the Bygd, must steer to the S.W. Gardar is the name of the Episcopal residence at the bottom of Erik's-firth. There is a church consecrated to St. Nicholas. There are twelve churches in Greenland in the East Bygd, four in the West Bygd."

* We may hence infer that the cathedral is one and the same with that magnificent church dedicated to St. Nicholas, which Ivar Bardsen mentions as situated at Foss, one of the royal farms, or demesnes. For Gardar is not named by Ivar Bardsen, nor Foss, in the Flateyan MS.; and it would appear from Biörn Jonsen's Chorography, that the Episcopal residence was on an arm of Rafnsfiord, where Ivar Bardsen places Foss.

† The word Jökel (*Icel.* Jökul) signifies a mountain perpetually covered with ice and snow; it occurs only in works treating of Iceland, &c.—*Trans.*

journey at eighty-four miles (which is taking it at the lowest computation), and place the Jökel at the most northernly extremity of the said island, we shall make out Hvidsærk to have been situated South of Cape Farewell, many miles out to sea; for the distance from the most northerly extremity of Spitzbergen to Cape Farewell is about 1664 miles, whereas twenty-one days' journey, at eighty-four miles, amounts to 1764. Again, if the second of the said Jökels be supposed to have been situated at Spitzbergen, we are then to look for Hvidsærk at the distance of seven days' journey from it, which would bring Hvidsærk as high up as lat. 69°, even allowing the day's journey in this instance to be 108 miles, instead of eighty-four, and the Jökel to have been at the most southerly, instead of at the most northerly, extremity of Spitzbergen.

It is therefore evident, that, according as we place the first or the second of the Jökels above-mentioned at Spitzbergen, Hvidsærk, according to Eggers' version, comes to be situated far out in the ocean, to the South of Cape Farewell, or on the East coast of Greenland, in lat. 69°, neither of which results is compatible with the theory which assigns the East Bygd to the East coast. But where shall we then place these Jökels? Not at Nova Zembla; for this island, if it was not considered as an integral part of Biarmaland, must, from its situation, have been the beginning of those uninhabited tracts said to lie North of Biarmaland, reaching all the way to Greenland, where the Jökels lay. Nor can they be assigned to any spot on the East coast of Greenland itself; for the most northerly land on that coast of which we have any knowledge, Gale Hamke's Land, in lat. 75°, is but about 1080 miles from Cape Farewell; so that, if the Jökels did lie on this coast, the ancients must have been acquainted with it to the distance of 680 miles farther North than we are; that it is to say, they must have been acquainted with it to within a very brief distance of the pole itself, nay, all the way to the pole, and even beyond it; if we suppose Hvidsærk to have been situated in the 64th or 65th degree of latitude *.

As it thus is clear, that no point can be found along the whole East coast of Greenland, from which it is a twenty-one days' journey to the northernmost extremity of the land, much less a twenty-one days' journey to another point on the same coast, lying in the parallel of Iceland; nay, as we have seen that a twenty-one days' journey commencing at the very northernmost point of Spitzbergen, would bring us far beyond Cape Farewell,—the only inference to be drawn is, that the Gripla has been misunderstood by Eggers, and his translation, above cited, therefore erroneous.

To those who read the Gripla with attention, it must, I should suppose, be obvious, that its whole bent and purport is to determine the situation of Greenland, and particularly of the Bygd, in respect to other countries, Now, for the same reason that our men of science are, as far as I am

---

* If we go the reverse way from Hvidsærk, placing it in lat. 65°, the second Jökel, which is 680 miles (seven days' journey) from it, will come to lie at Traill's Island. From this point, the coast, as far as we have any knowledge of it, trends due North. Supposing that it continues to run on in that direction, then the first Jökel, being fourteen days' journey from the second, or 1344 miles North of Traill's Island, will be carried nobody knows where, for Traill's Island itself, is but 1068 miles distant from the Pole.

aware, unanimous in thinking, that the expression in the Gripla, "and he that would not miss the Bygd must steer to the S. W.," is to be understood in the sense (and in no other) in which Eggers has understood it, namely, that he who would not miss the Bygd, must steer in the direction of S.W. *from Iceland*, where the author of the Gripla lived, and neither from Bavaria, Saxony, Russia, nor the aforesaid Jökels in Greenland themselves, which we have been already told trend to the S.W.; I conceive that the two distances above laid down, of fourteen and seven days' journey, are likewise to be understood as calculated from Iceland, and not from Jökel to Jökel, as Eggers and others, both before and since his time, imagined. I would, accordingly, render the passage cited thus:

" From Biarmaland lie uninhabited tracts all the way to the country which is called Greenland. And inlets run therein (into the land), and the land stretches towards the S.W., and there are Jökels and Firths, and islands lying outside the firth. To (towards, beyond) the one Jökel, the way has not been explored, to (towards, beyond) the second is half a month's run, to (towards, beyond) the third is a week's run; this one (the third) is nearest to Bygd, and is called Hvidsærk," etc.

Thus interpreted, the meaning of the passage evidently is, that the Bygd lay in the direction of S.W. from Iceland; and that from this island to Hvidsærk was a seven-days' journey; consequently, Hvidsærk must have been somewhere in the vicinity of Cape Farewell, which is exactly 580 miles distant S.W. of Snefieldsjökel.

This is further confirmed by what follows immediately after, " Tha víkur Landinu til Nordurs," (" then the land stretches away to the North"), for from no point along the whole tract of the East coast, where the Bygd has been supposed to lie,—in fact, from no point but Cape Farewell,—can the land be said to stretch away towards the North.

To conclude, I shall now briefly enumerate the various facts, as far as I am acquainted with them, that seem to substantiate Eggers' opinion in regard to the position of the East Bygd in the district of Juliana's-hope.

1. That, during my sojourn, of a year and a half, on the East Coast, I discovered no vestiges whatever of ancient Icelandic colonization; either ruins, of which several hundred are to be found on the West coast, both at the mouths and in the interior of the various firths, and on the islands lining the coast; or bell-metal, of which fragments are still frequently picked up in the district of Juliana's-hope; or stones with inscriptions, of which we have obtained several, of late, from the West coast; or iron, which Egede affirms was, even in his time, sought for by the native Greenlanders, in and about the ruins on the West coast; or any other trace whatever.

2. That the natives of the East coast, though, like those of the West, they not unfrequently take up their quarters in the interior of the firths, have never seen, or heard of, ruins in their country*.

---

* That the East Greenlanders differ in some respects from the natives of the West, in regard to personal appearance, is no proof of their descent from Icelandic ancestry; for, though the children of Greenlanders by Europeans, of whom, during the last hundred years, there has been no scarcity, usually differ somewhat from those of unmixed blood in cast of features and in form, particularly in the colour of their eyes and hair, yet *their* children, or grandchildren, by intermarriage with natives, lose again every indication of their European parentage, insomuch, that I

3. That on the East coast, as high up as lat. 65° 20', no hot springs are to be found, whereas three such exist in the island of Oanartok, in the district of Juliana's-hope. Ivar Bardsen, indeed, makes mention of several holms, or small islets with hot springs in Rafn's-fiord, but this may very easily be an error of the transcriber. It is no proof of the fallacy of my position, that pot-stone is not to be found in the islands of the district of Juliana's-hope. An island that produces none whatever now, may very well have produced it in abundance four centuries ago, particularly if what Ivar Bardsen tells us be true, that the old colonists used to make vessels of it of the capacity of ten or twelve barrels*; besides, probably, exporting a good deal. The inhabitants of the district of Juliana's-hope, now amounting to 2,000 souls, still consume a considerable quantity of it yearly, in the manufacture of their lamps and kettles.

4. That hares and rein-deer, said to have been staple articles of food among the colonists of the East Bygd, are not to be found on the East coast, as high up as I have explored it; whereas both abound in the district of Juliana's-hope.

5. That there are but few islands and sounds along the East coast, whereas the old chorographers speak of there being many islands in the East Bygd.

6. That it is said in the narrative of Erik Raude's voyage; "that, having arrived off Mid-jökel, or Blaasærk †, in Greenland, *he sailed to the south-ward along the land*, looking out for an inhabitable spot, and afterwards *to the West about Hvarf*,"—an expression, which, in the present state of our knowledge of the East coast, is altogether unintelligible, if by the East Bygd we do not understand the district of Juliana's-hope.

7. That it is said in Biörn Jonsen's Chorography, " Grænland horfer i Utsudr, synst er Herjolfsnes," (Greenland faces the S.W., its most south-erly point is Herjolfsnæs), words that have no meaning, unless the East Bygd lay in the district of Juliana's-hope.

8. That it is said in the Gripla, " Fyrir einn Jökulin gieta ther ey ransakad, fyrir annan er hálvs Mánadar ferd, fyrir thridja vikuferd, er sá næstur Bygdinne er heiter Hvítserkur," (" to the one Jökel the way has not been explored; to the second is half a month's journey; to the third a week's journey; this third is next the Bygd, and is called Hvidsærk")—a passage which cannot be interpreted so as to make sense of it, unless the distances therein laid down be calculated from Iceland, in which case the Bygd comes to be the district of Juliana's-hope.

9. That the Gripla proceeds to tell us; " Thá víkur Landinu til Nordurs, enn sá ey vill missa Bygdina, stefni hann i Utsudr" (" the land then stretches away to the North, and he that would not miss the Bygd, must

have known many Greenlanders descended thus from Europeans, who were not to be distinguished from genuine Esquimaux. From the slight fortuitous resemblance of these Eastlanders to Europeans, therefore, no inference can be drawn. Or, if we needs must hazard a conjecture with regard to them, I would suggest, as a more likely pedigree, that they may be descended from the crews of the Dutch whalers, wrecked off the East coast in 1777, many of whom effected their escape to the shore.

* An unlikely story, by the way.
† I do not take this Mid-jökel (or Blaasærk) to be either of those of which the Gripla makes mention.

steer to the S.W.")—which, taken in connexion with what precedes, shows
that Hvidsærk is Cape Farewell, and the Bygd, therefore, the district of
Juliana's-hope; for there is no point along the East coast, as high up as
lat. 65°, where the land stretches towards the North.

10. That we read in the Kongs-Skugg-Siá (*Speculum Regale*); " Enn
their Isar liggia meir i Landnordur edur til Nordurs fyrir Landinu,
helldur enn til Sudurs og Utsudurs *eda til Vesturs;* ok fyrir Thví skal
um Land sigla hver. er vill Landinu ná, til thess hann er umkominn alla
thessa Isavon, ogs igla thaden til Landsins," ("but this ice lies more in the
direction of North and North-East from the land, than of South, South-
West, *or West;* for which reason, he that would reach the land, must sail
round it, till he pass all the ice, and then sail in for the land.") A passage
showing, in the first place, that the Bygd lay on the West coast, for otherwise
there would have been no mention of ice at and about Gunbiörn's Skerries*, round which the navigator was to sail (as is said in one of Ivar
Bardsen's sailing directions) but the whole land†.

11. That it is stated in Ivar Bardsen's sailing directions,—"and the day
before the said Hvarf is seen, another mountain covered with snow will be
seen, which is called Hvidsærk,"—words, of which it is not easy to understand the meaning, unless we take Hvidsærk to be Cape Farewell, and
Hvarf to be Cape Egede, or some other mountain West of Cape Farewell.

12. That the conformity between Ivar Bardsen's account of the Bygd,
and Arctander's description of the firths and ruins in the district of Juliana's-hope cannot be explained on any other supposition, than that those
places are identical.

13. That the distance between the East and West Bygds, as given both
by Ivar Bardsen and Biörn Jonsen, corresponds accurately with what we
know of the West coast, assuming Juliana's-hope to be the East Bygd.

14. That on the West coast there are, at least, thirty-three firths, or
arms of firths, where ruins are to be found, of which twenty are in the
district of Juliana's-hope‡; a circumstance harmonizing with the accounts
of Biörn Jonsen and Arngrim Jonsen, respectively—the former assign-
ing to the East Bygd twenty-four firths or arms of firths (on some of which,
meanwhile, there probably were no settlements), and the latter nine or ten
to the West Bygd.

15. That ruins, bearing every indication of being those of churches,

---

* Ivar Bardsen, probably, knew as little about Gunbiörn's Skerries as we do
now. At one moment we find the old geographers placing them at the distance of
but a few miles from the North Cape; at another, South of Reykianæs; at another,
mid-way between Iceland and Greenland.

† In sailing now-a-days from Iceland to Juliana's-hope, we should by no means
shape a straight course for Cape Farewell; but, as it is laid down in the *Speculum
Regale,* keep away to the distance of from fifty to eighty miles South of that promontory, and then steer West to about the same distance (the state of the ice permitting) before hauling in for the shore.

‡ Namely, in the district of Juliana's-hope, Illoa, the firths of Friederichsthal,
Tessermiut, Sermelik, Ounartsk, Agluitsok with its three arms, Kangerdlueitsiak,
Igaliko with its two arms, Kakortok and Tartow (a branch of it), Kangerdluarsuk,
Tunnudliorbik with its two arms, Sermelik, and Immartinek; North of the district
of Juliana's-hope, Arsut with its two arms, a firth in the vicinity of Frederick's-
hope, whose name I have forgotten, Krabbë-firth, Fish-firth, Amaraglik, with its
two arms, and Ikertok at Holsteinsborg.

have been discovered at six or seven different places on the West coast*, whereas we know that the West Bygd had but four churches.

When we weigh deliberately all these arguments, and, at the same time keep in mind that the sailing directions above spoken of are, at best, apocryphal, that they have been written down, for the most part, from oral tradition, that they were not collected and published till a century after all intercourse with Greenland had ceased, that they were put together by Walckendorff, who entertained a preconceived opinion relative to the situation of the two Bygds (an opinion which it was very natural for him to entertain, as he knew nothing of the true site of Çape Farewell, and did not dream, perhaps, of Greenland having any West coast at all†), and that the different copies extant of these Instructions are at variance, while, on the contrary, the Gripla and Biörn Jonsen's Chorography bear every indication of authenticity,—it seems to me, that we can arrive at no other conclusion than this, that the East Bygd never did lie on the East coast of Greenland.

Eggers' location of the different firths, sounds, and islands, I believe to be upon the whole correct, and in particular, the discovery of the gravestone at Ikigeit, by the missionary, Mr. de Fries, in 1830, gives much probability to his conjecture, that Ikigeit is Herjolfsnæs, for the Flatey MS. expressly states, that the first church in the East Bygd stood at Herjolf's Firth, which, in all likelihood, derived its name from the same person with Herjolf's-næs. Directly opposite Ikigeit, at the distance of half a mile South of Friederichsthal, is a small cove with sandy bottom, and sandy beach. It might very well serve as a harbour for small craft, and may possibly be the "Sandhavn" of the ancients. That Mathias's-land (Akia) is their "Langey," its conformation, and the ruins there discovered seem to testify. Partlet Islands, between Dutchman's Isle (Irsarut), and Juliana's-hope, may, in that case, be the four Lamb Islands, mentioned by Ivar Bardsen. "Lamb-eyar-sund" will then be the channel between Partlet Islands and Akia, and "Fossa-sund," either Nardlunek, one of the entrances for ships to Juliana's-hope, (improperly called by the colonists, "Skovfiord," i. e. Wood-firth), or the sound from Partlet to Kangerdluarsuk and Tunnudliorbik, between the mainland on the one hand, and the islands of Kilatut, Kingiktok, and Akuliarisek on the other. "Solarfiall" is, possibly, the Illimansak of the Greenlanders (the mountain Narksak), a lofty, isolated mountain, constantly shone on by the sun, (when the sun is visible), and "Hardsteinaberg," a mountain in the vicinity of Narksak, at Tunnudliorbik, where Mr. Motzfeldt, some years ago, found some rock crystal, a mineral known to be extremely hard. "Korsey," I take to be Alluk (or another of the islands near it), where Polar bears resort, and where Mr. Vahl, in the Spring of 1829, actually killed one of those formidable monsters. "Hafsbotnar," finally, I take to be the imaginary bay,

* Namely, Ikigeit on the firth of Friederichsthal, Igaliko, Kakortok, Tunnudliorbik (here perhaps two), Amaraglik, and Ujararsoak, on the firth of Good-hope.

† The existence of Zeno's chart does not invalidate this statement, for it was constructed by him, probably, in the middle of the sixteenth century. Long after Walckendorff's time, we find the charts and maps of this part of the world so full of errors, that one can only know by the names, what seas and countries they were meant to represent. To be convinced of this, a glance at Matthias Schacht's MS. *Collectanea Grönlandia*, in the Arne-Magnean Collection, will suffice

or gulf, between East Greenland and Spitzbergen ; and " Svalbard," some place or other in the northern tracts of the East coast of Greenland ; perhaps at Scoresby's Sound, perhaps somewhat farther North. In regard to the first of the Jökels mentioned in the Gripla, I dare not hazard a conjecture; but the second I take to be Spitzbergen, for the distance between the northernmost extremity of this island and Snefieldsjökel is 800 miles, or fourteen days' journey, exactly as is stated in the Gripla.

As the old Chorographies that have come down to us are exceedingly deficient*, I consider it, for the rest, an unprofitable labour try to fix the site of every firth, or church. To arrive at any satisfactory results on that head, our surest guides are the remarkable remains at Tunnudliorbik, Igaliko, and Agluitsok, for at one or other of these spots, Gardar, or Foss, probably one and the same place,) is, in all likelihood, to be sought. Here dwelt the bishops, the chief public functionaries, and perhaps many other personages whose names have come down to us in history ; and here divers of them, doubtless, have been consigned to earth. A careful and minute examination of these ruins, therefore, is greatly to be desired ; for until *they* speak to us in a voice not to be misunderstood, it is in vain to hope that men will relinquish opinions long cherished, and which form, as it were, a part and parcel of their very being. Nor will this consummation, it is hoped, be long deferred. The Royal Society of Northern Antiquaries having now turned its attention to the subject, the most interesting and important results may be, ere long, expected†; results which, I am satisfied, will at length remove all doubt, and substantiate, incontestably, the fact asserted first by Eggers, that the East Bygd is the district of Juliana's-hope, and that the East coast of Greenland has never been inhabited by a colony of Europeans.

* The most voluminous of them is Ivar Bardsen's ; but it is scarcely to be called the most authentic; for Bardsen assigns but eight churches to the East Bygd, whereas the Gripla mentions twelve, the names of all of which are given in the Flatey MS. That Ivar Bardsen, as lay-superintendent of the diocese, must have been well acquainted with the affairs of the church in Greenland, is clear : but, from his account of " Himinraki," and " Œllum-leingri," and the phrase, " they say," or " it is said," so frequently occurring in his work, it is very evident that, as to other matters, he was less well informed. He observes, for instance, immediately after making mention of Erik's Firth,—" now, it is said, the course lies to the island further West." The meaning of this expression is, I should suppose, that he who, from Erik's Firth, purposed going further West, e. g., to the West Bygd, must shape a course " to the islands," that is to say, take the shortest route among the islands, instead of following the course of the mainland, which, North and West of Erik's Firth, appears to have been thinly peopled. This observation, meanwhile, seems to confirm Eggers' conjecture respecting the identity of Erik's Firth and Tunnudliorbik ; for, in going from thence to Arsut, or Frederick's-hope, the course does lie among the islands all the way West to Nunarsoit.

† This Society is on the point of publishing a work, to be entitled " The Historical Monuments of Greenland," comprising all the old accounts extant concerning Greenland, the history of the Icelandic colonies there planted, the voyages of discovery from thence to America, in the tenth and eleventh centuries, etc. Many of the MSS. intended to be included in it, have never yet been published, others have been, some of these even oftener than once (there have been, for example, three editions already printed of the Landnama-book), but most of them incorrectly. Much valuable information, that has hitherto been a dead letter to the literary world, will, it is confidently expected, by this work be brought to light.

No. II.

BOTANY AND ZOOLOGY.

A.—Plants.

During my stay on the East coast, I collected a number of plants, some of which I preserved and brought home with me. Our distinguished countryman, Professor Hornemann, has since been kind enough to classify them, as follows :—

Found in Queen Maria's Valley :

Hippuris vulgaris, Linn., varietas tetraphylla.
Veronica saxatilis, L., high up among the cliffs.
Elymus arenarius, L.
Alchemilla alpina, L.
Polygonum viviparum, L.
Epilobium origanifolium, L., high up among the cliffs.
———— *latifolium*, L.
———— *angustifolium*, L., var. denticulata *.
Erica cærulea, Willdenow.
Vaccinium uliginosum, L †.
Saxifraga stellaris, L.
Cerastium alpinum, L.
Potentilla nivea, L., varietas. Perhaps a new species; the under-surface of its leaves not white ‡.
———— *retusa*, Retz, high up among the cliffs.
Rubus saxatilis, L., ditto. ditto.
Euphrasia officinalis, L., of eight inches' length §.
Bartschia alpina, L., high up among the cliffs.
Arabis alpina, L.
Erigeron alpinus, L.
———— ———— var. uniflora, Spreng.
Gnaphalium alpinum, L., high up among the cliffs.
———— *sylvaticum*, L., var. furcata, Wahlenb., high up among the cliffs.
Betula nana, L., high up among the cliffs.
Carex, sp. without flower.
Salix glauca, L.
———— *herbacea*, L.
Equisetum arvense, L.
Aspidium fragile, Swarts.
Lycopodium alpinum, L.

* Less than on the West coast.　† The leaves larger than on the West coast.
‡ Has not yet been found on the West coast.
§ On the West coast, of from one to three inches length.

N

At the island of Kemisak :

Veronica saxatilis, L.
Alchemilla alpina, L.
Campanula rotundifolia, L., var. uniflora.
Epilobium latifolium, L.
Polygonum viviparum, L.
Saxifraga cæspitosa, var. grœnlandica, Retz.
—— *stellaris*, L., var. pygmæa*.
Stellaria humifusa, Rottbœll.
Cerastium alpinum, L.
Lychnis alpina, L.
Ranunculus hyperboreus, L†.
Thymus serpyllum, L., var. prostrata.
Bartschia alpina, L.
Draba Muricella, Wahlenb.
Leontodon taraxacum, L., variet.
Erigeron alpinus, L.
—— —— var. uniflora.
Hieracium alpinum, L.

B.—MAMMALIA, BIRDS, AND FISH.

I HAVE given the Greenland names of these as communicated by natives, and added the scientific synonymes from O. Fabricius's *Fauna Grœnlandica.* For the more modern (those in brackets) I am indebted to Professor Reinhardt.

MAMMALIA :

Ursus maritimus, white bear; Nennok.
Canis familiaris, dog; Kemmek.
Canis lagopus, arctic, or white fox; Terienniak.
Phoca vitulina, common seal; Kassigiak.
—— *hispida*, rough seal; Neitsek.
—— *Grœnlandica*, black-sided, or harp-seal, saddle-back; Atak.
—— *barbata*, bearded seal; Uksuk.
—— *cristata*, hooded seal; Neitsersoak.
Trichechus rosmarus, walrus; Auvek.
Delphinus albicans, white whale, or beluga; Kelelluak.

BIRDS :

Falco islandicus, Iceland falcon; Kirksoviarsuk.
Vultur (Aquila) albicilla, cinereous eagle; Nektoralik.
Strix nyctea, snowy owl; Opik.
Emberiza nivalis, snow bunting; Koparnauarsuk.
Corvus corax, raven; Tullugak.
Tetrao lagopus, ptarmigan; Akeiksek.

---

* Not yet found on the West coast. The flower and fruit are, as in many Greenland plants, large in proportion to the stalk and leaves.
† Larger than on the West coast.

Colymbus (Mergus) glacialis, great northern diver ; Tudlik.
————— *septentrionalis*, red-throated diver ; Karksauk.
Uria (Colymbus) grylle, doveky, or black guillemot; Serbak.
Alca pica (Uria Brünichii), Brunnich's guillemot (Loom) ; Akpa.
————— *(Uria) alle*, little auk, or roach ; Akpalliarsuk.
Procellaria glacialis, fulmar petrel, or mallemuk ; Kakordluk.
Larus glaucus, glaucous gull, or burgomaster; Naia.
————— *tridactylus*, Kittiwake gull ; Tattaruk.
Cataracta parasitica (Lestris parasiticus), arctic jager ; Isingak.
Sterna hirundo (arctica), common tern, or sea-swallow ; Imerkoteilak
Pelicanus carbo (Carbo cormoranus), cormorant ; Okaitsok.
Anas (Anser) bernicla, brent goose ; Nerdlek.
— *hiemalis (glacialis) Clangula glacialis*, Northern garrot, or long-
tailed duck ; Aglek.
— *histrionica*, harlequin-duck ; Tornaviarsuk.
— *mollissima*, eider-duck ; Mittek, Avok.
— *spectabilis*, king-duck ; Kingalik.

Besides which, I found the following—perhaps new contributions to the
Greenland Fauna :

Cygnus musicus (Bechstein), swan. Two of these, probably a male
and female, were seen by me in the spring of 1830,
near Cape Farewell, and one of them shot. The
skin I brought to Denmark, where it is still preserved in the Royal Museum. The natives could
not tell me the name of them in their language,
whence I conclude that they are rare in Greenland.
———— ——— Aualortalik ; a specimen likewise in the Museum.
———— ——— Akterkok ; a rare aquatic bird, resembling an eider-
duck. One of them was caught near the iceblink
of Colberger Heide.
———— ——— Avok. An Albino eider-duck. But one seen at the
Kitsiksut Islands, off Nunarsoit. The skin brought
home, and in the Museum.

FISH :

Cottus Gobio (tricuspis, Mus. Reg.), river bull-head ; Kaniok.
Perca Norvegica (Sebastes Norvegicus, Cuv.), Norwegian perch ; Sul-
lupaugak.
Salmo (carpio a. alpinus), red char ; Ekalluk.
————— *arcticus (Mallotus arcticus*, Cuv.), capelin of the Newfound-
land fishery ; Angmaksak.
Gadus callarias, torsk ; Saraudlit.
————— *barbatus*, pout ; Ogak.
Pleuronectes cynoglossus (Hippoglossus pinguis), halibut ; Kalleraglik.
Squalus carcharias (Scymnus borealis, Scoresby), Greenland Shark ;
Ekallurksoak.

The above I have myself seen during my sojourn on the East coast.
Those that follow I mention on the authority of the natives, and by their
Greenland names :

MAMMALIA :

—— —— Ardluk.
—— —— Ardlurksoak.

BIRDS :

— — Anarak.
— — Akparnak.
— — Kakordlungnak.
— — Killangak.
— — Kuksuk.
— — Kerrak.
— ᴗ Najardluk.
— — Nyaliksak.
— — Paik.
— — Siutitôk.
— — Tukavajok.

FISH :

— — Abapokitsok.
— — Akpaliakitsok.
— — Annardlek.
— — Ekallugak.
— — Ekallukâk.
— — Kapiselirsoak.
— — Kebleriksok.
— — Igarsok.
— — Kaniordluk.
— — Kanikitsok.
— — Ingmingoak.
— — Kigutelik.

No. III.

TEMPERATURE OF THE SEA,

AS OBSERVED ON MY VOYAGE TO GREENLAND IN THE YEAR 1828.

Date.	Lat. at Noon.	Greenwich Longitude at Noon.	Six A.M.	Noon.	Six P.M.	SITUATION AND REMARKS.
April 9	56·16	12·20 E.	36·0	38·0	38·0	In the Cattegat.
10	57·39	11·12	35·7	38·0	40·8	Cattegat—Skagerak.
11	57·56	7·10	37·5	38·5	44·0	Skagerak—NorthSea
12	59·33	1·39	44·0	45·0	44·5	North Sea.
13	59·18	2· 7 W.	45·8	45·6	46·2	North Sea—Atlantic.
14	59·49	6· 2	49·5	49·6	49·6	
15	60· 3	8·31	49·5	49·0	48·6	
16	59·51	12·27	49·0	49·0	49·0	
17	59·27	15·28	48·5	48·1	48·6	On Alof Cramer's Banks.
18	58·40	18·50	49·2	48·8	49·2	
19	58·33	20·32	49·0	49·5	50·3	
20	58·54	24·21	50·5	49·3	49·2	
21	59·26	24·44	48·6	49·2	49·8	
22	58·59	25· 1	49·2	49·0	49·5	
23	59·23	26·14	48·4	48·5	48·0	
24	59·17	27·38	48·6	49·2	48·2	
25	58· 2	31·21	48·0	48·0	48·0	
26	58· 0	30·34	48·6	48·0	48·0	
28	59· 3	29· 0	48·0	47·8	47·8	
29	58·39	28·35	48·0	47·5	48·8	
30	58·34	28·25	48·5	49·8	48·8	
May.. 1	59· 9	29·49	48·2	47·8	47·2	
2	59· 1	32·57	47·1	47·2	45·6	
3	58· 7	35·26	46·2	45·0	45·4	
4	57.52	36·17	45·4	45·4	45·2	
5	57·35	36·36	46·0	46·1	46·4	
6	57· 7	40·40	43·7	44·1	42·2	
7	58.52	41·25	42·8	43·1	42·4	
8	58· 8	40·48	43·2	43·2	43·2	
9	57·43	43· 6	43·0	42·4	40·0	
10	58·55	44·36	41·8	39·8	39·6	Some ice in sight.
11	57·55	44·20	40·9	38·8	38·8	
12	57· 1	43·44	40·8	42·4	42·8	
13	57·38	43·38	42·8	41·6	39·6	
17	55·50	46· 5	42·8	41·3	41·4	
18	56·22	48·17	40·0	40·6	40·3	
19	56·16	50·51	38·6	40·0	40·2	
20	56·33	52· 9	39·5	40·4	40·0	
21	57·39	51·31	39·9	38·6	38·3	
22	59· 0	50·39	39·7	38·6	38·8	
23	59·39	48· 4	39·6	42·0	39·6	{ At noon,—a considerable quantity of ice two miles distant.
24	59·30	48·26	38·4	38·2	38·0	
25	59·37	48·25	38·2	39·6	39·6	} Among ice.
26	60· 3	49·39	37·6	38·5	34·5	

No. IV. MAGNETIC OBSERVATIONS.

These Observations were made with a good Azimuth Compass, of Lous's construction.

A. VARIATION OF THE COMPASS.

Year and Date	True Time (h ′ ″)	Lat. N.	Long. W. Green.	Double altitude of lower limb of the Sun	Bearing	Sun's Azimuth	Variation N.W.	Medium	No. of Obs.	Situation, and Remarks
1829, July 28	...	65 17	38 30	44 0 15	N. 38 3 w.	N. 92 49 w.	...	54 46	10	On the ice, 200 fathoms from land.
Aug. 4	...	64 58	39 24	47 53 50	N. 45 14 w.	N. 101 18 w.	...	56 4	5	
—	...	64 58	39 42	39 42 0	S. 28 50 E.	S. 94 42 E.	...	56 28	5	150 fathoms from land.
1830, July 22	...	64 3	40 32	20 bearings of a point whose azimuth was determined.				54 45	20	
May 15	...	63 42	40 17	50 ...	...	...	...	55 0	50	150 fathoms from land.
— 21	...	63 37	40 23	20 ...	...	...	54 37	54 39	20	
1829, July 11	...			73 13 40	S. 8 29 E.	N. 116 50 E.	54 41	54 39	10	
1830, June 23	...	63 32	40 26	20 bearings of a point whose azimuth was determined.				54 22	20	150 fathoms from land.
1829, July 8	...	63 12	40 58	49 5 40	N. 34 58 w.	N. 88 53 w.	53 23	53 55	6	
— 3	...	62 52	41 34	89 4 24	S. 10 21 w.	N. 136 56 E.	53 18	53 20	8	
— 3	...			20 bearings of a point whose azimuth was deter.				53 20	20	
1828, May 28	...	62 0	50 0	43 0 0	N. 28 0 w.	N. 84 34 w.	56 38	56 25	3	
— 28	...			42 29 15	N. 27 45 w.	N. 84 8 w.	56 23	56 25	3	
— 28	...			41 44 0	N. 27 8 w.	N. 83 28 w.	56 20	56 25	3	
June 3	...			7 corresp. bearings to the same altitude of the Sun.			56 18	56 25	7	
1829, — 24	...	61 52	42 16	56 3 0	N. 40 26 w.	N. 92 46 w.	...	52 20	10	
— 22	...	61 46	42 8	52 53 50	N. 37 20 w.	N. 89 40 E.	...	52 20	10	
— 18	...	61 33	42 22	46 17 0	N. 31 0 w.	N. 83 35 w.	...	52 35	10	
1828, Aug. 26	...	61 10	48 43	29 55 0	N. 43 10 w.	N. 96 24 w.	53 14	53 14	40	150 fathoms from land.
1829, June 12	...	60 59	42 40	40 bearings of a point whose azimuth was determined				51 48	40	
1831, Feb. 28	...		46 19	bearings of a point whose azimuth was determined			52 29	52 29	60	
July 5	5 9 38	60 50	48 22	38 22 20	N. 34 26 w.	N. 89 8 w.	...	54 42	12	
1829, May 7	...	60 28	43 4	bearings of a point whose azimuth was determined				50 57	10	
— 17	...			34 34 0	N. 39 0 w.	N. 89 48 w.	50 48	50 57	30	
April 26	...	60 9	43 0		N. 42 12 w.	N. 93 2 w.	51 6	50 50	10	
1828-29	...	60 8	45 17	bearings of a point whose azimuth was determined				51 4	50	
April 6	...	60 4		Corresponding bearings to the same altitude of the Sun.				49 43	50	
1828, July 10	...	60 0	44 59	57 20 0	S. 34 16 E.	N. 95 14 E.	...	50 30	5	
1830, July 1	...	63 22	41 0	bearings of a point whose azimuth was determined.				54 22	20	

B.—OBSERVATIONS OF THE INTENSITY OF THE MAGNETIC FORCE.

NEEDLE No. I. (belonging to the Royal Society of Sciences.)——Tried at Copenhagen, before I set out : on my expedition to the East Coast was much injured by rust, and in the year 1831 had wholly lost its power.

Year and Date.	Lat. N.	Long. from Greenw.	Arc	Tempe-rature.	No. of Vibr.	Interval.	No. of Obs.	Remarks, &c.
	° ′	° ′	°					
1828, Mar. 18	55 41	12 36 E.	40	+ 7·5	300	720· 8		In a room, 5 or 6 feet from the fire-place.
July 8	60 8	45 17 w.		10·0		892· 4	1	
— 8	...	...		10·0		892· 8	1	
Dec. 20	...	...		10·0		913·89	1	In an earth-and-stone hut.
— 20	...	...		1·0		930·99	1	
1829, Jan. 15	...	...		1·5		929· 4	1	
Feb. 5	...	...		15·0		920· 0	1	
1828, July 10	60 0	44 59		10·5		915· 0	1	
— 12	60 17	44 59		10·5		915· 1	1	
Aug. 31	60 48	47 30		11·0		955· 0	1	
June 28	60 43	46 0		20·0		928· 5	1	
July 29	60 49	46 6		10·0		949· 3	1	
Aug. 27	61 10	48 47		7·0		966· 6	1	
June 8	62 0	50 0		13·0		981· 5		

NEEDLE No. II. (belonging to Commodore Wleugel).——Tried at Copenhagen, before I set out : on my expedition to the East Coast was injured by rust, and lost a good deal of its power : was subsequently proved in 1831, both in Greenland, and after my return to Copenhagen.

Year and Date.	Lat. N.	Long. from Greenw.	Arc	Tempe-rature.	No. of Vibr.	Interval.	No. of Obs.	Remarks, &c.
1828, Mar. 23	55 41	12 36 E.	20	...	100	344· 8		
July 10	60 0	44 59 w.		+10·5		458·45	2	In a room, 5 or 6 feet from the fire-place.
— 8	60 8	45 17		10·0		449· 4	2	
— 12	60 17	44 59		12·0		459·25	2	
June 28	60 43	46 0		16·0		465·43	1	
July 29	60 49	46 6		10·0		478· 5	1	
1831, Feb. 25	60 43	46 0		1·0		462· 8	3	
June 14	...	...		9·0		478· 6	4	These, perhaps, not to be compared with the foregoing.
Aug. 8·	60 42	46 45	40	9·0		478· 9	1	
June 8	60 55	48 39	20	2·5		486· 5	2	
— 25	62 0	50 0		8·0		501· 0	3	
Sept. 29	55 41	12 36 E.		15·0		387· 4	2	

NEEDLE No. III. (belonging to the Office of the Royal Hydrographer).——Was sent me in the year 1831, by Captain Zahrtmann. Tried at Copenhagen, and in Greenland.

Year and Date.	Lat. N.	Long. from Greenw.	Arc	Tempe-rature.	No. of Vibr.	Interval.	No. of Obs.	Remarks, &c.
1831, June 25	62 0	50 0 w.	40	+ 6·0	150	808·51	2	
Aug. 8	60 42	46 46	40	8·0		765· 1	1	
— 8	...	...	90	8·0		1046· 9	1	
Sept. 29	55 41	12 35 E.	40	15·0		627· 9	1	

C.—DIP OF THE NEEDLE.

THE instrument made use of was sent me in the year 1831, shortly before I left Greenland. Of some thirty Observations made with it, I here note three, the correctness of which I can vouch for ; though, in consequence of a defect in the instrument, I could only read off the dip by one of the poles of the needle.

1831, August 8th, Dip...80° 20′		Inverted Pole......79° 50′	
	80 00		80 00
	80 15		80 00
	80 12		79 57

Dip of the Needle...............Medium............80 04

No. V

TABLE OF LATITUDES AND LONGITUDES

OF VARIOUS POINTS ON THE COASTS OF GREENLAND.

[*M.* means Meridian altitude; *Chr.*, Long. by Chronometer; *Occ.*, Occultation of a star; *L.*, Lunar observation; △, determined trigonometrically; *Mtn.*, Mountain; *C.*, Cape; *F.*, Firth.]

NAMES OF PLACES.	N. Lat.	Long. W. of Greenwich.
Adler, *C.* (Kangek)	*M.* 61° 50′	41°45′
Akuliarisorsoak, *Mtn.*	△ 60 42	△ 45 09
Alluk, *Island*	*M.* 60 09	42 55
Aluik, *Island*	*M.* 64 19	39 55
Aneretok, *F.*	*M.* 61 32	42 20
Queen Anna, *C.*	66 24	53 20
Arfesearbik, *Island*	*M.* 60 12	42 55
Arsut, *Commercial Establishment* . . .	*M.* 61 10	*Chr.* 48 28
Asiouit, *Naze*	*M.* 62 40	42 00
Auarket, *F.*	*M.* 61 17	42 35
Aurora's *Harbour*	*M.* 60 49	*Chr.* 47 42
Bernstorff's *F.* (Kangerdlurksoak) . . .	63 40	40 18
Billè, *C.* (Kangek)	62 01	42 00
Princess Caroline Amelia's*Harbour* (Amitoarsuk)	*M.* 63 15	41 15
Prince Christian's *Sound*, eastern entrance (Ika-risarsoak)	*M.* 60 04	43 00
Christian's Hope, *Colony*	*M.* 68 49	*Chr.* 51 00
Christian, *C.* (Kangek)	*M.* 59 49	*Chr.* 44 05
Claushavn, *Commercial Establishment* . .	*M.* 69 07	*Chr.* 50 55
Coarse-toothed Comb, v. Redekam		
Colberger Heide, *Iceblink*	*M.* 64 10	40 07
Comfort, *C.* (Omenak)	61 49	49 50
Crown-prince's *Island, Commercial Establishment*	*M.* 68 57	*Chr.* 53 10
Danel's *Islands*	65 30	36 45
Dannebrog's *Island* (Beacon) . . .	65 18	38 30
Discord, *C.* (Kangek)	*M.* 60 54	42 29
Egede, *C.* (Kangek)	△ 60 10	△ 45 21
Egede's-minde, *Colony*, (Ausiset) . . .	*M.* 68 43	*Chr.* 52 45
Endeavour, v. Pröven		
Farewell, *C.* (Omenarsorsoak) . . .	△ 59 49	43 54
Fischer, *C.* (Kaningesakasik) . . .	61 05	△ 42 30
Fishernæs, *Colony*	63 04	— —
Frederick's-hope, *Colony* (Pamiut) . . .	*M.* 62 00	*L.* 50 01
Friederichsthal (Narksarmiut)	*M.* 60 00	*Chr.* 44 38
Goodhavn, *Colony* (Garsuk) . . .	*M.* 69 14	53 24
Gabel's *Island*	*M.* 64 22	39 35
Good-hope, *Colony* (Nouk), determined by the Missionary, Mr. Ginge	*M.* 64 10	*L.* 51 42
Griffenfeldt's *Island* (Omenak) . . .	*M.* 62 55	41 29

Names of Places.	N. Lat.	Long. W. of Greenwich.
Gyldenlöve's F.	64°22'	40°12'
Hare, *Island* (northernmost point) . .	*M.* 70 29	*Chr.* 54 32
Holm's *Naze*	*M.* 65 15	38 30
Holsteinsborg, *Colony* (Amertlok) . .	66 50	— —
Hornemann's *Island*	65 10	38 40
Hundë (Dog) *Island, Commercial Establishment*	*M.* 68 50	*Chr.* 53 01
Hvidsadel	64 59	38 57
Jacobshavn, *Colony*	*M.* 69 13	*Chr.* 50 56
Ikatamiut, *Naze*	*M.* 63 37	40 17
Ingiteit, *F.*	61 09	42 30
Itiblieitsiak	*M.* 60 53	*Chr.* 48 00
Juel, *C.* (Kangek)	*M.* 63 14	40 50
Juliana's-hope, *Colony* (Kakortok) .	*M.* 60 43	*Occ.* 46 01
Ivimiut, *Island*	*M.* 61 52	42 32
Kakortok Church	*M.* 60 50	*Chr.* 45 48
Kakortok, *Naze,* at Sennerut . .	*M.* 61 00	*Chr.* 47 55
Kakortok, *Naze,* at Juliana's-hope .	△ 60 42	△ 46 03
Kajartalik, *Harbour* . . .	61 10	,48 30
Kajartalik, *Island*	*M.* 61 02	42 35
Kangerdluluk, *F.*	61 03	42 34
Kemisak, *Island*	*M.* 63 37	40 18
Kikkertak, *Island*	*M.* 60 04	*L.* 43 02
Kikkerteitsiak, *Island* . . .	△ 60 47	△ 47 25
Kinarbik, *Naze*	*M.* 62 46	41 40
Kingitoarsuk, or Kingitorsoak, *Island* .	72 55	56 05
Klokkerhuk, *Commercial Establishment* .	*M.* 69 32	51 06
Koarak	*M.* 59 59	*Chr.* 44 36
Korsoak	*M.* 60 17	44 41
Kunnak, *Mtn.*	△ 61 15	△ 48 25
Kutek	*M.* 60 45	42 36
Lichtenau, *Missionary Establishment* .	*M.* 60 31	45 30
Lichtenfels, *Ditto* Ditto . .	63 04	— —
Lindenow's *F.*	*M.* 60 28	43 10
Lövenorn, *C.*	*M.* 64 30	39 30
Malingiset, *Island* . . .	*M.* 62 20	42 08
Malenefield	△ 60 46	△ 48 04
(Queen) Maria's Valley . . .	*M.* 63 31	41 40
Moltke, *C.* (Kangek) . . .	*M.* 63 31	40 25
Mösting, *C.* (Kangek) . . .	*M.* 63 42	40 11
Nah-ah, *Mtn.*	*M.* 59 59	44 36
Narksak, *Commercial Establishment* .	△ 60 54	△ 46 00
Narksakfield (Illimansak) . . .	△ 60 59	△ 45 52
Narrow Sound, *v.* Smalle-sund		
Nenneetsuk, *Naze* . . .	*M.* 60 28	43 04
Nennortalik, *Commercial Establishment* .	*M.* 60 08	*Occ.* 45 16
Niakornak, *Naze,* or Christian Fourth's *Island*	60 14	44 08
Niakornak, *Commercial Establishment* .	*M.* 70 47	*Chr.* 53 24
Nicolai's *Naze*	△ 60 28	△ 45 27

O

NAMES OF PLACES.	N. Lat.	Long. W. of Greenwich.
Noursoak, *Naze*	*M.* 60°25′	43°04′
Nukarbik	*M.* 63 22	40 50
Nunarsoit (highest summit) Cape Desolation (Kidlaueit)	Δ 60 47	Δ 43 05
Okkiosorbik	*M.* 61 34	42 21
Omenak, *Colony*	*M.* 70 41	*Chr.* 51 59
Oxefiord, *F.*	64 35	39 40
Ounartok, *Island*	Δ 60 28	*Chr.* 45 20
Pisiksalik, *Naze*	*M.* 60 45	*Chr.* 47 00
Pröven, *Commercial Establishment* . .	Δ 60 27	Δ 45 32
Pröven, *Ditto* *Ditto* . .	*M.* 72 21	*Chr.* 55 20
Puisortok, *Iceblink* . . .	61 59	42 02
Puisortok, *Ditto*	64 28	39 55
Ranzau, *C.*	61 46	42 00
Redekam, *Mtn.* (Kidlaueit) . . .	Δ 60 53	Δ 45 41
Rittenbenk, *Colony*	*M.* 69 41	*Chr.* 51 12
Römer's *Island*	*M.* 64 58	39 38
Rud's *Island*, S. extremity (Kikkertarsoak) .	*M.* 62 07	42 08
Sardlok, *Island*	Δ 60 32	Δ 46 01
Schumacher's *Island*	64 55	39 37
Sehested's *F.*	63 05	41 38
Serketnoua, *Naze*	*M.* 60 59	*L.* 42 35
Sermenoua, *Ditto*	*M.* 61 55	42 07
Sermesok (highest point) . .	Δ 60 17	Δ 45 11
Skram's *Islands*	*M.* 64 47	39 36
Smalle-sund	61 34	49 18
Sneedorff's *Island*	*M.* 64 58	*L.* 39 20
Sugar-loaf (Sukkertop), *Colony* . .	65 20	— —
Sugar-loaf (Sukkertop), Old (*Coquin Sound*) .	65 38	53 00
Svartehuk, *Naze*	*M.* 71 38	55 33
Taterat, *Naze*	61 15	42 34
Taterat, *Island*	*M.* 63 49	40 10
Thorvaldsen, *C.* (Agleruset) .	Δ 60 42	*Chr.* 47 55
Thorstein Icelander (Omenarsuk) .	Δ 60 48	Δ 48 26
Tordenskiold, *C.* (Kunuranak) .	61 25	42 15
Torsukatek (entrance into) . .	60 48	48 13
Trollë, *C.*	61 10	42 28
Turn-back, *C. v.* Vend-om		
Twins, *Isle* of	*M.* 63 42	40 11
Udlosietit, *Island* (S.E. point) . .	*M.* 62 30	42 02
Ukusiksak, *Island*	*M.* 63 57	40 15
Ujararksoak	*M.* 60 10	43 32
Uppernavik, *Colony* . . .	*M.* 72 48	*Chr.* 55 54
Uppernavik, *Naze* . . .	*M.* 61 11	*Chr.* 48 12
Vahl's *Island*	65 10	38 30
Vallöe, *C.* (Kangek) . . .	60 37	42 41
Vend-om, *Island* . . .	*M.* 65 14	38 35
West (Vester-), *Island* . . .	*M.* 68 38	53 30
Œrsted's *Island*	*M.* 65 05	38 46

DETAILS OF THE EXPERIMENTS ON THE INTENSITY OF THE MAGNETIC FORCE,

ADVERTED TO IN APPENDIX No. IV., B.

THE object of these experiments is to ascertain the intensity of the magnetic force, which is different at different places, varying with the observer's distance from the magnetic pole. It is ascertained by noting the number of vibrations, in a given time, of a magnetic needle suspended by a silken fibre. Though I can vouch for the correctness of my observations, I fear they will, nevertheless, prove but of little service to science, the needles being, in regard to the intensity of their magnetic force, very variable.

1828. JUNE 28th.

NEEDLE No. I.
Observed every 2t0h Vibration.

34ᵐ 12ˢ 0		
35 15 3	63ˢ 3	
36 18 0	2 7	
37 20 7	2 7	
38 23 2	2 5	
39 25 0	1 8	
40 26 5	1 5	
41 28 5	2 0	
42 30 2	1 7	
43 31 5	1 3	
44 33 0	1 5	
45 34 7	1 7	
46 36 0	1 3	
47 37 7	1 7	
48 39 0	1 3	
49 40 5	1 5	

NEEDLE No. II.
Observed every 2nd Vibration.

0ᵐ 41ˢ 0	9ˢ 3	3ᵐ 38ˢ 3	9ˢ 3
50 3	2	47 5	2
59 5	5	57 0	5
9 0	5	6 0	0
18 5	2	15 2	2
27 7	3	24 7	5
37 0	5	33 8	1
46 5	2	43 3	5
55 7	3	52 5	2
5 0	3	2 0	5
14 3	4	11 2	2
23 7	3	20 5	3
33 0	5	30 0	5
42 5	0	39 0	0
51 5	5	48 5	5
1 0	0	57 5	0
10 0	5	6ᵐ 6 8	3
19 5	5		
29 0	5		

1828. JULY 8th.

NEEDLE No. I.
Observed every 20th Vibration.

19ᵐ 11ˢ 3	60ˢ 4	53ᵐ 15ˢ 0	60ˢ 5
20 11 7	0 3	54 15 5	0 2
21 12 0	0 0	55 15 7	0 1
22 12 0	59 5	57 15 8	59 7
23 11 5	9 7	57 15 5	9 5
24 11 2	9 6	58 15 0	9 7
25 10 8	9 5	59 14 7	9 5
26 10 3	9 2	0 14 2	9 6
27 9 5	9 3	1 13 8	9 2
28 8 8	9 2	2 13 0	9 5
29 8 0	9 0	3 12 5	9 0
30 7 0	9 3	4 11 5	9 5
31 6 3	9 2	6 11 0	9 0
32 5 5	9 0	6 10 0	8 8
33 4 5	9 2	7 8 8	8 9
34 3 7		8 7 7	

1828. JULY 8th.

NEEDLE No. II.
Observed every 2nd Vibration.

21ᵐ 24ˢ 0	8ˢ 5	23ᵐ 56ˢ 8	8ˢ 8	26ᵐ 29ˢ 7	8ˢ 9
32 5	9 2	6 0	9 2	38 5	8 8
41 7	9 1	14 7	8 7	47 5	9 0
50 8	8 9	23 7	9 0	56 8	9 3
59 7	9 3	32 5	8 8	5 7	8 9
9 0	9 0	41 5	9 0	14 8	9 1
18 0	9 0	50 8	9 3	23 7	8 9
27 0	8 8	0 0	9 2	32 5	8 8
35 8	9 2	8 5	8 5	41 5	9 0
45 0	9 0	17 7	9 2	50 5	9 0
54 0	9 0	26 5	8 8	59 3	8 8
3 0	9 3	36 0	9 5	8 2	8 9
12 3	8 7	45 0	9 0	17 0	8 8
21 0	9 0	53 5	8 5	26 0	9 0
30 0	8 7	2 8	9 3	35 3	9 3
38 7	9 3	12 0	9 2	44 0	8 7
48 0		20 8	8 8	28ᵐ 53 5	9 5

1828. JULY 8th.

NEEDLE No. II.

Observed every 2nd Vibration.

39ᵐ 24ˢ 2	8ˢ 8	41ᵐ 56ˢ 5	9ˢ 0	44ᵐ 29ˢ 0	9ˢ 0
33 0	9 0	5 7	9 2	37 8	8 8
42 0	9 0	14 8	9 1	47 0	9 2
51 0	9 0	23 0	9 2	56 0	9 0
0 3	9 3	32 2	9 2	4 7	8 7
9 2	8 9	41 5	9 3	14 0	9 3
18 3	9 1	50 3	8 8	22 5	8 5
27 0	8 7	59 5	9 2	31 8	9 3
35 8	8 8	8 0	8 5	40 5	8 7
45 0	9 2	17 0	9 0	49 5	9 0
53 7	8 7	26 2	9 2	58 5	9 0
2 5	8 8	35 0	8 8	7 7	9 2
11 5	9 0	44 0	9 0	16 5	8 8
20 5	9 0	53 0	9 0	25 2	8 7
29 8	9 3	2 3	9 3	34 3	9 1
38 5	8 7	11 0	8 7	43 5	9 2
47 5	9 0	20 0	9 0	46ᵐ 52 5	9 0

1828. JULY 10th.

NEEDLE No. I.
Observed every 20th Vibration.

37ᵐ 3ˢ 7	62ˢ 3
6 0	1 8
7 8	1 5
9 3	1 4
10 7	1 3
12 0	1 0
13 0	0 8
13 8	0 5
14 3	0 9
15 2	0 8
16 0	0 5
16 5	0 8
17 3	0 7
18 0	0 5
18 5	0 2
52ᵐ 18 7	

[NEEDLE No. II.
Observed every 2nd Vibration.

16ᵐ 36ˢ 5	9ˢ 0	20ᵐ 35ˢ 2	9ˢ 2	28ᵐ 51ˢ 3	9ˢ 2	32ᵐ	50ˢ 0	9ˢ 0
45 5	9 5	44 3	9 1	0 5	9 3		59 2	9 2
55 0	8 7	53 2	8 9	9 8	9 2		8 3	9 1
3 7	9 5	2 5	9 3	19 0	9 2		17 2	8 9
13 2	9 3	12 0	9 5	28 2	9 2		26 5	9 5
22 5	9 3	21 0	9 0	37 5	9 3		36 0	9 0
31 7	9 3	30 0	9 0	46 5	9 0		45 0	9 0
41 0	9 0	39 3	9 3	56 0	9 5		54 0	9 3
50 0	8 8	48 5	9 2	5 0	9 0		3 3	9 2
58 8	9 2	57 5	9 0	14 0	9 0		12 5	9 5
8 0	9 3	6 5	9 0	23 3	9 3		22 0	9 0
17 3	9 4	16 0	9 5	32 7	9 4		31 0	8 8
76 7	9 3	25 2	9 2	42 0	9 3		39 8	9 2
36 0	9 2	34 3	9 1	51 0	9 0		49 0	9 2
45 2	8 8	43 5	9 2	0 2	9 2		58 2	8 8
54 0	9 5	52 5	9 0	9 3	9 1		7 0	9 3
3 5	9 3	1 7	9 2	18 5	9 2		16 3	9 1
12 8	9 2	10 8	9 1	27 5	9 0		25 4	8 8
22 0	9 0	20 0	9 2	36 7	9 2		34 2	9 3
31 0	9 3	29 2	9 2	45 8	9 1		43 5	9 5
40 3		38 3	9 1	55 0	9 2		53 0	9 2
49 2	9 3	47 5	9 2	4 5	9 5		2 2	9 1
58 5	9 2	56 5	9 0	13 5	9 0		11 3	9 2
7 7	9 1	5 2	8 7	22 5	9 0		20 5	9 2
16 8	9 2	24ᵐ 14 7	9 5	31 7	9 2			
26 0				41 0	9 3	36ᵐ	30 0	9 5

1828. JULY 12th.

NEEDLE No. II.
Observed every 2nd Vibration.

NEEDLE No. I.
Observed every 20th Vibration.

25ᵐ 33ˢ 5	9ˢ 5	29ᵐ 32ˢ 8	9ˢ 1	35ᵐ 2ˢ 5	9ˢ 3	39ᵐ 1ˢ 8	9ˢ 6
43 0	9 3	41 7	8 9	11 8	9 2	11 0	9 2
52 3	9 2	51 0	9 3	21 0	9 2	20 0	9 0
1 5	9 0	0 5	9 5	30 2	9 2	29 5	9 5
10 5	9 2	9 5	9 0	39 5	9 3	38 5	9 0
19 7	9 3	18 3	8 8	48 7	9 5	47 7	9 2
29 0	9 2	28 0	9 7	58 2	8 8	57 0	9 3
38 2	9 3	37 0	9 0	7 0	9 3	6 0	9 0
47 5	9 2	46 0	9 0	16 3	9 2	15 2	9 2
56 8	9 2	55 2	9 2	25 5	9 0	24 3	9 1
6 0	9 0	4 3	9 1	34 5	9 5	34 0	9 7
15 0	9 5	13 5	9 2	44 0	9 2	43 0	9 0
24 5	9 0	22 7	9 2	53 2	9 3	51 7	8 7
33 5	9 5	31 8	9 1	2 5	9 0	1 0	9 3
43 0	8 8	41 3	9 5	11 5	9 0	10 2	9 2
51 8	9 2	50 2	8 9	20 7	9 3	19 0	8 8
1 0	9 3	59 5	9 3	30 0	9 3	28 5	9 5
10 3	9 2	8 5	9 0	39 3	8 9	37 3	8 8
19 5	9 0	17 7	9 2	48 2	9 1	47 0	9 7
28 5	9 2	27 0	9 3	57 3	9 2	56 2	9 2
37 7	9 3	36 0	9 0	6 5	9 5	5 0	8 8
47 0	9 2	45 2	9 2	16 0	9 0	14 3	9 3
56 2	8 8	54 3	9 1	25 0	9 2	23 5	9 2
5 0	9 5	3 5	9 2	34 2	9 1	32 8	9 3
14 5	9 2	33ᵐ 12 5	9 0	43 3	8 9	42ᵐ 42 0	9 2
23 7				52 2			

NEEDLE No. I. Observed every 20th Vibration.

28ᵐ 4ˢ 9	61ˢ 9
6 8	1 7
8 5	1 5
10 0	1 2
11 2	1 1
12 3	1 1
13 2	0 9
14 3	1 1
15 2	0 9
16 0	0 8
16 8	0 8
17 5	0 7
18 0	0 5
18 7	0 7
19 3	0 6
43ᵐ 20 0	0 7

1828. JULY 29th.

NEEDLE No. I.
Observed every 20th Vibration.

58ᵐ 40ˢ 2	64ˢ 8
45 0	3 8
48 8	3 7
52 5	3 8
56 3	3 3
59 5	3 5
3 0	3 0
6 0	2 7
8 7	3 3
12 0	3 0
15 0	3 0
18 0	3 0
21 0	3 0
24 0	2 8
26 8	2 7
14ᵐ 29 5	

NEEDLE No. II.
Observed every 2nd Vibration.

28ᵐ 34ˢ 5		31ᵐ 17ˢ 5	9ˢ 5	34ᵐ 0ˢ 0	9ˢ 5
44 0	9ˢ 5	27 3	9 8	9 7	9 7
53 5	9 5	36 5	9 2	19 2	9 8
3 2	9 7	46 0	9 5	29 0	9 3
13 0	9 8	56 0	10 0	38 3	9 5
22 7	9 7	5 5	9 5	47 8	9 7
32 0	9 3	15 0	9 5	57 5	9 5
42 0	10 0	24 2	9 2	7 0	9 5
51 3	9 3	34 0	9 8	16 5	9 5
1 0	9 7	44 0	10 0	26 0	9 5
10 5	9 5	53 5	9 5	35 7	9 7
20 2	9 7	3 0	9 5	45 0	9 5
30 0	9 8	12 3	9 3	54 5	9 8
39 5	9 5	21 7	9 4	4 3	9 7
49 0	9 5	31 3	9 6	14 0	9 5
58 5	9 5	41 0	9 7	23 5	9 5
8 0	9 5	50 5	9 5	36ᵐ 33 0	9 5

1828. AUG. 27.

NEEDLE No. I.
Observed every 20th Vibration.

37ᵐ 38 2	66ˢ 3
44 5	5 7
50 2	4 8
55 0	4 5
59 5	4 8
4 3	4 2
8 5	4 0
12 5	4 0
16 5	4 3
20 8	4 7
24 5	4 2
28 7	4 1
32 8	3 7
36 5	4 2
40 7	4 1
53ᵐ 44 8	

1828. Aug. 31st.

NEEDLE No. I.

Observed every 20th Vibration.

30m	6s 3		
	11 0	64s	7
	15 7	4	7
	20 2	4	5
	24 0	3	8
	27 8	3	8
	31 5	3	7
	35 0	3	5
	38 3	3	3
	41 7	3	4
	45 0	3	3
	48 2	3	2
	51 6	3	4
	55 0	3	4
	58 0	3	0
46m	1 3	3	3

1828. DECEMBER 20th.

NEEDLE No. I.

Observed every 20th Vibration.

Arc.					
40°	41m	37s 0	63s	0
34		40 0	2	5
30		42 5	2	0
27		44 5	2	5
23		47 0	2	2
20		49 2	2	3
17		51 5	2	0
15		53 5	1	8
13		55 3	2	2
11		57 5	1	7
10		59 2	2	1
9		1 3	1	7
8		3 0	1	5
7		4 5	1	7
6		6 2	1	8
5	57m	8 0		

Arc.					
40°	49m	41s 0	62s	3
36		43 3	1	7
31		45 0	1	5
28		46 5	1	0
25		47 5	1	2
23		48 7	1	0
20		49 7	0	8
18		50 5	0	7
15		51 2	0	8
14		52 0	0	5
12		52 5	0	5
11		53' 0	0	3
10		53 3	0	4
9		53 7	0	3
8		54 0	0	5
7	4m	54 5		

1829. Jan. 15th.

NEEDLE No. I.

Observed every 20th Vibration.

Arc.				
40°	35m	17s 5	62s	5
		20 0	2	5
29		22 5	2	7
		25 2	2	1
22		27 3	2	2
		29 5	2	5
17·5		32 0	2	2
		34 2	2	6
		36 8	1	7
10		38 5	1	5
		40 0	1	5
8		41 5	1	7
		43 2	1	6
6		44 8	1	7
		46 5	1	8
4	50m	48 3		

1829. FEB. 5th.

NEEDLE No. I.

Observed every 20th Vibration.

Arc.				
40°	40m	5 2	62s	3
		7 5	1	8
34		9 3	1	9
26		11 2	1	6
		12 8	1	2
		14 0	1	3
15		15 3	1	4
		16 7	1	3
11		18 0	1	2
		19 2	1	1
7		20 3	0	9
		21 2	1	3
5		22 5	1	2
		23 7	0	8
3		24 5	0	8
2	55m	25 3		

1831. FEBRUARY 5th.

NEEDLE No. II.

Observed every 10th Vibration.

28m	14s 0	47s	2
	1 2	5	1
	46 3	5	2
	31 5	5	5
	17 0	5	8
	2 8	6	2
	49 0	6	6
	35 6	6	2
	21 8	7	2
	9 0	7	8
35m	56 8		

11m	13s 5	47s	2
	0 7	5	6
	46 3	5	2
	31 5	5	5
	17 0	5	8
	2 8	6	0
	48 8	5	9
	34 7	6	7
	21 4	7	3
	8 7	7	5
18m	56 2		

1831. FEB. 25th.

NEEDLE No. II.

Observed every 10th Vibration.

23ᵐ	43ˢ	5	47ˢ	3
	30	8	5	5
	16	3	5	1
	1	4	5	3
	46	7	5	6
	32	3	5	9
	18	2	6	1
	4	3	7	0
	51	3	7	4
	38	7	7	7
31ᵐ	26	4		

1831. JUNE 8th.

NEEDLE No. II.

Observed every 20th Vibration.

48ᵐ	32ˢ	8	97ˢ	4	1ᵐ	12ˢ	1	97ˢ	9
	10	2	7	4		50	0	7	2
	47	6	7	1		27	2	7	1
	24	7	7	3		4	3	6	9
	2	0	5	8		41	2	7	0
56ᵐ	38	8			9ᵐ	18	2		

1831. JUNE 14th.

NEEDLE No. II.

Observed every 10th Vibration.

Arc.

20°	24ᵐ	53ˢ	5	48ˢ	0	37ᵐ	17ˢ	5	48ˢ	0
		41	5	8	2		5	5	7	9
16		29	7	7	5		53	4	7	7
		17	2	8	0		41	1	7	8
14		5	2	8	0		28	9	8	1
		53	2	7	6		17	0	7	6
12		40	8	7	9		4	6	8	1
		28	7	7	8		52	7	7	7
10		16	5	7	8		40	4	7	6
		4	3	7	7		28	0	8	0
7	32ᵐ	52	0			45ᵐ	16	0		

Arc.

20°	48ᵐ	10ˢ	2	48ˢ	2	1ᵐ	45ˢ	5	48ˢ	0
		58	4	7	8		33	5	8	1
		46	2	8	1		21	6	7	6
		34	3	7	7		9	2	8	0
15		22	0	8	0		57	2	8	0
		10	0	8	0		45	2	8	0
		58	0	7	5		33	2	8	0
11½		45	5	8	0		20	7	7	5
		33	5	7	8		8	8	8	1
		21	3	7	4		56	4	7	6
8	56ᵐ	8	7			9ᵐ	44	2	7	8

1831. JUNE 25th.

NEEDLE No. I.

Observed every 10th Vibration.

Arc.

40°	55ᵐ	52ˢ	7	54ˢ	6	17ᵐ	12ˢ	2	55ˢ	0	1ᵐ	26ˢ	5	54ˢ	1
		47	3	4	8		7	2	4	8		21	2	4	
		42	1	4	4		2	0	4	4		15	3	3	9
24		36	5	4	1		56	4	3	9		9	2	3	8
		30	6	4	1		50	3	4	1		3	0	3	8
		24	7	3	6		44	4	4	0		56	8	3	9
14		18	3	3	9		38	4	4	0		50	7	3	4
		12	2	3	8		32	4	3	6		44	1	3	4
		6	0	3	7		26	0	3	8		37	5	3	7
9		59	7	3	8		19	8	3	5		31	2	3	5
		53	5	3	7		13	3	3	1		24	7	3	3
		47	2	3	6		6	4	3	6		18	0	3	4
6		40	8	3	5		0	0	3	6		11	4	3	4
		34	3	3	4		56	6	3	6		4	8	3	6
		27	7	3	5		47	2	3	6		58	4	3	5
25	9ᵐ	21	2			30ᵐ	40	8			14ᵐ	51	9		

1831. JUNE 25th.

NEEDLE No. II.
Observed every 10th Vibration.

14m 53s 8	50s 2		28m 27s 2	50s 3		46m 21s 0	50s 2		
44 0	0 4		17 5	0 0		11 2	0 3		
34 4	0 4		7 5	0 4		1 5	0 1		
24 8	0 0		57 9	0 0		51 6	0 1		
14 8	0 0		47 9	0 0		41 7	0 2		
4 8	0 0		37 9	0 0		31 9	0 1		
54 8	0 0		27 9	49 9		22 0	0 0		
44 8	0 0		17 8	9 2		12 0	0 0		
34 8	0 0		8 0	9 0		2 0	0 0		
24 8	0 0		58 0	9 2		52 0	49 9		
23m 14 8			36m 48 2			54m 41 9			

1831. AUG. 8th.

DIPPING NEEDLE
In the Magnetic Meridian. Observed every 10th Vibration.

26m	14 s8	28s 2
43 0	8 6
11 6	7 4
39 0	8 2
7 2	7 5
34 7	8 1
2 8	7 5
29m 30 3	

1831. AUGUST 8th.

NEEDLE No. II.
Observed every 10th Vibration.

Arc.		
40° 6m 42s 7	49s 3	
32 0	8 4	
20 4	8 0	
28 8 4	8 0	
56 4	8 0	
44 4	7 6	
20 32 0	7 6	
19 6	7 4	
7 0	7 4	
54 4	7 2	
15 41 6	7 1	
28 7	7 3	
16 0	7 2	
3 2	7 1	
50 3	7 3	
6' 18m 37 6		

NEEDLE No. III.
Observed every 10th Vibration.

Arc.		
40° 33m 48s 7	52s 6	
41 3	1 7	
33 0	1 4	
24 4	1 0	
15 4	1 1	
6 5	1 1	
57 6	0 7	
48 3	0 8	
39 1	0 7	
29 8	0 9	
20 7	0 8	
11 5	0 7	
2 2	0 5	
52 7	0 8	
43 5	0 3	
46m 33 8		

Arc.		
90° 50m 1s 6	59s 1	
78 0 7	6 8	
70 57 5	5 1	
60 52 6	4 1	
52 46 7	3 3	
45 40 0	2 8	
40 32 8	2 0	
35 24 8	1 9	
32 16 7	1 7	
28 8 4	1 6	
24 0 0	1 2	
21 51 2	1 1	
18½ 42 3	0 9	
17 33 2	0 8	
15 24 0	0 8	
13 14 8	1 2	
11 6 0	0 4	
10 56 4	0 8	
9 47 2	0 6	
7° 37 8	0 7	
7m 28 5		

1831. SEPTEMBER 29th.

NEEDLE No. II.

Observed every 10th Vibration.

10ᵐ 4ˢ 7	38ˢ 8	40ᵐ 9ˢ 2	39ˢ 0	7ᵐ 30ˢ 3	42ˢ 0
43 5	9 0	48 2	9 1	12 3	2 4
22 5	8 8	27 3	8 7	54 7	2 6
1 3	9 0	6 0	8 5	37 3	1 9
40 3	8 7	44 5	8 8	19 2	2 1
19 0	8 5	23 3	8 9	1 3	1 7
57 5	8 6	2 2	8 8	43 0	2 2
— .	8 6	41 0	8 4	25 2	1 5
14 7	8 5	19 4	8 6	6 7	1 7
53 2	9 0	58 0	8 5	48 4	2 2
32 2	8 3	36 5	8 8	30 6	1 2
10 4	9 1	15 3	8 4	11 8	1 6
49 5	8 5	53 7	8 8	53 4	1 9
28 0	8 5	32 5	8 2	35 3	1 5
6 5	8 5	10 7	8 7	16 8	1 4
19ᵐ 45 0		49ᵐ. 49 4		17ᵐ 58 2	

(Right group: **NEEDLE No. III.** Observed every 10th Vibration.)

THE result of these Observations (Table IV. B.) is deduced by simply taking the difference between the first and last of them, without making any correction, or reduction. After the said table had left the press, I received from Professor Hansteen, whose experiments in terrestrial magnetism have gained him a well-merited celebrity, some valuable and interesting remarks upon this head, which I here communicate for the benefit of future travellers, regretting that I myself was not acquainted with the mode of calculation therein recommended in time to profit by it :

" IN reference to Captain Sabine's observations, I have shown the defects of that process*, as well in our own ' Magazine of Sciences,' as in ' Poggendorff's Annalen,' where I have likewise given correct formulas of reduction, and laid down better modes of observation. In the said process, use is made but of the first and last of the series of observations, all the intermediate ones being passed by without notice. I will point out the proper method of calculating such an observation, taking, as my example, that made at Juliana's-hope on the 14th of June, 1831, with needle No. II."

No.	Arc.	Time.	No.	Arc.	Time.		
0	20	24 53 6	100	° 7	32 52 0		100 vibr. = 7 58 5 = 478 5
10	—	25 41 5	90	—	32 4 3	Conse-	80 „ = 6 22 8 = 382 8
20	16	26 29 7	80	10	31 16 5	quently the	60 „ = 4 46 8 = 286 8
30	—	27 17 2	70	—	30 28 7	time of	40 „ = 3 11 5 = 191 5
40	14	28 5 2	60	12	29 40 8		20 „ = 1 35 6 = 95 6
50	—	28 53 2					

" All the observations, after the 50th, are here set down, it will be seen, in an inverted order, and the differences noted between those standing in the same horizontal line.

" If we suppose all the observations to have been made with equal accuracy, it is evident that they have an equal claim to notice in the process of calculation built on them. But if an error in observation of, for example,

* That followed by me.

half a second, have been committed in the deduction of each of these results, it is easy to comprehend, that the interval of one vibration will be determined twice as accurately by taking 40, as by taking 20 vibrations; three times as accurately by taking 60; four times as accurately by taking 80, and so on; we must therefore multiply the above results, beginning with the uppermost, and going downwards, respectively by 5, 4, 3, 2, and 1; and we then obtain—

Time of 500 vibrations	= 2392 5	
„ 320 „	= 1531 2	Which 5262″ 7, being divided by 1100,
„ 180 „	= 860 4	would give the nearest approximation
„ 80 „	= 383 0	to the true time of one vibration
„ 20 „	= 95 6	$= t = 4''\ 7843.$
Time of 1100 vibrations	= 5262 7 =T.	

" But this is neither the time of a vibration in an arc of 20°, or in an arc of 7°, but is too little for the former, and too much for the latter. Had we in this manner calculated the time of one vibration out of the first 50, we should have found it much greater, and if out of the last 50, much less (the time of the first 50 being, to wit, 3′ 59·7″, and that of the last 50, 3′ 58″·8). If, therefore, we would give numbers that may be accurately compared, we must reduce the time to vibrations in infinitely small arcs. But this reduction depends as well on the first arc, as on the law by which these decrease; as also on the number of vibrations observed, and, finally, on the intervals between the vibrations (for example, whether we have observed every 2nd, every 10th, or every 20th). Now, as this correction is somewhat difficult to compute, as a new formula must be taken for every change in the mode of observation, and when it has been obtained, the value of its numbers must be calculated, it is one of the worst defects of this unsatisfactory process, that he who follows it either takes no note whatever of the length of the arc, and therein commits a gross error, or, if he attempt to compute the correction of the same, is led into an interminable series of calculations, inasmuch as no certain rule or method is therein followed, but at one moment an arc of 20°, at another an arc of 40°, is taken; at one moment every 2nd, at another every 10th, at another every 20th vibration, is observed; at one moment a stop is made at the 50th or 60th, at another at the 70th or 100th, or 150th or 300th,—for every one of these diversities occurs in this series of observations. If, on the contrary, a certain fixed rule be adhered to, throughout, we are enabled once for all, to make out a small logarithmic table of corrections, and to obtain the whole correction by a single subtraction.

" To revert to our example:—When, out of 100 vibrations, every 10th is observed, and these be calculated as above, I find, that when the arc, as in this instance, decreases to the half (= 10°) at the 80th vibration, the 1100 vibrations, if the experiment began with an arc of 20°, occupy the same time with 1103·85 in infinitely small arcs; and, if it began with an arc of 30°, with 1108·71, and consequently the nearest approximation to the true time of one vibration in an infinitely small arc $= \frac{5262.''\ 7}{1103\ 85} = 4''·7675$. If any further correction be required for temperature, this may be made as follows:

log. $T = 3$ 72121 $t = 4'' 7553.$
log. 1103"85 $= 3$ 04291

0 67830 ⎰ This t is reduced to infinitely small
Corr. for $+ 9°. 5 = -112$ ⎱ arcs and 0° temperature.

log. $t = 0$ 67718

" If all the observations made were made in this manner that is to say, if, of 100 vibrations, every 10th were observed, and the elongation of the arc at the beginning noted, as well as at what precise vibration this decreased to the half, I have made out tables of divisors for the reduction* as well for cases where the elongation of the arc at the beginning is 20° as where it is 30°, by means of which the calculation of the whole set of observations may be made in a forenoon; whereas, according to the other method, a multitude of different tables is required.

" The arcs form, as near as possible, a geometrical progression. This important result, on which the whole process of reduction depends, I have been gratified to find confirmed by your experiment with needle No. III., on the 18th of August, 1831, at Ikarisarsuk, which begins with an arc of 90°. I myself had but tried it in an arc of 40°. If, to wit, to first arc $= e$, the second becomes $= m e$, the third $= m^2 e$, the fourth $= m^3 e \ldots$ the nth, $m^n - {}^1 e$, where m is a proper fraction, which very nearly $= 1$. In this observation, I find the log. $m = 9·9940895$, and consequently $m = 0·986483$. If we now take this to be the value of m, and calculate the size of every 10th arc accordingly, we obtain : —

e

No.	Observed.	Computed.	Difference.
	°	°	°
0	90	90 00	0 00
10	78	78 55	+ 0 55
20	70	68 55	— 1 45
30	60	59 83	— 0 17
40	52	52 22	+ 0 22
50	45	45 58	+ 0 58
60	40	39 78	— 0 22
70	35	34 72	— 0 28
80	32	30 30	— 1 70
90	28	26 45	— 1 55
100	24	23 08	— 0 92
110	21	20 14	— 0 86
120	18·5	17 58	— 0 92
130	17·0	15 34	— 1 66
140	15	13 39	— 1 61
150	13	11 69	— 1 31
160	11	10 20	— 0 80
170	9	8 90	— 0 10
180	7	7 77	+ 0 77

" Beginning at the 80th vibration, the arcs as computed are about 1° too small; but this is of no material consequence, as the arc has already by this time decreased to 30°.

* Vide pages 198 and 199.

" In order to see if the resistance of the air has not some effect on the time of vibration in such large arcs, I have divided this observation into two parts, calculating the first 100 vibrations in arcs of from 90° to 24° by themselves and the last 100 in arcs of from 24° to the end likewise by themselves, and obtained as follows:—

THE FIRST 100 VIBRATIONS.			THE SECOND 100 VIBRATIONS.		
$e = 90°$.	Mult. by		$e = 24°$	Mult. by	
100 Vibr. $= 8\ 58\ 4 = 538\ 4$	5	2692 0	$8\ 28\ 5 = 508\ 5$	5	2542 5
80 —— $= 7\ \ 7\ 7 = 427\ 7$	4	1710 8	$6\ 46\ 6 = 406\ 6$	4	1626 4
60 —— $= 5\ 19\ 2 = 319\ 2$	3	957 6	$5\ \ 4\ 9 = 304\ 9$	3	914 7
40 —— $= 3\ 32\ 2 = 212\ 2$	2	424 4	$3\ 23\ 2 = 203\ 2$	2	406 4
20 —— $= 1\ 46\ 1 = 106\ 1$	1	106 1	$1\ 42\ 0 = 102\ 0$	1	102 0

Divis. $= 1157\ 67 = D'$ } $5890''9 = T$
     Sum.

Divis. $1103\ 55 = D'$ } $5592'\ 0 = T'$
     Sum.

log. T. $= 3\ 77018$
log. D. $= 3\ 06358$
log. $t = 0\ 70660$
     $t = 5''\ 0887$

log. T' $= 3\ 74757$
log. D' $= 3\ 34279$
log. $t' = 0\ 70478$
     $t' = 5''\ 0674$

" It appears from this, that in such large arcs the resistance of the air does add something to the time of a vibration; for the time occupied by 100 such infinitely small arcs is seen, in the case of the first 100, to be $= 508''\ 87$, and in that of the last $100 = 506''\ 74$, thus giving a difference of $2''\ 1$.

" All three of the needles have lost a good deal of their magnetic power; but how much, it is impossible for me to ascertain, until I am in possession of the details of the observations made with them at Copenhagen, in 1828, previous to your departure. For as I have remarked above, the deduction for the arc of vibration varies with the number, and is likewise different according as every 2nd, or every 10th vibration is observed. The time of 100 vibrations of No. II., appears to have changed from 345" to 387", or 42". That this is an effect of its contracting rust, I do not believe, as I have known an instance of a needle being so encrusted with it, as to make it necessary to have it ground away, without losing its force in any sensible degree. No safe deductions can therefore be made from these observations, in consequence of this considerable alteration. In the meanwhile I shall calculate them with all the accuracy possible, if I am furnished with the details of those made in Copenhagen in 1828.

" In the expectation that it may prove useful either to yourself at some future day, or to others whom you may have an opportunity of instructing, I here enclose a small book, wherein occurs (as an example of my method,) an observation made at Christiania, with the calculation deduced from it*, which method I shall now explain more fully. To facilitate my calculations, I have always steadily followed one and the same method, to wit:—
1. The arc at the beginning of the observation has been uniformly $= 20°$; except in high latitudes, where the horizontal power of the needle is very small · and where, therefore, if an arc of 20° were taken, the last vibra-

* Vide page 199.

tions would be so small, as to be with difficulty perceptible : in such case I have taken $e = 30°$. Larger arcs than this I have never found it necessary to have recourse to; that they give less precise results is attested by your own observation made at Ikarisarsuk. 2. I have always taken note of that vibration at which the arc has become reduced to the one-half of what it was at first $(= \frac{1}{2}e)$; this vibration is denoted in the table by the letter x; and in the example cited, where $e = 20°$, and $\frac{1}{2}e = 10°$, coincides with the 80th vibration, $x = 80$. 3. I have always observed every 10th vibration, a rule, by following which, one has time to note one observation before the occurrence of the next. 4. I have always carried on the observation to 360; this is, indeed, quite an arbitrary number; but as far as this the vibrations may without difficulty be observed ; and the more one does observe, the more correct of course will be the means afterwards obtained. In this respect, however, every one will do best to follow his own fancy. If he goes on to 300, it is, perhaps, all that it is required ; the last arcs in that case are not so small, and the result obtained nearly as exact. 5. I have taken the difference between the numbers in the first and fourth vertical columns that are marked with Sec.; consequently, between 0 and 300, between 10 and 310, 20 and 320....60 and 360 ; and thus obtained seven values of 300 vibrations, of which I have then taken the mean $=$ T'. 6. At the beginning and end, the temperatures, as shown by a thermometer enclosed in the box, are noted. 7. From log. T'. is subtracted the correction, according to Table I., for the mean of the two temperatures, and the correction, according to Table II. (Method 1), for the just value of e and x, and the log. T. thereby obtained, which is the amount of time of 300 vibrations in infinitely small arcs. This process is extremely easy, and can be got through with in a few minutes ; the almost equal values of the first, second, and third hundred vibrations, and the almost equal seven values of 300 vibrations, give one at once a check on the correctness of the observations.

" Second Method.

" If one does not like to make the observation so prolix, one may terminate it at the 290th inclusive, and take the mean of the numbers in the first and third column, whereby he will obtain ten values of 200 vibrations. In the example annexed, the following values of 200 vibrations are thus obtained, $9' 11'' 2 - 5'' 6 = 9' 5'' 6$; $38'' 4 - 32'' 8 = 5'' 6$, etc.

9′ 5″ 6	Log. T′=2·73642	
5 6	Cor. for + 17 = — 200	2nd Method $\begin{cases} x = 80 \\ e = 20 \end{cases}$
5 3	— — Arc = — 48	
5 2	Log. T. =2· 73394	
5 4		
5 0		
5 0		T = 541″ 93
4 6		$\frac{1}{2}$ T = 270 96
4 1		300 Vibr. =812″ 89
4 5		Accord. to } 812 96 *vid. page*
Mean—9′ 5″ 43		1st Method } 199.
T′=545″ 03		Difference 0″ 07

" THIRD METHOD.

" IF one chooses to take only 100 vibrations, and is desirous to obtain the most exact value that can be thence deduced, he must proceed as above directed. As an example, I again give here the observation made at Christiania:—

												Mult. by			
0	5 6	100	38 4	4	32 8	=272 8	5	1364 0		log. T′ = 3·47777
10	32 8	90	4′ 11 6	3	38 8	=218 8	4	875 2		Cr. for 17° — 200
20	1′ 0 3	80	44 4	2	44 1	=164 1	3	492 3		$\begin{Bmatrix} x = 80 \\ e = 20° \end{Bmatrix}$ +8·95709 3d Meth.
30	27 6	70	3 16 8	1	49 2	=109 2	2	218 4		
40	54 6	60	49 2		54 6	= 54 6	1	54 6		Log. T = 2·43286
50	2 ... 21″ 9					Sum T′ 3004″ 5

T = time of 100 Vibr. = 270″ 93
3 T = 300 Vibr. = 812 79

" We have accordingly found the time of 300 vibrations:—

" According to the 1st Method = 812″ 96
    „   „   2nd do.   := 812 89
    „   „   3rd do.   = 812 79

" You will thus perceive, that the first and second are much more easy modes of calculations than the third. According to the theory of probabilities it may be proved, that, in respect of the correctness of their results, these three methods stand to one another as 793·7 : 632·4 : 148·4; or, in other words, that the error in their results are conversely as $1 : 4\frac{1}{3} : 5\frac{1}{3}$. Consequently, the method adopted by me is the most exact of the three. If, on the contrary, we observe 100 vibrations, and calculate them in the manner adopted by you, the degree of exactness in the result obtained (under supposition of a reduction for the size of the arc) will = 100; i. e., it will stand to the above as $1 : 1'484 : 6'324 : 7'937$; in other words, my method is eight times as accurate, or, the observations in either case being equally good, the chances of an error in the result obtained by my method, $\frac{1}{8}$ of those by yours.

" I have endeavoured to obtain general formulas of reduction for infinitely small arcs, where n vibrations are observed, and the time of every kth noted. If, in these we substitute the value of n (e. g., 100, 150, 200, &c.) and for k (e. g., 2, or 10, or 20), the reduction is obtained. The one formula is to be employed when $\frac{n}{k}$ is an even, the other when $\frac{n}{k}$ is an odd, number. As, however, these formulas would probably terrify you by reason of their prolixity, I shall not insert them here, but, when time permits, apply them to your observations, of which I have taken a copy.

CORRECTION FOR THE TEMPERATURE.

t.	Cor.	t.	Cor.	t.	Cor.	t.	Cor.	t.	Cor.
1°	12	6°	71	11°	129	16°	188	21°	247
2	24	7	82	12	141	17	200	22	259
3	35	8	94	13	153	18	212	23	271
4	47	9	106	14	165	19	224	24	282
5	59	10	118	15	177	20	235	25	294

APPENDIX. 199

CORRECTION FOR THE ARC.

	1st Method. Mean of 7 values of 300 Vibrations between 300 & 360.		2nd Method. Mean of 10 values of 200 Vibrations between 200 & 290.		3rd Method. Probable value of 100 Vibrations when a mean is taken of 100, 80, 60, 40, 20 Vibrations.		
x	e 20	30	e 20	30	20	e 30	x.
60	−26	− 59	−30	− 76			60
70	−33	− 74	−39	− 89	+8 95723	+8 95550	70
80	−40	− 90	−48	−108	+8 95709	+8 95518	80
90	−47	−105	−56	−127	+8 95696	+8 95490	90
100	−54	−121	−65	−147	+8 95685	+8 95465	100
110	−60	−136	−73	−165	+8 95676	+8 95443	110
120	−67	−151	−81	−189	+8 95667	+8 95424	120
130	−73	−166	−89	−201			130

e, denotes the elongation of the arc at the beginning of the observation; x, the number of vibration at which the arc $= \frac{1}{2}e$.

CHRISTIANIA.

1832. 17th of JULY.   Needle No. I.   Therm.

Beg. 11 2 A.M.   + 15 6
End. 11 22 ,,   + 18 3
Noon. = + 17 0

Arc.	Sec.	Arc.	Sec.	Arc.	Sec.	Sec.	Time of 300 Vibr.
20	5 6		38 4		11 2	43 2	13 37 6
	32 8		6 0		38 4	10 5	37 7
	0 3		33 2		5 6	37 8	37 5
15	27 6		0 5		32 8	5 0	37 4
	54 6		27 6		0 0	32 0	37 4
	21 9		54 8		26 9	59 4	37 5
	49 2	5°	22 0		54 2	26 4	37 2
	16 8		49 2		21 4		
10	44 4		16 8		48 5	Mean 13 37 47	
	11 6		44 0		16 1	T′ = 817 47	

log. T′ = 2·91247
Corr. for Arc = ,, 40 $x = 80$, 1st Method.
,, ,, +17° = ,, 200
log. T = ¦2·91007
T = 812″ 96.

THE END.

LONDON:

JOHN W. PARKER, ST. MARTIN'S LANE.

For EU product safety concerns, contact us at Calle de José Abascal, 56–1°,
28003 Madrid, Spain or eugpsr@cambridge.org.

 www.ingramcontent.com/pod-product-compliance
Ingram Content Group UK Ltd.
Pitfield, Milton Keynes, MK11 3LW, UK
UKHW010335140625
459647UK00010B/617